ST. MARY'S COLLEGE OF EDUCATION
LIBRARY

HIGH TALK

MISCELLANY

HIGH TALK

The philosophical poetry of W. B. Yeats

ROBERT SNUKAL

CAMBRIDGE

AT THE UNIVERSITY PRESS

1973

34035

Published by the Syndics of the Cambridge University Press
Bentley House, 200 Euston Road, London NWI 2DB
American Branch: 32 East 57th Street, New York, N.Y.10022

Library of Congress Catalogue Card Number: 72–87440

ISBN: 0 521 20057 I

Printed in Great Britain
by W & J Mackay Limited, Chatham

Contents

Preface   *page* vii

1 Borrowings   1

2 Towards a reading of the poems: beginnings   18

3 Symbol and symbolism   39

4 Art, history and the phenomenal world   84

5 Freedom and necessity   125

6 History as necessity   161

7 'Among School Children'   182

8 Conclusions   230

Appendix A: 'The Genealogical Tree of
Revolution'   238

Appendix B: Thomas Taylor's edition of
Porphyry's essay, 'On the Cave of the Nymphs,
in the thirteenth book of the Odyssey'   240

Appendix C: 'The Oracle'   263

Index   266

Acknowledgments   270

Preface

Most, although not all, of what has been published in the last thirty years about Yeats has attempted to deal with the whole body of his work. Such an approach was a natural reaction in the immediate circumstances – which were that Yeats's work could now be treated as a whole (since he was dead,) and that by the time of his death it was clear that he was one of the more important literary figures of the century.

One useful consequence of this sort of attention has been to illuminate his relative stature; Yeats's importance has loomed larger just in so far as the failure of his critics to encompass his work has become clear. So the failure of his critics, is, paradoxically, their success. When a writer's work is clearly seen to be so important that a single book, however compendious and however good, cannot provide an accurate account, it is possible to begin to give individual works a kind of attention that is impossible when the object is to say all that can be said about the work as a whole. This book attempts to elucidate a relatively small number of Yeats's poems. I have chosen poems which are, I believe, worth close attention and which illuminate each other.

Two of Yeats's more important themes were his rejection of transcendental answers to questions about the nature of human experience, and his 'romantic' belief that reality is a human creation. It is at once obvious that both these themes are not purely literary, but are closely related to questions which are normally regarded as philosophical questions. Yeats's knowledge of Kant provided him with an epistemological theory that supported his 'romantic' stance, and which rejected the transcendentalism of most of the philosophical positions normally described as idealism.

Kant's philosophical writings are notoriously difficult: so difficult that philosophers are still divided about whether he should be described as a peculiar sort of idealist, or a peculiar sort of empiricist. I have followed Yeats's practice of referring to him as an idealist, although I myself am not convinced that it would not be better to call him an empiricist. Chapter 1 of the book is intended as a guide for the uninitiated through these troubled waters. I regret that the journey is necessary, since I am not a philosopher, and the help that I can offer the reader is limited. But I have done what I can to deal briefly and cogently with material which will be difficult for those readers who are not familiar with the philosophical issues that are raised in the rest of the book.

October 1972   R. S.

I

Borrowings

The Romantic movement seems related to the idealist philosophy; the naturalistic movement, Stendhal's mirror dawdling down a lane, to Locke's mechanical philosophy, as simultaneous correspondential dreams are related, not merely where there is some traceable influence but through their whole substance, and I remember that monks in the Thebaid, or was it by the Mareotic Sea, claimed 'to keep the ramparts', meaning perhaps that all men whose thoughts skimmed the 'unconscious', God-abetting, affected others according to their state, that what some feel others think, what some think others do. When I speak of idealist philosophy I think more of Kant than of Berkeley, who was idealist and realist alike, more of Hegel and his successors than of Kant, and when I speak of the romantic movement I think more of Manfred, more of Shelley's Prometheus, more of Jean Valjean, than of those traditional figures, Browning's Pope, the fakir-like pedlar in *The Excursion*.[1]

This passage expresses, as do many others, Yeats's fundamental allegiance to romanticism in poetry, and to idealism in philosophy. It also expresses his belief that 'idealism' and 'romanticism' are related in some special way. The nature of the relationships Yeats found between them becomes clear only when the rather special way Yeats is using these two terms is explained. I shall claim that an understanding of Yeats's use of the terms 'romantic' and 'idealist' and the relationship between idealism and romanticism, provides an insight into a number of Yeats's poems, and to the proper interpretation of his work as a whole.

Perhaps the easiest way to understand Yeats's use of 'romanticism' is to see it as directly opposed to the most popular interpretation of the Aristotelian ideal of *mimesis* or imitation. Yeats rejects the notion of art as a reflection or photograph of what is. That is, he has in mind an art which creates, rather than reflects, reality. By 'romantic' he refers not to subject-matter or style, but to a particular complex of beliefs about poetry which were first

[1] W. B. Yeats, 'Bishop Berkeley', *Essays and Introductions* (New York: The Macmillan Company, 1961), p. 404.

I

formulated in English by Wordsworth and Coleridge, especially Coleridge.

By 'idealism' Yeats means the epistemological and metaphysical doctrines which claim that the universe we discover about us is in some sense a product of the human mind. Any philosophical or quasi-philosophical position which seemed to imply that objective reality was mind-dependent, Yeats would call idealist. This is not quite the usual meaning of the word. The philosophical term 'idealist' usually refers to someone who believes, as did Plato, that the ideal is the real. That is, Plato and others like Plato claimed that there are some things that differ from the ordinary things which are reported to us by our senses. These things are immaterial and in some way prior to, or above, material things. Or it may mean someone who believes, as did Berkeley, that all those things which seem real are ideas. According to Berkeley, these ideas were in the mind of God and were thus 'objective'. Hence Yeats says Berkeley is both realist and idealist alike. Both of these idealist theories displeased Yeats because they left the human mind a passive vehicle for perception – a camera or a mirror – in the same way as did most forms of realism.

When Stendhal described a masterpiece as a 'mirror dawdling down a lane' he expresses the mechanical philosophy of the French eighteenth century. Gradually literature conformed to his ideal; Balzac became old-fashioned; romanticism grew theatrical in its strain to hold the public; till, by the end of the nineteenth century, the principal characters in the most famous books were the passive analysts of events, or had been brutalised into the likeness of mechanical objects.[1]

Yeats, in the passage quoted at the beginning of this chapter, specifically repudiates Berkeley's idealism, and even more important, does not mention Plato, because the philosophies of both these men proclaim an exterior reality just as intransigent as the exterior reality of philosophical realism; they too require only a mirror, albeit a supra-sensual mirror, to shadow forth the whole of reality. Instead of the idealism of Plato and Berkeley, Yeats says that he is concerned with the idealism of Kant and Hegel and their successors.[2] Kant, and those who followed him, are not idealists in either

[1] W. B. Yeats, 'Fighting the Waves', *Wheels and Butterflies* (London: Macmillan & Company, 1924), p. 73.

[2] The people Yeats wants to include here are Bradley and McTaggart in England, Croce and Gentile in Italy, and Fichte, Hegel, Schopenhauer and Nietzsche in Germany. All these men are mentioned often in the prose of the period.

of these senses. In fact, few philosophers would be willing to call
Kant an idealist at all. Since Kant's position and what Yeats made
of it is central to the argument, I shall expand upon the relevant
areas of Kant's thought.

Locke had claimed that there were two kinds of 'qualities' possessed by things – primary qualities and secondary qualities. The
secondary qualities, such as colour, smell etc., were interpretations,
made by the human senses, of real things. The primary qualities of
extension, solidity and motion were, however, actual properties of
things. This is, in effect, the metaphysics of science – reality is
matter in motion. And Whitehead's remark that a world of odour-
less and colourless particles did not leave much place for poetry is
echoed by Yeats:

I can see in a sort of nightmare vision the 'primary qualities' torn from the
side of Locke, Johnson's ponderous body bent above the letter to Lord
Chesterfield, some obscure person somewhere inventing the spinning-
jenny, upon his face that look of benevolence kept by painters and engrav-
ers, from the middle of the eighteenth century to the time of the Prince
Consort, for such as he, or, to simplify the tale –

> Locke sank into a swoon;
> The Garden died;
> God took the spinning-jenny
> Out of his side.[1]

But Locke was followed by Berkeley and Hume, who saw no
difference between primary and secondary qualities, and so shook
the whole structure of British empirical epistemology. Berkeley
simply used his scepticism to set up his own idealism. Once all
those things reported by the senses were ideas in the mind of God,
the problem he had created disappeared. Since Hume had no such
easy access to God's ideas he developed a radical scepticism which
played a more important role in determining the direction of western philosophy.

According to Hume both primary and secondary qualities were
mere representations of things by the human senses. Locke would
have said that an apple merely appeared to taste sweet, and merely
appeared to be red; but that it did not only appear to be solid and
extended, but was *in reality* solid and extended. Hume pointed out
that there was no more reason to suppose an apple to be in reality
solid and extended than to suppose it to be red and sweet.

[1] Yeats, 'The Words Upon the Window-pane', *Wheels and Butterflies*, p. 24.

Further, Hume was able to show that certain kinds of inductive arguments, for example, those linking cause and effect, were suspect. Hume's comments on causation and the rules of induction could be translated into this – only *a priori* truths are necessary, and all *a posteriori* or inductive judgments could have at best varying degrees of probability. All probable judgments depend on the premise that future instances will resemble past instances. But this premise is itself an *a posteriori* judgment (that is, it is not logically necessary). As a result of the fact that one had no right to assume that future events would indeed resemble past events, no collection of instances, however large, ever entitle us to conclude that in the future this event (say a causal sequence e.g., extreme heat when applied to flesh produces a burn), would repeat itself. Since most of the conclusions of science, and for that matter of ordinary life, are inductive, Hume's arguments question the validity of almost everything men think, and make thinking itself (except about mathematics etc.) almost an impossibility.

Of course, so radical a scepticism seems to be self-defeating. The immediate reaction to Hume's view is that since we do, in fact, seem to be able to think successfully about the world, Hume must be mistaken. This was Kant's reaction. But since Kant's philosophy is notoriously difficult I will not try to continue with my own explanation, but will take the easier way out – easier both for myself and the reader, and quote the simplest and most cogent brief explanation of Kant's philosophy I know.

Kant's most important book is *The Critique of Pure Reason* (first edition, 1781; second edition, 1787). The purpose of this work is to prove that, although none of our knowledge can transcend experience, it is, nevertheless, in part *a priori* and not inferred inductively from experience. The part of our knowledge which is *a priori* embraces, according to him, not only logic, but much that cannot be included in logic or deduced from it. He separates two distinctions which, in Leibniz, are confounded. On the one hand there is the distinction between 'analytic' and 'synthetic' propositions; on the other hand, the distinction between '*a priori*' and 'empirical' propositions. Something must be said about each of these distinctions.

An 'analytic' proposition is one in which the predicate is part of the subject; for instance, 'a tall man is a man', or 'an equilateral triangle is a triangle'. Such propositions follow from the law of contradiction; to maintain that a tall man is not a man would be self-contradictory. A 'synthetic' proposition is one that is not analytic. All the propositions that we know only through experience are synthetic. We cannot, by a mere analysis of concepts, discover such truths as 'Tuesday was a wet day' or 'Napoleon was a great general'. But Kant, unlike Leibniz and all other previous philosophers, will not admit the converse, that all synthetic propositions are only known through experience. This brings us to the second of the above distinctions.

An 'empirical' proposition is one which we cannot know except by the help of sense-perception, either our own or that of someone else whose testimony we accept. The facts of history and geography are of this sort; so are the laws of science, whenever our knowledge of their truth depends on observational data. An 'a priori' proposition, on the other hand, is one which, though it may be *elicited* by experience, is seen, when known, to have a basis other than experience. A child learning arithmetic may be helped by experiencing two marbles and two other marbles, and observing that altogether he is experiencing four marbles. But when he has grasped the general proposition 'two and two are four' he no longer requires confirmation by instances; the proposition has a certainty which induction can never give to a general law. All the propositions of pure mathematics are in this sense *a priori*.

Hume had proved that the law of causality is not analytic, and had inferred that we could not be certain of its truth. Kant accepted the view that it is synthetic, but nevertheless maintained that it is known *a priori*. He maintained that arithmetic and geometry are synthetic, but are likewise *a priori*. He was thus led to formulate his problems in these terms:

How are synthetic judgments *a priori* possible?

The answer to this question, with its consequences, constitutes the main theme of *The Critique of Pure Reason*.

Kant's solution of the problem was one in which he felt great confidence. He had spent twelve years in looking for it, but took only a few months to write his whole long book after his theory had taken shape. In the preface to the second edition he compares himself to Copernicus, and says that he has effected a Copernican revolution in philosophy.

According to Kant the outer world causes only the matter of sensation, but our own mental apparatus orders this matter in space and time, and supplies the concepts by means of which we understand experience. Things in themselves, which are the causes of our sensations, are unknowable; they are not in space or time, they are not substances, nor can they be described by any of those other general concepts which Kant calls 'categories'. Space and time are subjective, they are part of our apparatus of perception. But just because of this, we can be sure that whatever we experience will exhibit the characteristics dealt with by geometry and the science of time. If you always wore blue spectacles, you could be sure of seeing everything blue (this is not Kant's illustration). Similarly, since you always wear spatial spectacles in your mind, you are sure of always seeing everything in space. Thus geometry is *a priori* in the sense that it must be true of everything experienced, but we have no reason to suppose that anything analogous is true of things in themselves, which we do not experience.

Space and time, Kant says, are not concepts; they are forms of 'intuition'. (The German word is '*Anschauung*', which means literally, 'looking at' or 'view'. The word 'intuition', though the accepted translation, is not altogether a satisfactory one.) There are also, however, *a priori* concepts; these are the twelve 'categories', which Kant derives from the forms of the syllogism. The twelve categories are divided into four sets of three: (1) of quantity: unity, plurality, totality; (2) of quality: reality, negation, limitation; (3) of relation: substance – and – accident, *cause – and – effect*, reciprocity; (4) of modality; possibility, existence, necessity. These are subjective in the same sense in which time and space are – that is to say, our mental constitution is such that they are applicable to whatever we experience, but there is no reason to suppose them applicable to things in themselves. As regards cause, however, there is an inconsistency, for things in themselves are regarded by Kant as causes of sensations, and free volitions are held by him to be causes of occurrences in space and time. This inconsistency is not an accidental oversight; it is an essential part of his system.

A large part of *The Critique of Pure Reason* is occupied in showing the fallacies that arise from applying space and time or the categories to things that are not experienced. When this is done, so Kant maintains, we find ourselves troubled by 'antinomies' each consisting of thesis and antithesis.

In the first, the thesis says: 'The world has a beginning in time, and is also limited as regards space.' The antithesis says: 'The world has no beginning in time, and no limits in space; it is infinite as regards both time and space.'

The second antinomy proves that every composite substance both is, and is not, made up of simple parts.

The thesis of the third antinomy maintains that there are two kinds of causality, one according to the laws of nature, the other that of freedom; the antithesis maintains that there is only causality according to the laws of nature.

The fourth antinomy proves that there is, and is not, an absolutely necessary Being.

This part of the *Critique* greatly influenced Hegel, whose dialectic proceeds wholly by way of antinomies.[1]

Now it is clear that Kant's notions are very different from those of Plato and Berkeley. The earlier Idealists were primarily concerned with ontological and metaphysical problems, and Kant has put both ontology and metaphysics aside in order to concentrate on

[1] Bertrand Russell, *History of Western Philosophy* (London: George Allen & Unwin, 2nd ed., 1963), pp. 679–81.

epistemology. Yeats's interest in Kant derived from the nature of Kant's solution. With just a slight twist Kant's views can be turned into Yeats's insistence that the world is a product of the human mind. Space, time, the laws of causality, etc., are all forms of thought which create the world.

In the passage from Yeats quoted at the head of this chapter, romanticism in poetry and idealism in philosophy are equated, because both start from the view that the reality we perceive is the common creation of the human mind, and because both place great stress on the mind as the ground of experience and as constitutive of experience. Both provide freedom from the tyranny of fact which materialism and the earlier idealism of Plato and Berkeley alike seem to impose on the human mind. Both materialism and the idealism of Plato and Berkeley reduce mental activity to a mere mirroring of what is simply given.

I feel that an imaginative writer whose work draws him to philosophy must attach himself to some great historic school. My dreams and much psychic phenomena force me into a certain little-trodden way but I must not go too far from the main European track, which means in practice that I turn away from all attempts to make philosophy support science by starting with some form of 'fact' or 'datum'...[1]

Yeats's search for evidence to support his revolt against any theory of perception that guaranteed the validity of our knowledge of the external world only at the cost of reducing the perceiving mind to a cipher lay behind his involvement with spiritualism and his deep interest in Eastern philosophies. Despite his lack of familiarity with mathematics, he even read mathematicians and works about mathematics in the hope of finding his views confirmed. Because he found Eddington's position on these matters more congenial than Russell's he wrote to T. Sturge Moore that Eddington was the better mathematician. In another instance he found Henry Adam's interpretation of Poincaré's mathematics most congenial.

The mathematician Poincaré, according to Henry Adams, described space as the creation of our ancestors, meaning, I conclude, that mind split itself into mind and space. Space was to antiquity mind's inseparable 'other', coincident with objects, the table not the place it occupies. During the seventeenth century it was separated from mind and objects alike, and

---

[1] *W. B. Yeats and T. Sturge Moore, their Correspondence 1901–1937*, ed. Ursula Bridge (London: Routledge & Kegan Paul Ltd., 1953), p. 149.

thought of as a nothing yet a reality, the place not the table, with material objects separated from taste, smell, sound, from all the mathematicians could not measure, for its sole inhabitants, and this new matter and space, men were told, had preceded mind and would live after... yet... Berkeley ...established forever the subjectivity of space. No educated man today accepts the objective matter and space of popular science, and yet deductions made by those who believed in both dominate the world, and make possible the stimulation and condonation of revolutionary massacre and the multiplication of murderous weapons by substituting for the old humanity with its unique irreplaceable individuals something that can be chopped and measured like a piece of cheese; compel denial of the immortality of the soul by hiding from the mass of the people that the gravediggers have no place to bury us but in the human mind.[1]

Yeats's fascination with spiritualism, Eastern theology, and Poincaré's mathematics arose from the same desire to re-assert the mind's domination of the world about it as did his interest in Kant's philosophical views.

However, in certain respects Kant must have seemed to Yeats far too conservative. Like the German philosophers of the nineteenth century Yeats found the noumenal world of things-in-themselves an unnecessary postulate.

> And I declare my faith:
> I mock Plotinus' thought
> And cry in Plato's teeth,
> Death and life were not
> Till man made up the whole,
> Made lock, stock and barrel
> Out of his bitter soul,
> Aye, sun and moon and star, all,
> And further add to that
> That, being dead, we rise,
> Dream and so create
> Translunar Paradise.
>
> from Stanza III of 'The Tower'[2]

The major difference between Kant and the neo-Kantians arose because of the most glaring inconsistency in Kant's system. According to Kant, all our experience is in space and time. To continue

---

[1] W. B. Yeats, *Explorations* (New York: The Macmillan Company, 1961), pp. 435–6.

[2] *The Collected Poems of W. B. Yeats* (London: Macmillan and Co. Ltd., 1963 reprint of 1950 2nd ed.), p. 223.

Russell's analogy, we might say the blue spectacles are permanent; we can never get them off. Kant pointed out that this meant we could never know anything that was not in the phenomenal world, and he believed that this did away with the possibility of metaphysical knowledge, or with any knowledge about noumenal reality. But it soon became obvious that Kant's position was based upon a glaring paradox. It was a basic tenet of his philosophy that there was a noumenal reality behind the phenomenal. Our knowledge must be knowledge of the phenomenal world, the world of time and space. Kant's theory insisted that there was a noumenal world, a world of things-in-themselves, that provided the material of the phenomenal world. But since we could never get out of space and time he had no right to suppose a noumenal reality in the first place. For it was logically impossible to know anything not in space and time. One of the more popular reactions of the philosophers who succeeded Kant was simply to do away with the noumenal world, with the thing-in-itself. They substituted instead the notion that the collective human mind (usually called the Absolute or Absolute Ego) was all in all. This is a very strange notion, and one that I do not understand. At best it seems to mean that the mind, acting collectively, creates the world, and acting individually, receives what it previously created as sense data. In any case, Yeats seems to have been aware of the difficulty of Kant's position and on certain occasions even seems to be more neo-Kantian than Kantian. Writing to T. Sturge Moore about a book that Moore had recently published, Yeats objects to certain of Moore's views because he feels they contradict certain Kantian and neo-Kantian principles:

One sentence of yours I hoot at. You have taken it from some rascally philosopher science has corrupted and who, as Blake charged against his predecessors, insists on mystery, as the priests do, to enslave his betters. Hegel set free the human soul when he declared (the 'thing in itself', this theological echo had just been proved unnecessary) that 'there is nothing that is not accessible to intellect.' One must qualify this sentence but it still keeps sufficient truth. Your sentence dismissed the great philosophical systems, as the priests do, as works of imagination, and yet the logic of Kant and that built upon his conclusions cannot be so dismissed, unless it first be disproved, and that seems to me beyond us both. If one assumes, as I think you told me your brother did... that mind and matter are one in a 'prior' state, mind his still its secret entrance there.[1]

[1] *Yeats–Moore Correspondence*, p. 146.

In another letter in his correspondence with Moore, Yeats writes of Coleridge's 'restatement' of Kant. Coleridge's views correspond closely with those of the earlier neo-Kantians, especially Schelling. His debt to the early nineteenth-century German philosophers is well-known, and some of the material in the middle chapters of the *Biographia Literaria* is almost a paraphrase of Fichte, Schelling and Kant. The point that Yeats wants to bring out by referring to Coleridge seems to be this; according to Kant the limitations placed upon human knowledge arose because of our inability to come to grips with the noumenal world. The antinomies arose because what was true of the phenomenal world was not true of the noumenal world. Once we realised that one argument was true of the noumenal and the other was true of the phenomenal world, the contradiction disappears. This is, I think, what Yeats means by claiming that Kant thought the antinomies were 'regulative'. When Yeats goes on to say that Coleridge and the 'Platonists' think that the antinomies are 'constitutive', he means that since they reject the notion of the 'thing-in-itself', what they end up saying is that at one stage in its creation of the world the ego posits one side of the antinomy (that is, the noumenal world) and at another its opposite (the phenomenal world). The noumenal and phenomenal worlds are thus seen to be both the projections of the ego. In this strange and difficult passage Yeats even goes so far as to suggest that this is the meaning of what his 'instructors' are dictating to him as *A Vision*.

You say 'experience or our senses and emotions never set before us the one or render us conscious of it.' You mean either that 'regularity', 'universality', 'unity' are mere names and classifications (Berkeley), or that they are a priori forms or rules of the mind which only came into 'existence' through experience (Kant). Coleridge re-stated Kant in terms of Plato and argued that they were 'constitutive' not merely 'regulative', and he would be supported by various Platonists today. The mind is its own object and sees itself as the necessary truths. The mathematical scientists who say that all must vanish except a mathematical consciousness must think so too. If Kant is right the antinomy is in our method of reasoning; but if the Platonists are right may one not think that the antinomy is itself 'constitutive', that the consciousness by which we know ourselves and exist is itself irrational? I do not yet put this forward as certainly the thought of my instructors, but at present it seems the natural interpretation of their symbols. I shall wait at least twelve months before I publish. What are the gyres? Antiquity had both symbols. Is Satan truly an archangel?[1]

1 *Ibid.*, p. 131.

Yeats is being both playful and serious in this passage. This is typical of the way he treated all the philosophical ideas he became fond of. They are, as were the 'communications' from his instructors, 'metaphors for poetry'. He does not take philosophy completely seriously, but regards it as an adjunct to poetry. Whenever it threatens to usurp the place of poetry, Yeats turns it into a joke. However, Yeats was extremely concerned with the Kantian antinomies. In the strange document he called 'The Genealogical Tree of Revolution' (see Appendix A, p. 238) he divides modern thought into two main streams – each stream represents one way of resolving the antinomies – and poses a third possibility which is, I take it, his own view, and which is based upon his belief that the antinomies cannot be resolved. Further, in the section of *A Vision* entitled 'Stories of Michael Robartes and His Friends: An Extract From a Record Made by His Pupils' we find the following passages.

I found myself upon the third antinomy of Immanuel Kant, thesis: freedom; antithesis: necessity; but I restate it. Every action of man declares the soul's ultimate, particular freedom, and the soul's disappearance in God; declares that reality is a congeries of beings and a single being; nor is this antinomy an appearance imposed upon us by the form of thought but life itself which turns, now here, now there, a whirling and a bitterness.

After an age of necessity, truth, goodness, mechanism, science, democracy, abstraction, peace, comes an age of freedom, fiction, evil, kindred, art, aristocracy, particularity, war. Has our age burned to the socket?

Death cannot solve the antinomy: death and life are its expression. We come at birth into a multitude and after death would perish into the One did not a witch of Endor call us back, nor would she repent did we shriek with Samuel: 'Why hast thou disquieted me?' instead of slumbering upon that breast.

The marriage bed is the symbol of the solved antinomy, and were more than symbol could a man there lose and keep his identity, but he falls asleep. That sleep is the same as the sleep of death.[1]

and

Love contains all Kant's antinomies but it is the first that poisons our lives. Thesis, there is no beginning; antithesis, there is a beginning; or, as I prefer: thesis, there is an end; antithesis, there is no end. Exhausted by the cry that it can never end, my love ends: without that cry it were not love but desire, desire does not end. The anguish of birth and that of death cry

[1] W. B. Yeats, *A Vision* (New York: The Macmillan Company, 1961), p. 52.

out in the same instant. Life is not a series of emanations from divine reason such as the Cabalists imagine, but an irrational bitterness, no orderly descent from level to level, no waterfall but a whirlpool, a gyre.[1]

In this chapter I am primarily concerned with demonstrating at which point Yeats borrows from Kant, and it is my intention to leave for a later chapter the necessary attempt to discover what he made of the Kantian ideas he used. But, with reference to the first quotation, which deals with the antinomy of freedom and necessity, I would like to point out that Kant originally was concerned with the problem of freedom of the will in the sense that, according to the laws of cause and effect, which were supposed to operate in every instance in the phenomenal world, every event had a cause and thus there could be no freedom of the will. Kant claimed that this antinomy arose because the self was 'noumenal'. The activity of the self, willing, was beyond cause and effect. Thilly and Wood summarise this part of Kant's philosophy as follows:

Looked at through the spectacles of sense and understanding, man is a part of nature; in this aspect he has an empirical character, he is a link in a chain of causes and effects. But in reality man is an intelligible or spiritual being. To such a being the sense forms do not apply; such a being can originate acts. That man is cognizant of this power is attested by the fact that he holds himself responsible for his decisions and actions. Whenever we think of an act as a phenomenon, it must have a cause; as such it cannot be re-garded as spontaneously initiated. This interpretation cannot, however, be extended to the reason; we cannot say that the state in which reason determined the will was preceded by another state, and so on, for reason is not a phenomenon, and is not subject to the conditions of sensibility, such as time, space, causality. We cannot interpret its causality in the natural way, that is, expect a cause for everything it does. Reason, or the intelligible, or man as he is in himself, is the permanent condition of all his voluntary acts. A man's character, considered in its empirical aspect, is only the sensuous schema of his character considered in its super-sensuous aspect. The empirical is thus the way in which we image man or phenomenalize him.

Whether his position is tenable or not, Kant's meaning is quite clear. Every voluntary act is the direct expression of man's intelligible character, of pure reason: hence, man is a free agent, he is not a link in the chain of natural causes. Yet the act itself, when viewed as a phenomenon, is abso-lutely determined. Man in his intelligible aspect is a free agent, he origin-

[1] *Ibid.*, p. 40.

ates acts; but when these acts are perceived by a mind they are woven into a web of causation and are the effects of particular impulses, ideas, education, natural disposition, and so on.[1]

The neo-Kantians dropped the notion of the thing-in-itself while trying to maintain the main tenets of Kant's position. As an example of the sort of thing that resulted, consider these sentences from Russell:

Kant's immediate successor, Fichte (1726–1814), abandoned 'things in themselves', and carried subjectivism to a point which seems almost to involve a kind of insanity. He holds that the Ego is the only ultimate reality, and that it exists because it posits itself; the non-Ego, which has a subordinate reality, also exists only because the Ego posits it.[2]

Once the reader of Yeats's more abstruse prose has some idea of the intellectual antecedents of Yeats's more obscure notions they begin to seem less purely the result of his dabbling in spiritualism and more a continuation, however obscured, of the ideas which were current among the philosophers of the nineteenth century. For example, the passage entitled 'The Seven Propositions' which is first quoted by Ellmann in *The Identity of Yeats* owes as much (if not more) to Kantian and neo-Kantian speculation as it does to the spiritualism that interested Yeats at the beginning of the century

(I) Reality is a timeless and spaceless community of Spirits which perceive each other. Each Spirit is determined by and determines those it perceives, and each Spirit is unique.

(II) When these Spirits reflect themselves in time and space they still determine each other, and each Spirit sees the others as thoughts, images, objects of sense. Time and space are unreal.

(III) This reflection into time and space is only complete at certain moments of birth, or passivity, which recur many times in each destiny. At these moments the destiny receives its character until the next such moment from those Spirits who constitute the external universe. The horoscope is a set of geometrical relation between the Spirit's reflection and the principal masses in the universe and defines that character.

(IV) The emotional character of a timeless and spaceless spirit reflects itself as its position in time, its intellectual character as its position in space. The position of a Spirit in space and time therefore defines character.

---

[1] F. Thilly and L. Wood, *A History of Philosophy* (New York: Holt, Rinehart and Winston, 1956) p. 434.
[2] Russell, *History of Western Philosophy*. p. 690.

(V) Human life is either the struggle of a destiny against all other destinies, or a transformation of the character defined in the horoscope into timeless and spaceless existence. The whole passage from birth to birth should be an epitome of the whole passage of the universe through time and back into its timeless and spaceless condition.

(VI) The acts and nature of a Spirit during any one life are a section or abstraction of reality and are unhappy because incomplete. They are a gyre or part a gyre, whereas reality is a sphere.

(VII) Though the Spirits are determined by each other they cannot completely lose their freedom. Every possible statement or perception contains both terms – the self and that which it perceives or states.[1]

These propositions assume that the noumenal souls are responsible for the whole of the phenomenal world. In this they not only resemble the ideas of Kant and Fichte, but also bear a close resemblance to Hegel's idea of history as the unfolding of the Absolute (Ego) in the world. However, Yeats and Hegel differ in that Yeats's primary interest is in the role of the individual soul, and Hegel's interest is in the collective mind, or the Absolute. Thus, when Yeats restates Kant's third antinomy, it is not the phenomenal world which threatens the soul's freedom, but instead it is the collective mind which posits the phenomenal world and that limits individual freedom. 'Every action of man declares the soul's ultimate, particular freedom, and the soul's disappearance in God; declares that reality is a congeries of beings and a single being.'

The nature of the neo-Kantian position necessitates that there be some confusion about the nature of what is variously called Ego (note the capital E), the Absolute, or God. It is never clear whether or not the Absolute (the Ego, or God) has a separate ontological status. It is never clear whether reality is One being, the Absolute, or whether reality is a number of souls, who taken together, are the Absolute. As the last few quotations from Yeats indicate, he too does not make his views on this clear. In the passage from *A Vision* on the third antinomy the noumenal world is a single being, a Hegelian Absolute, yet in 'The Seven Propositions' this Absolute turns out to be a 'community of spirits'. But, when Yeats does use words like 'God', he seems to be more likely to mean a collection of

[1] Unpublished papers – first quoted in Richard Ellmann, *The Identity of Yeats* (New York: Oxford University Press, 1964), p. 236.

beings rather than one being. In fact, Yeats's notion of God, or the Absolute, is best summed up in the tag which he often quoted from Blake, 'God only acts or is in existing beings or men.'[1]

I do not think that it is possible to compare the kind of things that Kant and his successors were saying, and the kind of things Yeats said, without reaching the conclusion that something very similar is involved. In the passage from *A Vision* which discusses the third antinomy and in his 'Seven Propositions', Yeats has formulated a queer metaphysic which, although idiosyncratic, is definitely the result of his acquaintance with Kantian and neo-Kantian speculation.

'The Seven Propositions' are, as Ellmann realised, a continuation of the symbology of *A Vision*. In *A Vision* the central symbol is the cone or 'gyre'. By plotting the gyres of personality we can know all we need to know of a person's psychological make-up, and the historical gyres are just as informative about the nature of any period – past, present, or future. When Yeats first describes the gyre he defines it in the following manner:

A line is a movement without extension, and so symbolical of time – subjectivity – Berkeley's stream of ideas – in Plotinus it is apparently 'sensation' – and a plane cutting it at right angles is symbolical of space or objectivity. Line and plane are combined in a gyre which must expand or contract according to whether mind grows in objectivity or subjectivity.

And he footnotes this passage with

Giovanni Gentile summarises Kant on time and space as follows: 'Kant said that space is a form of external sense. He meant that we represent nature, that is what we call the external world and think of as having been in existence before our knowledge and spiritual life began, in space, that we represent the multiplicity of the objects of our internal experience, or what we distinguish as diverse and manifold in the development of our spiritual life, not in space but in time.' (*Theory of Mind as Pure Art*, chap. 1/ix, H. Wildon Carr's translation.) He thinks these definitions which seem to separate time and space from one another require restatement. It will be seen, however, when I come to what I have called the Four Principles, that my symbols imply his description of time as spatialising act.[2]

Yeats believed in a cyclical movement in history and in personal immortality. The central idea behind *A Vision* is that each '*daimon*' or spirit projects itself into time and space an infinite number of

---

[1] *Yeats–Moore Correspondence*, p. 80.   [2] Yeats, *A Vision*, p. 70.

times, and that its position in time and space during each incarnation determines its character. From the gyres we can read this position in time and space, and thus the character of the *daimon* in that particular reincarnation. The sum total of these individual projections determines the nature of events and thus if we could read the pattern of these projections in general we would be in a position to establish the nature of each historic period. The connection between Yeats's historiography and Hegel's, although complicated, is quite clear. I do not know how seriously Yeats took all this, nor how seriously he intended his readers to take it, but the controlling image is once again considerably influenced by Kantian and neo-Kantian terminology and eschatology.

Both Yeats's theory of history and Hegel's centre in the premise that history is a function of consciousness. In neither theory is it perfectly clear just whose consciousness is under discussion. But the Hegelian theory seems, on the whole, to be that the Absolute realises itself through the individual, and this absolute, in its search for self-realisation, determines and controls the individual consciousness. Yeats's theory seems to be geometrically opposed. The *Zeitgeist*, instead of being an independent principle which operates through the individual and determines the course of history and the life of the individual, is no more than the product or function of all individual consciousnesses. While Yeats and Hegel both believed that it was consciousness or ego which constituted ultimate reality, Hegel's absolute was a monistic consciousness which determined and directed all other consciousnesses, while Yeats's theory saw the consciousness of an age as simply the sum of the independent and self-determined egos. Yeats's ambivalent attitude towards Hegel arose because, while they shared the belief that reality was consciousness, Yeats could not stomach Hegel's determinism and lack of respect for the individual ego.

The purpose of this chapter has been to establish that Yeats was influenced by his reading of Kant and the neo-Kantians, and to show which of their views he utilised. I have not tried to show that Yeats 'believed' in Kantianism, or that he was a Kantian. To begin with I do not know what kind of evidence would be necessary to substantiate such a claim. But more important I do not believe that Yeats was a Kantian, or that his philosophical views can be characterised in this manner. Yeats was primarily concerned with writing poetry. He found the issues documented in the previous pages cogenial for a number of reasons. First, he was not the sort of romantic who is interested in a private world. Kant provided a way of thinking that allowed Yeats to maintain his belief in the sovereignty of the human intellect and the common human imagination, without diluting his sense of a common reality. Secondly, Kant's work provided him with an adequate account of the importance of intellect, and an adequate account of the limits placed on the intellect. The consequence of the theory was that this sense of the reality of the phenomenal world did not make it necessary for him to abandon his sense of the unknowable, the mystery behind events. And most important, the philosophy that he called 'idealist' seemed to give the individual soul its proper emphasis.

> Considering that...
> The soul recovers radical innocence
> And learns at last that it is self-delighting,
> Self-appeasing, self-affrighting,
> And that its own sweet will is Heaven's will...
>
> from 'A Prayer for my Daughter'
> (*Collected Poems*, pp. 213–14)

But although Yeats found these views congenial, here, as always, he refuses to let himself be forced into a position which, by its rigidity, by its formal aspects, would interfere with what must always be the primary concern of the poet – a lively and active attempt to get at the raw materials of experience:

My imagination was for a time haunted by figures that, muttering 'The great systems', held out to me the sun-dried skeletons of birds, and it seemed to me that this image was meant to turn my thoughts to the living bird. That bird signifies truth when it eats, evacuates, builds its nest, engenders, feeds its young; do not all intelligible truths lie in its passage from egg to dust? Passages written by Japanese monks on attaining Nirvana, and one by an Indian, run in my head. 'I sit upon the side of the mountain and look at a little farm. I say to the old farmer, "How many times have you mortgaged your farm and paid off the mortgage?" "I take pleasure in the sound of the rushes." No more does the young man come from behind the embroidered curtain amid the sweet clouds of incense; he goes among his friends, he goes among the flute-players; something very nice has happened to the young man, but he can only tell it to his sweetheart.' 'You ask me what is my religion and I hit you upon the mouth. Ah! Ah! The lightning crosses the heavens, it passes from end to end of the heavens. Ah! Ah!'[1]

[1] Yeats, *A Vision*, p. 214.

Towards a reading of the poems: beginnings

The interpretation of the later poetry of Yeats provides certain difficulties which, although not unique, are more than usually troublesome. By the time Yeats reached middle age he was very widely read, and the vast knowledge he had accumulated began to find its way into his poetry. This might not be a problem had Yeats's poetry been discursive. However, his poetry is almost always organised around a series of central images that dominate the minds of his readers to such an extent that the poems escape the close scrutiny which is necessary in order to discover their intellectual subtlety. Even when it is recognised that Yeats is writing poetry which is intellectual in nature, the resulting interpretations are often no more successful. The academic habit of searching for 'sources' and 'influences', although illuminating, may be as misleading as it is informative. Yeats's intellect was of the highest order; and his borrowings were never allowed to determine the meaning of his poetry.

Whenever Yeats used an image or idea from the vast lore he had accumulated, he adapted it to his purpose. More than most poets, he was that kind of intellectual who derives pleasure from the juxtaposition of seemingly disparate ideas, or from standing an idea on its head. As a result his poetry is highly intelligent, often difficult, and even more often, amusing, even when it is most serious. In order to read poetry of this sort what is most necessary is close attention to the text of the poem, for Yeats's meaning is rarely the same as the 'meaning' which his sources might lead one to expect.

I would like to illustrate the difficulties that arise in reading this kind of poetry by interpreting the four poems that form the end of the volume *Words for Music Perhaps* (*Collected Poems*, pp. 305–7).

XXII

TOM THE LUNATIC

Sang old Tom the lunatic
That sleeps under the canopy:

'What change has put my thoughts astray
And eyes that had so keen a sight?
What has turned to smoking wick
Nature's pure unchanging light?

'Huddon and Duddon and Daniel O'Leary,
Holy Joe, the beggar-man,
Wenching, drinking, still remain
Or sing a penance on the road;
Something made these eyeballs weary
That blinked and saw them in a shroud.

'Whatever stands in field or flood,
Bird, beast, fish or man,
Mare or stallion, cock or hen,
Stands in God's unchanging eye
In all the vigour of its blood;
In that faith I live or die.'

XXIII

TOM AT CRUACHAN

On Cruachan's plain slept he
That must sing in a rhyme
What most could shake his soul:
'The stallion Eternity
Mounted the mare of Time,
'Gat the foal of the world.'

XXIV

OLD TOM AGAIN

Things out of perfection sail,
And all their swelling canvas wear,
Nor shall the self-begotten fail
Though fantastic men suppose
Building-yard and stormy shore,
Winding-sheet and swaddling-clothes.

XXV

THE DELPHIC ORACLE UPON PLOTINUS

Behold that great Plotinus swim,
Buffeted by such seas;
Bland Rhadamanthus beckons him,
But the Golden Race looks dim,
Salt blood blocks his eyes.

> Scattered on the level grass
> Or winding through the grove
> Plato there and Minos pass,
> There stately Pythagoras
> And all the choir of Love.

It is usually claimed that these poems represent several moods; that the first is Yeats being Berkeleyan, and that the third and fourth are Yeats being a Platonist. The second gets relatively little attention because it cannot be so easily classified. I hope to be able to demonstrate that these poems are a unity, and that they are not, in whole or in part, Berkeleyan or Platonic, but that the Platonic and Berkelyan ideas which Yeats uses are being twisted and juggled to produce something that is closer to the Kantian ideas which were documented in the first chapter, but is, in the final analysis, idiosyncratic.

As for the first poem, it is usually remarked that Yeats has Berkeley in mind, the justification for this inference being that the last stanza, with its reference to 'God's unchanging eye', sounds like what every philosophical text says Berkeley said. But, if you read those textbooks it is soon obvious that whatever stands in God's eye should not stand in all 'the vigour of its blood' if Yeats is indeed following Berkeley. For Berkeley's theory stated that God's perceiving things simply guaranteed the normal process of events; according to Berkeley God's eye might well be unchanging, but the things perceived by God would decay and change nevertheless. This is one of the things Yeats objected to when he claimed that Berkeley was realist and idealist alike – the theory did not seem to alter anything. To quote the well-known limerick:

> There was a young man who said, 'God
> Must think it exceedingly odd
> If he finds that this tree
> Continues to be
> When there's no one about in the Quad.'

and the reply

> Dear Sir, your astonishment's odd;
> I am always about in the Quad.
> And that's why the tree
> Will continue to be,
> Since observed by yours faithfully, God.

The tree will decay and die too – absolutely nothing is changed.

The most probable source of the last stanza of Yeats's poem, if it is sources we are looking for, is the idea of the *Anima Mundi* in the writings of Henry More. There is at least one Ph.D thesis on the poetry of Yeats that remains to be done, and that is to trace the influence of that singular group of men, the Cambridge Platonists, on their more singular reader, W. B. Yeats. In any event, compare the last stanza of this poem with Stanza XIV of Canto I of Henry More's 'Psychozoia or The Life of the Soul'.

> 'Whatever stands in field or flood,
> Bird, beast, fish or man,
> Mare or stallion, cock or hen,
> Stands in God's unchanging eye
> In all the vigour of its blood;
> In that faith I live or die.'

with

> Not that his forms increase, or that they die:
> For Aeon-land, which men Idea call,
> Is nought but life in full serenity,
> *Vigour of life is root, stock, branch, and all;*
> *Nought here increaseth, nought here hath its fall:*
> *For Æons Kingdoms always perfect stand,*
> *Birds, Beasts, Fields, Springs, Plants, Men and Minerall*
> *To perfectness nought added be there can.*
> This Aeon also hight/Autolacon and On.[1]

But Aeon-land is not this world, but a world which, in More's ontological scale is between the world of the forms of Plato and the sensible world. Yeats's fields are less Elysian than this. More is talking about *Anima Mundi*; Yeats's poem is about this world.

These considerations preclude our getting any help in reading the poem from either More or Berkeley, and suggest that the best place to look for Yeats's meaning is Yeats's poem and not his sources. There are a number of statements in the poem which, once reconciled, provide the meaning involved in the poem. In the last stanza we are told that whatever stands, stands because it is 'in God's unchanging eye'. Yet in the first two stanzas of the poem Tom was not aware of this:

> 'What change has put my thoughts astray
> And eyes that had so keen a sight?

[1] Henry More, The *Philosophical Poems of Henry More* (Manchester: Manchester University Press, 1931), p. 16.

What has turned to smoking wick
Nature's pure unchanging light?

'Huddon and Duddon and Daniel O'Leary,
Holy Joe, the beggar-man,
Wenching, drinking, still remain
Or sing a penance on the road;
Something made these eyeballs weary
That blinked and saw them in a shroud.

The 'pure unchanging light' of nature is, one may assume, the equivalent of God's unchanging eye. But in the first stanza we have also learned that this light is the light of Tom the Lunatic's eye – which has only temporarily been obliterated by the 'change'. In the second stanza we learn that this change has made Tom's eyeballs weary, and as a result, he fails to see things properly. The point seems to be that the 'unchanging light' of nature is the same light that previously shone through Tom's eyes; and this light reveals, not ideas in the kingdom of Aeon, but the full phenomenological glory of the fields and floods of the spatio-temporal world. Despite Tom's occasional lapses from the celebration of the vigour and energy of the temporal world, God is continually aware of this vigour and energy. And the light illuminating the glories of this world to God is available to Tom; when his eyeballs are not wearied he, too, is aware of the vigour and energy of the animals and men. However, the poem means something more than this. There is a passage in the Yeats–Moore correspondence which is relevant. When Sturge Moore wrote to Yeats that:

Berkeley had resort to God to explain objective reality; God went on thinking and so his thoughts remained just as the objective reality does; in fact there was only a verbal difference between the two. It matters little whether I call a tree a tree or God's thoughts of a tree if both have exactly the same properties. The only objection to doing the latter is that it is less simple and less concise.

Yeats replied:

I agree...about the later Berkeley who was a Platonist. My Berkeley is the Berkeley of the Commonplace Book, and it is this Berkeley who has influenced the Italians. The essential sentence is of course 'things only exist in being perceived' and I can only call that perception God's when I add Blake's 'God only acts or is in existing beings or men.'[1]

[1] *Yeats–Moore Correspondence*, pp. 78–80.

The relevance to the poem seems to be that God, that is the sum of existing beings or men, continues to guarantee the fecundity of the universe. Tom has fallen out of step – he has failed to look at the world correctly, to see with nature's pure light (or God's eye if we remember that God only is or acts in existing beings or men). It should be noted that Tom the Lunatic's views are closer to what has been described as a Kantian position than to that usually ascribed to Berkeley or to the Platonists. In fact when Yeats gets through revising Berkeley, Berkeley turns out to be more Kantian than Berkeleyan. In the final analysis, of course, Yeats's poem defies classification.

The same kind of intellectual playfulness is at work in the three poems which follow 'Tom the Lunatic'. In these poems, however, the source material being used is not from Berkeley or the Cambridge Platonists but Plato. But more important, in these three poems Yeats's intellectual revisions are made by reversing the direction of certain characteristic Platonic images, rather than by explicit statements on points of doctrine such as were found in the previous poem.

Probably the easiest way to discover Yeats's attitude to Platonism is to call attention to the severe attack on Plato and Plotinus made in the section from 'The Tower' which was quoted in Chapter I (p. 8). As we saw then, Yeats's idealism is not the idealism of either Plato or Plotinus, although Plotinus is often closer to Yeats's position than any of the philosophers who preceded Kant except Berkeley. In this respect the note on 'The Tower' which he published along with the poem (*Collected Poems*, p. 533) is extremely interesting:

When I wrote the lines about Plato and Plotinus I forgot that it is something in our own eyes that makes us see them as all transcendence. Has not Plotinus written: 'Let every soul recall, then, at the outset the truth that soul is the author of all living things, that it has breathed the life into them all, whatever is nourished by earth and sea, all the creatures of the air, the divine stars in the sky; it is the maker of the sun; itself formed and ordered this vast heaven and conducts all that rhythmic motion – and it is a principle distinct from all these to which it gives law and movement and life, and it must of necessity be more honourable than they, for they gather or dissolve as soul brings them life or abandons them, but soul, since it never can abandon itself, is of eternal being.'?

Yeats was eclectic in all things, and especially in his borrowings when he is dealing with philosophical or quasi-philosophical subjects. What he gets from Kantianism is a general direction and not a dogma. As a result, his philosophical views cannot be called categorically anti-Platonic. What can be said with certainty, however, is that Yeats consistently refuses any commerce with the popular mixture of Christianity and Plato which is served up as Platonism in most discussions of ideas in literature. The distinction I am drawing, between what Plato, Plotinus, and the other neo-Platonists actually said, and the generalised and sometimes misleading views which are ascribed to them, is, I think of great importance in reading Yeats. The beautiful passage which Yeats quotes in connection with 'The Tower' does not fit what has come to be accepted as Platonism nor does it fit with most of what Plato and Plotinus believed. But it does fit with the general tendency of Yeats's thought, and as a result some of the same images that Plotinus employed are used by Yeats in the very passage of 'The Tower' which repudiates Plato and Plotinus.

It is often assumed that because Yeats uses Platonic and neo-Platonic images, he must necessarily be a Platonist. What happens when this kind of 'evidence' is used to show that Yeats is usually, or even sometimes a Platonist, can be found in almost every critical work on the poetry. Even the best of Yeats's critics continually fall into this trap. Consider this comment on 'Old Tom Again' in Ellmann's *The Identity of Yeats* (p. 232):

While Yeats frequently takes the position, as in the last of the Gregory poems, that the world, lamentable though it is, exists, he sometimes suggests, with Blake or the Hindu seers, that this world is a fiction, and death mere fantasy. So he declares in 'Old Tom Again':

> Things out of perfection sail,
> And all their swelling canvas wear,
> Nor shall the self-begotten fail
> Though fantastic men suppose
> Building-yard and stormy shore,
> Winding-sheet and swaddling-clothes.

This is the opposite position of that of 'The Tower' where life and death are real precisely because 'fantastic men' have imagined them so.

What Ellmann implies is that here Plato is preferred to Kant and Berkeley. But a careful look at the poem will show that 'Old Tom Again' is anti-Platonic in much the same way as the passage from

'The Tower' and the first poem in the series. However, because the two middle poems of the series are the most closely connected poems in the group a short comment should be made about 'Tom at Cruachan' before returning to 'Old Tom Again'. 'Tom at Cruachan' is not a difficult poem. Its primary function is to inform us that what most delights the speaker of the previous poem and the one to follow is the production of the world. This agrees with what has been previously said about 'Tom the Lunatic' and provides a clue to what follows in 'Old Tom Again'.

In 'Old Tom Again' the 'perfection' which is referred to in the first line is the Kingdom of the stallion Eternity and the voyage being described is a voyage through the world which is the product of the mounting of Time by Eternity. The voyage is a voyage across water because Yeats is thinking of the neo-Platonic metaphor for life. This metaphor, which is also used in the poem which follows, 'The Delphic Oracle Upon Plotinus', supposed that life was a voyage through a rough and turbulent sea which was continually disturbed by storms of sensuality. At the end of the voyage was the neo-Platonic heaven, a supra-sensible world of forms which were immutable (and beyond our senses). Life was a progress into this heaven, and to fail to make the crossing, to fall back into the world of matter, was disastrous. To achieve a successful crossing and to enter the world of forms was a true second birth much like the Christian birth in Christ. In the two poems being discussed Yeats seems to be accepting the Platonic ontology. But in the first of these poems it is quite obvious that the production of the sensible world, which to Plato and Plotinus was a fall, is what interests and delights the speaker. The entry of Platonic forms into the spatio-temporal world produces the reality we experience – the 'foal of the world'.

In 'Old Tom Again' the speaker, who is a sensual strange old man, and the male counterpart of Crazy Jane in the same volume, continues where he has left off. 'Things' sail *out* of perfection, become sensible objects. This is, says Tom, like the skeleton of a sailing vessel filling out its canvases and moving before the wind. These self-begotten images – or souls, as we shall see when considering the last of the poems – will not fail because they have already achieved their objective and are in full sail. The 'self-begotten' have to sail out of perfection; they will themselves on their journeys, and are thus 'self-begotten'. And this Tom tells us, is true despite what the 'fantastic men' or Platonists, Christians etc., suppose. These men mistakenly think that the voyage from the building-yard (which is the equivalent to the coupling of 'Time' and 'Eternity' in the first stanza and which stands for entrance into the sensible world) to the stormy shore of death, is a voyage from the winding-sheet to swaddling-clothes. That is, they think of the voyage from the sensual to the supra-sensual as a voyage from death to life. And conversely they think the voyage from the supra-sensual (building-yard) to the sensual is a voyage from life into death. But, claims Tom, the voyage leads out of the skeletal world of pure forms to the life of the sensible world. For the platonist, the form is all important, and the canvas a mere distraction. For Yeats's lunatic the swelling canvas is the realisation of the form. The ship is only interesting under sail. To prefer to be becalmed in heaven, is, for Yeats and his 'lunatic', a truly fantastic desire. Ellmann misreads the poem because he does not recognise that Yeats's lunatic rejects a view that is not his own because he recognises how truly fantastic is the transcendentalist rejection of the world of the senses.

The last poem continues the image and further illustrates Yeats's ability to borrow from various sources, and to use diverse material in his own particular way. Porphyry had reported that the Delphic Oracle had declared that Plotinus had successfully crossed the sea of life and found his way to the Isle of the Blessed, which was inhabited by Plato, Rhadamanthus, Minos, Pythagoras and the choir of Love. This is, of course, one of the many variants of the traditional image which Yeats had used in the previous poems. It is important to note, however, that Plotinus, who is going in the opposite direction to the ships in the previous poem, is having a difficult time. Yeats's note on 'The Tower', quoted earlier, stated that Plotinus was not 'all transcendence', and in the poem at hand this is reflected by the fact that it is not only the turbulent sea which interferes with Plotinus's crossing but his own sensuality, his own 'salt blood'. The oracle does not tell us whether or not Plotinus succeeds in his crossing; that is a question which is answered in a later poem. Nor are we too sure that the object of Plotinus's energy is worth his trouble. Compared to the turbulence and energy of the seas of sense and sensuality Rhadamanthus looks 'bland' (hardly a satisfactory epithet from the standpoint of neo-Platonic orthodoxy) and the Golden Race 'looks dim', is almost obscured by Plotinus's own sensuality.

This group of poems reflects the anti-Platonic direction of Yeats's poetry; that is, they reflect Yeats's dislike for popular Platonic and Christian spirituality and other-worldliness. Although these poems utilise ideas and images from Plato, the neo-Platonists, Berkeley and Henry More, the poems which result are primarily concerned with the vigour and energy of the phenomenal world.

The 'fantastic men' form an orthodoxy that preaches the abandonment of the world. In the volume that these poems conclude, only 'Crazy Jane' and 'Tom the Lunatic', outcasts who live on the fringe of society, are able to challenge the orthodox wisdom of the Bishop and the Philosopher, and to insist that we follow our common sense and our senses and rejoice in this world. It is fitting that the last poem in the volume pictures Plotinus struggling to overcome the common impulse of humanity, struggling to overcome his 'salt blood'.

II

Yeats's usual strategy is not to write long discursive poems, but to utilise certain traditional myths, images and metaphors; and by changing these myths, metaphors and images to suggest his own usually unorthodox view. Of these myths none are more important in the poetry than the ideas of individual immortality and the repetitiveness of history. As was mentioned earlier Yeats connected these two ideas together, and made of them one idea. In his introduction to 'The Resurrection' he says:

Yet there is a third myth or philosophy that has made an equal stir in the world. Ptolemy thought the procession of the equinoxes moved at the rate of a degree every hundred years, and that somewhere about the time of Christ and Caesar the equinoctial sun had returned to its original place in the constellations, completing and recommencing the thirty-six thousand years, or three hundred and sixty incarnations of a hundred years apiece, of Plato's man of Ur. Hitherto almost every philosopher had some different measure for the Greatest Year, but this Platonic Year, as it was called, soon displaced all others; it was a Christian heresy in the twelfth century, and in the East, multiplied by twelve as if it were but a month of a still greater year, it became the Manvantra of 432,000 years, until animated by the Indian jungle it generated new noughts and multiplied itself into Kalpas.

It was perhaps obvious, when Plotinus substituted the archetypes of individual men in all their possible incarnations for a limited number of Platonic Ideas, that a Greatest Year for whale and gudgeon alike must exhaust the multiplication table. Whatever its length, it divided, and so did every unit whose multiple it was, into waxing and waning, day and night, or summer and winter. There was everywhere a conflict like that of my play between two principles or 'elemental forms of the mind', each 'living the other's life, dying the other's death'. I have a Chinese painting of three old sages sitting together, one with a deer at his side, one with a scroll open at the symbol of yin and yen, those two forms that whirl perpetually, creating and re-creating all things. But because of our modern discovery that the equinox shifts its ground more rapidly than Ptolemy believed, one must, somebody says, invent a new symbolic scheme. No, a thousand times no; I insist that the equinox does shift a degree in a hundred years; anything else would lead to confusion.

All ancient nations believed in the re-birth of the soul and had probably empirical evidence like that Lafcadio Hearn found among the Japanese. In our time Schopenhauer believed it, and McTaggart thinks Hegel did, though lack of interest in the individual soul has kept him silent. It is the foundation of McTaggart's own philosophical system.[1] Cardinal Mercier saw no evidence for it, but did not think it heretical; and its rejection compelled the sincere and noble Von Hugel to say that children dead too young to have earned Heaven suffered no wrong, never having heard of a better place than Limbo. Even though we think temporal existence illusionary it cannot be capricious; it is what Plotinus called the characteristic act of the soul and must reflect the soul's coherence. All our thought seems to lead by antithesis to some new affirmation of the supernatural. In a few years perhaps we may have much empirical evidence, the only evidence that moves the mass of men today, that man has lived many times; there is some not yet perfectly examined – I think of that Professor's daughter in Palermo. This belief held by Plato and Plotinus, and supported by weighty argument, resembles the mathematical doctrines of Einstein before the experimental proof of the curvature of light.

We may come to think that nothing exists but a stream of souls, that all knowledge is biography, and with Plotinus that every soul is unique; that these souls, these eternal archetypes, combine into greater units as days and nights into months, months into years, and at last into the final unit that differs in nothing from that which they were at the beginning: everywhere that antinomy of the One and the Many that Plato thought in his Parmenides insoluble, though Blake thought it soluble 'at the bottom of the grave'. Such belief may arise from Communism by antithesis, declaring at last even to the common ear that all things have value according to the clarity of their expression of themselves, and not as functions of changing economic conditions or as an excuse for some Utopia. There is perhaps no final happy state except in so far as man may gradually grow better; escape may be for individuals alone who know how to exhaust their pos-

---

[1] Schopenhauer, Hegel and McTaggart were neo-Kantian philosophers.

sible lives, to set, as it were, the hands of the clock racing. Perhaps we shall learn to accept even innumerable lives with happy humility – 'I have been always an insect in the roots of the grass' – and putting aside calculating scruples be ever ready to wager all upon the dice.

Even our best histories treat men as function. Why must I think the victorious cause the better? Why should Mommsen think the less of Cicero because Caesar beat him? I am satisfied, the Platonic Year in my head, to find but drama. I prefer that the defeated cause should be more vividly described than that which has the advertisement of victory.[1]

Yeats's reasons for taking this seriously, or at least as seriously as he did take it, are set out in his introduction to 'The Words Upon the Window-pane' (p. 20).

I suggest to the Cellars and the Garrets that though history is too short to change either the idea of progress or the eternal circuit into scientific fact, the eternal circuit may best suit our pre-occupation with the soul's salvation, our individualism, our solitude. Besides we love antiquity, and that other idea – progress – the sole religious myth of modern man is only two hundred years old.

As in *A Vision*, however, this idea is usually modified by Yeats's reading of Kantian and neo-Kantian philosophy. According to both Plato and Plotinus, one could escape from the wheel, could achieve a unity with the one, and thus lose personality and escape re-birth. In Yeats's cosmology, however, there is nothing beyond the human mind. The supra-sensual world is simply mind, and this mind cannot be confused with another greater being:

II

Many times man lives and dies
Between his two eternities,
That of race and that of soul,
And ancient Ireland knew it all.
Whether man die in his bed
Or the rifle knocks him dead,
A brief parting from those dear
Is the worst man has to fear.
Though grave-diggers' toil is long,
Sharp their spades, their muscles strong,
They but thrust their buried men
Back in the human mind again.[2]

Stanza II from 'Under Ben Bulben'
(*Collected Poems*, p. 398)

[1] Yeats, introduction to 'The Resurrection', *Wheels and Butterflies*, pp. 105–9.
[2] See Chapter I for the genesis of this idea in the prose.

Furthermore, Yeats's cosmology disdains the opportunity of release. The poem 'A Dialogue of Self and Soul' (*Collected Poems*, pp. 265–7) is based upon the choice between a noumenal and a phenomenal world, between a retreat into pure mind or the repeated fall into matter.

A DIALOGUE OF SELF AND SOUL

I

My Soul. I summon to the winding ancient stair;
    Set all your mind upon the steep ascent,
    Upon the broken, crumbling battlement,
    Upon the breathless starlit air,
    Upon the star that marks the hidden pole;
    Fix every wandering thought upon
    That quarter where all thought is done:
    Who can distinguish darkness from the soul?

My Self. The consecrated blade upon my knees
    Is Sato's ancient blade, still as it was,
    Still razor-keen, still like a looking-glass
    Unspotted by the centuries;
    That flowering, silken, old embroidery, torn
    From some court-lady's dress and round
    The wooden scabbard bound and wound,
    Can, tattered, still protect, faded adorn.

My Soul. Why should the imagination of a man
    Long past his prime remember things that are
    Emblematical of love and war?
    Think of ancestral night that can,
    If but imagination scorn the earth
    And intellect its wandering
    To this and that and t'other thing,
    Deliver from the crime of death and birth.

My Self. Montashigi, third of his family, fashioned it
    Five hundred years ago, about it lie
    Flowers from I know not what embroidery –
    Heart's purple – and all these I set
    For emblems of the day against the tower
    Emblematical of the night,
    And claim as by a soldier's right
    A charter to commit the crime once more.

My Soul. Such fullness in that quarter overflows
And falls into the basin of the mind
That man is stricken deaf and dumb and blind,
For intellect no longer knows
Is from the *Ought*, or *Knower* from the *Known* –
That is to say, ascends to Heaven;
Only the dead can be forgiven;
But when I think of that my tongue's a stone.

II

My Self. A living man is blind and drinks his drop.
What matter if the ditches are impure?
What matter if I live it all once more?
Endure that toil of growing up;
Ignominy of boyhood; the distress
Of boyhood changing into man;
The unfinished man and his pain
Brought face to face with his own clumsiness;

The finished man among his enemies? –
How in the name of Heaven can he escape
That defiling and disfigured shape
The mirror of malicious eyes
Casts upon his eyes until at last
He thinks that shape must be his shape?
And what's the good of an escape
If honour find him in the wintry blast?

I am content to live it all again
And yet again, if it be life to pitch
Into the frog-spawn of a blind man's ditch,
A blind man battering blind men;
Or into that most fecund ditch of all,
The folly that man does
Or must suffer, if he woos
A proud woman not kindred of his soul.

I am content to follow to its source
Every event in action or in thought;
Measure the lot; forgive myself the lot!
When such as I cast out remorse
So great a sweetness flows into the breast
We must laugh and we must sing,
We are blest by everything,
Everything we look upon is blest.

This poem expresses, as do 'Vacillation' and 'Under Ben Bulben', Yeats's belief that to choose escape from the wheel of death and life was to avoid human responsibility, and an act of cowardice. Furthermore, we may note that once again Yeats has employed traditional Platonic and neo-Platonic metaphors in order to deny the theological and philosophical position the mythology was used to illustrate. The notion of reincarnation was used by Plato and the neo-Platonists to illustrate the value of turning away from the things of the world. One of the ways which the myth was couched was in terms of sight; that is, to be aware of this world is to be blind to heaven. Often it was claimed that each man had two '*daimons*', and that in order to ascend to heaven the individual had to blind his 'natal *daimon*'. So both self and soul claim that it is valuable to be blind, but disagree about what it is that we should not see. Further, the living man who is blind is blind because he has drunk of the cup of oblivion. According to the myth each soul goes to heaven for a short period and when it leaves is forced to drink and thus forget the glories of heaven. Yeats playfully suggests that this libation is really the 'drop' which the stage Irishman enjoys so much. Instead of being a 'drop' which deprives us of the pleasure of heaven, and begins our journey downward into a life that must be lived through simply so we can return to heaven, Yeats's drop is a drop which frees us from the dream of heaven, and so provides us with the secular blessedness which is no more, and no less, than the acceptance of the conditions of life.

The point to the Platonic myth was that if you practised the right kind of blindness you would be forever liberated from the round of life and death and could remain permanently in heaven. Yeats insists that if you simply forget about heaven you are able to achieve a secular blessedness. That is, once you get rid of notions of permanence, of pure form, you are able to achieve a proper perspective.

> When such as I cast out remorse
> So great a sweetness flows into the breast
> We must laugh and we must sing,
> We are blest by everything,
> Everything we look upon is blest.

The poems 'At Algeciras – A Meditation before Death' and 'Mohini Chatterjee' were originally one poem in two sections, 'At

Algeciras – A Meditation Upon Death' being the first section and 'Mohini Chatterjee' the second.

AT ALGECIRAS – A MEDITATION UPON DEATH

The heron-billed pale cattle-birds
That feed on some foul parasite
Of the Moroccan flocks and herds
Cross the narrow Straits to light
In the rich midnight of the garden trees
Till the dawn break upon those mingled seas.

Often at evening when a boy
Would I carry to a friend –
Hoping more substantial ioy
Did an older mind commend –
Not such as are in Newton's metaphor,
But actual shells of Rosses' level shore.

Greater glory in the sun,
An evening chill upon the air,
Bid imagination run
Much on the Great Questioner;
What He can question, what if questioned I
Can with a fitting confidence reply.

(Collected Poems, p. 278)

MOHINI CHATTERJEE

I asked if I should pray,
But the Brahmin said,
'Pray for nothing, say
Every night in bed,
"I have been a king,
I have been a slave,
Nor is there anything,
Fool, rascal, knave,
That I have not been,
And yet upon my breast
A myriad heads have lain."'

That he might set at rest
A boy's turbulent days
Mohini Chatterjee
Spoke these, or words like these.
I add in commentary,
'Old lovers yet may have

33

All that time denied –
Grave is heaped on grave
That they be satisfied –
Over the blackened earth
The old troops parade,
Birth is heaped on birth
That such cannonade
May thunder time away,
Birth-hour and death-hour meet,
Or, as great sages say,
Men dance on deathless feet.'

(*Collected Poems*, pp. 279–80)

The first stanza of 'At Algeciras' is a symbol of the passage from life to death and back to life, of the familiar notion of reincarnation. It is an evocation of the death Yeats had begun to feel coming upon him. In the second stanza Yeats suggests that as a boy he was concerned with the actual physical world. Newton said that he felt that his theorising sometimes seemed to him a child's search for a pretty pebble or shell, an almost aesthetic and ethereal pursuit. Yeats claims that his youth was spent in search of the more substantial joy of the actual.

In the third stanza he says that in his old age ('Evening chill upon the air') he is concerned with heaven. He now sees his life from the position of the soul in the previous poem, and wishes it to be a justification for entrance into heaven. How shall he be judged by the 'Great Questioner'? (This phrase is probably ironically intended.)

What He can question, what if quest end I
Can with a fitting confidence reply.

This is the religious attitude, an attitude which sees human existence from the point of view of a transcendental God, a heaven and a heaven-ordained ethic. It is summed up in the first line of the next section of the original poem. 'I asked if I should pray'. To this question Yeats gets an answer which parallels the Platonic or Christian distaste of this world. Mohini Chatterjee's advice suggests an Eastern abnegation of desire that is much like the Platonic. Both the view that is indicated in 'At Algeciras' and the viewpoint of Mohini Chatterjee reject the world and worldly things as somehow unimportant. But in the last stanza Yeats reverses the

34

direction by suggesting that the very purpose of reincarnation is to satisfy man's desire for the things of this world. His 'commentary' reverses the direction of the poem.

> 'Old lovers yet may have
> All that time denied –
> Grave is heaped on grave
> That they be satisfied –'

Eternity is not the property of the transcendental realm but is simply the continuation of the physical world! Yeats's point in these three poems is that value cannot be divorced from this world (is not transcendental) but is to be discovered in and through the world of the senses. The eternity that Yeats finally salutes as the answer to the question posed at the end of 'At Algeciras', in the final stanza of 'Mohini Chatterjee', is similar to the answer of the Self in 'A Dialogue of Self and Soul'. This life is not judged in terms of the desire for an eternal life in a supra-sensual heaven. Instead, eternity is a function of our mental needs and desires, and provides the breathing space in which to satisfy our separate energies.

> 'Over the blackened earth
> The old troops parade,
> Birth is heaped on birth
> That such cannonade
> May thunder time away,
> Birth-hour and death-hour meet,
> Or, as great sages say,
> Men dance on deathless feet.'

No poem more fully illustrates this attitude than 'News for the Delphic Oracle'. Yeats's sources for this poem were probably numerous. However, two in particular ought to be mentioned. These are Thomas Taylor's edition of Porphyry's essay 'On the Cave of the Nymphs', and Henry More's poem 'The Oracle or A Paraphrastical Interpretation of the answer of Apollo, when he was consulted by Amelius whither Plotinus soul went when he departed this life' (see Appendixes B and C, pp. 240 and 263). In a sense this poem is a companion piece and explanation of the poem previously discussed, 'The Delphic Oracle Upon Plotinus'.

The title of the poem sets the mood. Yeats has decided to reveal to the Delphic Oracle what 'The Isle of the Blessed' is really like. The Isle is another version of the Heaven of 'A Dialogue of Self and

Soul'. As such it represents an escape from the phenomenal and the release from the senses that is the object of Platonic and neo-Platonic discipline. Yeats's attitude to all this is made quite clear in the first stanza, where the gods of 'The Delphic Oracle Upon Plotinus' are described as 'golden codgers' and found to share their island with the sensual and rowdy heroes of Irish mythology. Furthermore the whole of the first stanza is infused with a mood of drowsy sensuality. Plotinus comes to look about and then 'Lay sighing like the rest'. The atmosphere is more like that of a Dionysian rite or orgy than that of the supra-sensual and asexual heaven of Platonism. But it is the third stanza which most clearly demonstrates how Yeats plays with these Platonic ideas, and turns them to his own use.

> Slim adolescence that a nymph has stripped,
> Peleus on Thetis stares.
> Her limbs are delicate as an eyelid,
> Love has blinded him with tears;
> But Thetis' belly listens.
> Down the mountain walls
> From where Pan's cavern is
> Intolerable music falls.
> Foul goat-head, brutal arm appear,
> Belly, shoulder, bum,
> Flash fishlike; nymphs and satyrs
> Copulate in the foam.
>
> from 'News for the Delphic Oracle'
> (*Collected Poems*, p. 377)

Poussin's painting the *Marriage of Peleus and Thetis* is the source for the image in the first five lines of this stanza, but for Yeats's interpretation we must go to Taylor's edition of Porphyry's essay 'On the Cave of the Nymphs' (Appendix B, p. 240). In this essay the Cave of the Nymphs has the same topography, and many of the same inhabitants as Yeats's version of the Isle of the Blessed.[1] However, there is one significant difference; according to Taylor the cave located on the island had two gates, one which led up to the supra-sensible world, one leading back to the sensible world. Yeats's island cave has only one gate (Pan's cavern).

---

[1] Shelley's poem 'The Witch of Atlas' is also a possible source of some of the symbolism. Yeats, in his essay on Shelley's poem, claims that Shelley must have read Taylor's translation of the essay 'On the Cave of the Nymphs'.

In Taylor's edition sea-nymphs are, we are told, the Goddesses which preside over generation. Thetis is one of these, and Peleus is seen enraptured with her beauty. But, we are told that Thetis's belly 'listens'. What she is listening to is the music of generation; she carries her son Achilles in her belly. The poem ends with the dance of the divinities of generation in the foam of the sea of life; the symbolic copulation that was discussed earlier by Old Tom in 'Tom at Cruachan'. The poem then, is circular; we have in the first two stanzas a description of Plotinus's arrival at the isle, and immediately following the description of the voyage to the Isle, the descent into generation. The second gate, the gate which leads to heaven, has disappeared, and in this poem, as in the poems discussed earlier, the supra-sensible world, the world of the forms, has no separate reality, but becomes only the generative principles.

> 'The stallion Eternity
> Mounted the mare of Time,
> 'Gat the foal of the world.'

> ('Tom at Cruachan')

The last stanza of 'News for the Delphic Oracle' illustrates Yeats's poetry at its best. It is serious in the sense that Yeats is dealing with an important subject, but at the same time it is outrageously funny. And the humour and fun of the stanza in no way interfere with Yeats's purpose, but complement it. The poetry is difficult, in that it deals with complicated ideas; but it is not discursive. The idea lies behind the scene, and the scene can be appreciated, and a good deal of its significance realised, by anyone who is willing to read poetry. This is true even though they may not know Yeats's source material, or the genesis of the ideas in the poem. For example, Yeats's shift from the evanescent, ephemeral pleasure one would expect on the island – 'Her limbs are delicate as an eyelid' – to the perspective he prefers 'But Thetis' belly listens' – 'Belly, shoulder, bum' turns philosophy into flesh. The ability to provide the sensual equivalent of an argument, to prove it upon the pulse of the reader, is, it has been argued, the greatest achievement of the metaphysical poets of the seventeenth century.[1] Yeats, more than any other poet of this century, shares this gift.

[1] But there are few first-rate poets who could not be discussed in the same way.

A careful attention to Yeats's sources and to the philosophical and quasi-philosophical questions which provided the framework for many of these poems is, I believe, absolutely necessary to realise their meaning fully. However, this must be only a small part of the critic's task.

Yeats's methodology, his attempt to provide a concrete and sensual embodiment of his ideas, is a necessary consequence of the ideas themselves. To do otherwise is to produce a poem which is not so much a birth into this world as that dying into pure thought which Yeats abhorred. A critical approach which ignores the fact that Yeats's poetry is always concrete and sensual has confused birth and death, or at best has fallen prey to that particular kind of neo-Platonic thinking which, if it does not confuse one with the other, preaches a birth which is more like a death.

3

Symbol and symbolism

The ideas that were described in the first chapter as Kantian and neo-Kantian are not a separate part of Yeats's intellectual equipment. Yeats was intent on creating an intellectual superstructure that was not metaphysics or epistemology, nor yet a theory of history or aesthetics, but something which was all of these while at the same time a mythology. To attempt to do this, even to want to do this, reflects a turn of mind more synthetic than analytic, and an imagination more sensuous than abstract. Naturally what resulted was not the kind of philosophy that was likely to appeal to anyone whose philosophical training or inclination was that of the analytical, empirical school of early twentieth-century English philosophy. What T. Sturge Moore, earnestly attempting to maintain a philosophical dialogue with Yeats, and often asking his famous brother (G. E. Moore) for advice, made of Yeats's position is not clear. But one suspects the brothers Moore must often have been exasperated by passages like this:

You say Bertrand Russell says that Kant smashed his own philosophy by his doctrine of practical reason. So he does say, and what more can you expect from a man who has been entirely bald during the whole course of his life. He merely repeats a piece of common electioneering nonsense which writer has copied from writer for generations. The men who invented it had as much to do with philosophy as an Orange brass band on the twelfth of July has to do with religion.

From Buddha's time there have always been the two paths to reality, that of knowledge and that of will. (Zen Buddhism, like Blake and Kant thought the path of knowledge was closed, that of will open.) St. Paul's Christianity set up the path of will as against the quick path of knowledge; and from Kant have descended two great streams of thought, the philosophy of will in Schopenhauer, Hartmann, Bergson, James, and that of knowledge in Hegel, Croce, Gentile, Bradley and the like.[1]

This passage illustrates both Yeats's breadth of interest, and his

---

[1] *Yeats–Moore Correspondence*, p. 124.

ability to create a cosmic stew out of bits and pieces from unlikely sources.

However, although many of the relationships Yeats drew between the major areas of intellectual discourse may give the scholar pause, his attempt to find within them a common myth or rationale is not so implausible as might first seem. These beliefs often occur together (1) an idealistic metaphysic and epistemology (as discussed in Ch. 1); (2) the survival of the soul after death; (3) a cyclical theory of history; (4) a naturalistic theory of symbolism in the arts; (5) something that Yeats defines as 'spiritualism' and 'magic'; and (6) a relationship between the tradition of spiritualism and magic and eastern philosophy or religion.

Schopenhauer and Nietzsche, both neo-Kantians, held epistemological and philosophical positions of the sort discussed in Chapter 1, and both were interested and influenced by Eastern religious doctrines. Nietzsche believed in the survival of the soul after death and in reincarnation, and both these beliefs seemed to be intricately connected to his cyclical theory of history. In fact, Nietzsche's historical theory, like Yeats's, seems deliberately intended to provide the secular blessedness Yeats invokes in 'A Dialogue of Self and Soul', and is helpful in explicating poems like 'Lapis Lazuli'. All post-Kantian speculation that took as its starting point the nature and function of the noumenal soul, implied the survival of the soul after death, at least to the extent that the soul was thought to be a part of Absolute Ego, and to apply this kind of speculation to the arts was to hold what I have called later in this book a 'naturalistic' theory of symbolism in aesthetic speculation. Nietzsche, Schopenhauer and Croce all hold variants of this position.

What has been termed 'spiritualism' or 'magic' in the previous paragraph is the tradition of heterodox mysticism in the Western world. F. A. C. Wilson, in an attempt to provide more accurate description, has characterised this movement, which he says begins with the Kabala, Egyptian Theurgy, and Plotinus, and continues into the present through Swedenborg, Blake, the Rosicrucians, and Madame Blavatsky, as the 'subjective tradition in religion'. Wilson means, I suppose, both the belief that visionary experience is acquired through the self, in contact with a God that is immanent rather than transcendent, and that the immanent principle operates beyond the laws of cause and effect.

In this chapter, it is my intention to discuss Yeats's poetic theory and the most important single element in this poetic theory, Yeats's view of the nature of the imagination and the role of the symbol. Yeats's position on these questions, like his views of history and personal immortality, arises out of his myth. And it cannot be understood unless the role of the Kantian and neo-Kantian elements of the myth is understood. So I should like to begin by demonstrating the change worked in Yeats's ideas by the introduction of Kantian and neo-Kantian notions, specifically the changes in those ideas which were previously associated with Yeats's interest in the tradition of heterodox mysticism.

In Chapter 1 the nature of the noumenal soul in nineteenth-century German philosophy was documented, and Yeats's 'Seven Propositions' quoted as an example of his modifications of these views. Both the original Kantian and neo-Kantian position and Yeats's modification of it in the 'Seven Propositions' can be profitably compared with an early statement of Yeats's made in an essay entitled 'Magic', in which he states that he 'believes in the practice and philosophy of what we have agreed to call magic'. In the essay he states the three major tenets of his beliefs. These doctrines are:

(1) That the borders of our mind are ever shifting, and that many minds can flow into one another, as it were, and create or reveal a single mind, a single energy.
(2) That the borders of our memories are as shifting, and that our memories are a part of one great memory, the memory of Nature herself.
(3) That this great mind and great memory can be evoked by symbols.[1]

These ideas, which Yeats continually attributes to Swedenborg, Blake, and the Cambridge Platonists, to name only his most significant sources, were easily assimilated with the Kantian ideas presented in Chapter 1. With the introduction of Kantian and post-Kantian ideas, however, the earlier position grows in clarity. That is, the relationship between minds is more clearly defined. Furthermore, mind, instead of being simply another reality, becomes the creator of the phenomenal reality as well. Furthermore, both these positions are, in some respects, similar to the pyschology of Carl Jung. In the 'Seven Propositions', Yeats argues that reality is a function of the human mind, and in the proposition on magic, he argues that there are certain forms, or characteristic projections of the individual mind, which can bring it into contact with all

[1] Yeats, 'Magic', *Essays and Introduction*, p. 28.

minds. Both these ideas closely parallel Jung's notion of significant forms; the first being close to what Jung means by an archetype, the second to what he describes as a *mandala*. To establish the historical relationships between these three views would require a major effort in intellectual history and is beyond the scope of this book. But I think it important to note that Jung's psychology and the Kantian epistemology and metaphysics both have roots in the tradition of heterodox mysticism.

There seems to be little doubt that Kant borrowed from Swedenborg. Despite their temperamental differences, especially Kant's aversion to metaphysics, Kant's notion of the relationship of the noumenal to the phenomenal seems to copy Swedenborg's position on the relationship between the spiritual world and the ordinary world. A measure of this influence is the fact that Kant was one of only four people actually to purchase Swedenborg's *magnum opus, The Arcana Coelestia*, in its first printing; and Kant wrote a book (for the most part sardonically critical) on Swedenborg's visionary experience, entitled *Dreams of a Ghost-Seer Explained by Dreams of Metaphysics*.

Yeats may well have read this book. In any event, from a re-mark made by Yeats in his essay on Swedenborg, we may assume that he at least knew of it, and that he assumed that there was some connection between Kant and Swedenborg.

In his fifty-eighth year he [Swedenborg] was sitting in an inn in London, where he had gone about the publication of a book, when a spirit appeared before him who was, he believed, Christ himself, and told him that hence-forth he would commune with spirits and angels. From that moment he was a mysterious man describing distant events as if they were before his eyes, and knowing dead men's secrets, if we are to accept testimony that seemed convincing to Immanuel Kant.[1]

Jung's work, as is well known, takes as data the whole of the heterodox tradition; and seeks to provide a scientific explanation of the continual recurrence of specific images within this tradition, of the continual ability of these images to provide the same mean-ing to their interpreters. That is, Jung's generalisations, and the generalisations of his followers about the role of these symbols as archetypes of human experience, are built, in large measure, upon the role of these symbols within the mystical tradition and subsi-

[1] Yeats, *Explorations*, p. 33.

diary traditions such as medieval alchemy. While Jung and his followers (e.g. Northrop Frye in literary criticism) claim to be scientific, their ideas seem to be just as speculative as those of the 'heterodox mystical tradition'. Theories which claim that symbols are to be understood as the product of *Anima Mundi*, Absolute Ego, or the Collective Unconscious, seem to be equally speculative.

While it cannot be stated with certainty that Yeats was directly conversant with Jung's ideas, since he nowhere mentions Jung, it seems to me reasonable to assume that he would have been at least aware of the general outlines of Jung's position. Further, he was very much concerned with the relationship between myths as seen from the pyschological and anthropological points of view in such works as Frazer's *The Golden Bough*.

There was a fourth approach to the question of symbolism with which Yeats was conversant; and that was the French symbolist movement. Of the four this seems to have had the least noticeable effect on Yeats's theory and practice, and will be ignored in the rest of this chapter.

Because of the variety of approaches to myth and symbol which interested Yeats, and the seriousness which characterised his approach to any material which touched his art, his notion of symbolism is both complex and well-thought-out. However, Yeats's final position on this subject occurs most often in his poetry, and is given its fullest expression in the many poems he wrote about art.

II

Before I begin to discuss Yeats' use of the term 'symbolism' and the poems in which this becomes a major issue I shall try to get clear some at least of the issues from an independent standpoint. I do not intend to try to solve all the problems connected with the term; but to get one or two basic issues clear. In most discussions of literature what is meant by the terms 'symbol', 'symbolic', 'symbolism' and 'symbolist', is rarely clear. All these terms are fairly recent additions to the technical language of literary criticism. And because this criticism is a relatively new endeavour most of its technical terms lack clarity. Questions like: What are the characteristics of literary symbols which set them apart from ordinary symbols? How do these symbols signify? How does symbol differ from allegory? and What is the relationship between symbol, image and metaphor? should embarrass the literary critic. Usually, however, the words are used indiscriminately, and what parades as a technical vocabulary is most often an intuitive struggling after precision. John Unterecker, in his *A Reader's Guide to William Butler Yeats*, has at least acknowledged the problem:

At this point, definition is in order. 'Image', 'metaphor', and 'symbol', are terms which must be used so often in any discussion of Yeats' work that their meanings had better be pinned down in the very beginning as precisely as possible. All three words are of course intimately related.[1]

However, in his discussion of these three terms, he is unable to fulfil the task he sets himself. After defining 'sign' as 'the denotative level of a word'[2] he claims that both 'a' and 'coat' are signs. What 'a' might be a sign of is not clear. Further, he claims that 'image' is almost synonymous with 'sign'; the other two conditions which a sign must fill, in order to become an image, are that it involves the reader in a recollection of concrete or sensuous experience, or that it has the potential to become either a metaphor or a symbol. Neither of these restrictions remains, when analysed, a restriction at all. Almost any substantive can involve the reader in concrete or sensuous recollection, and almost any substantive can become one of the terms of a metaphor, or be employed as a symbol. His definition of 'metaphor' is not interesting; it is a slight expansion of the usual lexical definition. (He quotes Webster's *New Collegiate*.) However, the poverty of the normal critical vocabulary becomes most obvious when Unterecker tries to adumbrate the meaning of 'symbol'. Starting with the 'notion' of the work of art itself as 'non-discursive symbol', he says:

The distinction between metaphor and symbol is one between assigned and unassigned meaning. A metaphor always has at least two assigned meanings (its own sign value and the sign value of the object or idea it stands for). But symbol stands on one leg only; the other kicks at the stars. It exists with only its sign value as a fixed meaning. Its other meaning or meanings are unassigned. Any analogy we can construct for the symbol, any meaning we assign to it, is legitimate so long as we recognize that meaning is not its meaning. (Its meaning must always be more elusive than any value we can – with words – fix to it.) All that the meaning we assign

---

[1] Op. cit. New York: The Noonday Press, 1961, p. 33.
[2] But 'centaur' is a sign. That is, it has a connotation, but it does not denote anything.

to a symbol can ever be is either part of its meaning or one of its possible meanings. No symbol has a meaning.[1]

This is the abdication of criticism in a subjective riot of possible, always correct, interpretations and evaluations. What Unterecker's definition says, in effect, is that a symbol is nothing at all. Any 'sign' is a symbol if we wish to interpret it as such.

This passage is typical of contemporary criticism in that it reflects both our need to believe we have some sort of conceptual framework, and the almost hysterical recognition that we do not have one. Could anyone write a book which is to function as a 'reader's guide' to a poet who is frankly a symbolist poet if he really believed that 'no symbol has a meaning'? Unterecker is surely aware that if this is true then anything we say is just as good as anything else. It is important to get clear about the genesis of the problem. We don't need a conceptual framework in order to get on with most of our work as critics. We can, and do, argue with one another. What is more, the arguments usually amount to something; we change our minds, we are converted by someone's evidence, or we are successful in converting them with ours. So we do decide on what a 'symbol' means. The sort of thing that Unterecker says in the passage that has been quoted is a bone thrown in the direction of a large scientific dog. But the dog is peculiar in that it never gets down to cases – it always says something about poetry in general. So for the last three centuries poets and critics, and other interested parties (that is, most literate men), have thrown the in general dog an in general bone.

When Unterecker says a symbol has no meaning he is really involved in battle with the old enemy, science; probably the best way to demonstrate this is to look briefly at the relationship between philosophy and literary criticism in the period between the wars. Philosophy has always had a major impact on theories of criticism; Plato and Aristotle were philosophers, and critical theorists only by the way. But they are certainly the seminal figures for students of theories of literature. The only English critic who has been as important a critical theoretician is Coleridge, and he did his theoretical work as a part of a more general metaphysical theory, and thought of himself as a practising philosopher. But in the period between the wars English literary critics found contem-

1 Unterecker, *Reader's Guide to William Butler Yeats*, p. 34.

porary English philosophy uncongenial. Literary critics have always been interested in language, for poetry is, after all, language; and when they turned to contemporary English philosophy they found that their philosophers were now even more concerned with language than they had been previously. When they turned to philosophy, however, what they found was that the relationship between science and language was one of the primary areas of investigation, and that the doctrines which resulted resembled nothing so much as a continuation of the old split between literature and science, and that once again science was triumphant. One way of construing the empiricist, positivist attitudes about language was that they were intended to distinguish between meaningful or true linguistic usage, that is, scientific language, and meaningless language, that is, poetry and metaphysics. I hope to show that this is a misconception of the empiricist tradition. But, right or wrong, this view has been accepted by most of those English-speaking people who have been interested in critical theory; and because they have held this view they have been less and less interested in the mainstream of English philosophy, and more and more interested in continental metaphysics. I think that this is unfortunate and I will at least sketch how the work of contemporary English philosophers may be useful when considering the problems of Literary Theory. But this is getting ahead of the story and I want now to consider briefly just what the Logical Positivists, and especially the most famous English Positivist, A. J. Ayer, actually did say. Ayer's book, *Language, Truth and Logic*, appeared in 1936 and was the first book-length presentation in English of a theory of meaning that has been growing steadily more influential for almost two decades and was being propagated by Schlick, Carnap and others in the Vienna circle. But Ayer is correct in giving Berkeley, Russell, Wittgenstein, and especially Hume, pride of place in his introduction.

Like Hume, I divide all genuine propositions into two classes: those which, in his terminology, concern 'relations of ideas', and those which concern 'matters of fact'. The former class comprises the a priori propositions of logic and pure mathematics, and these I allow to be necessary and certain only because they are analytic. That is, I maintain that the reason why these propositions cannot be confuted in experience is that they do not make any assertion about the empirical world, but simply record our determination to use symbols in a certain fashion. Propositions concerning empirical matters of fact, on the other hand, I hold to be hypotheses, which can be probable, but never certain. And in giving an account of the method of their validation I claim also to have explained the nature of truth.

To test whether a sentence expresses a genuine empirical hypothesis, I adopt what may be called a modified verification principle. For I require of an empirical hypothesis, not indeed that it should be conclusively verifiable, but that some possible sense-experience should be relevant to the determination of its truth or falsehood. If a putative proposition fails to satisfy this principle, and is not a tautology, then I hold that it is metaphysical, and that, being metaphysical, it is neither true nor false but literally senseless. It will be found that much of what ordinarily passes for philosophy is metaphysical according to this criterion, and, in particular, that it can not be significantly asserted that there is a non-empirical world of values, or that men have immortal souls, or that there is a transcendent God.[1]

What the verifiability criterion of cognitive meaninglessness claimed was that only those sentences which expressed '*a priori*' propositions,[2] or propositions which were in principle verifiable, could be true or false, and furthermore, only sentences which expressed true or false propositions were meaningful. All this was to be 'scientific'. Ayer's book concludes with this paragraph:

It is indeed misleading to draw a sharp distinction, as we have been doing, between philosophy and science. What we should rather do is to distinguish between the speculative and the logical aspects of science, and assert that philosophy must develop into the logic of science. That is to say, we distinguish between the activity of formulating hypotheses and defining the symbols which occur in them. It is of no importance whether we call one who is engaged in the latter activity a philosopher or a scientist. What we must recognise is that it is necessary for a philosopher to become a scientist, in this sense, if he is to make any substantial contribution towards the growth of human knowledge.[3]

A common response to this among literate people who aren't philosophers or scientists has been a kind of reluctant acceptance coupled with a distaste for anyone barbaric enough to mention these issues in polite company. So what in effect has happened is that 'Logical Positivism' has become a term of abuse in literary

---

[1] A. J. Ayer, *Language, Truth and Logic* (New York: Dover Publications, 1936), p. 31.
[2] In the second edition Ayer tries to answer some of his critics by changing to talk about statements instead of about propositions.
[3] *Ibid.*, p. 153.

circles, while an analysis of critical problems that is based on the supposed consequences of the positivist criterion of meaning has become current, and can be traced through most of the important critical documents of the past forty years. Here is a typical passage of I. A. Richards's criticism:

This brief analysis may be sufficient to indicate the fundamental disparity and opposition between pseudo-statements as they occur in poetry and statements as they occur in science. A pseudo-statement is a form of words which is justified entirely by its effect in releasing or organising our impulses and attitudes (due regard being had for the better or worse organisations of these inter se); a statement, on the other hand, is justified by its truth, i.e., its correspondence, in a highly technical sense, with the fact to which it points.[1]

A cursory examination of Brooks's and Warrens's *Understanding Poetry* shows the same dichotomy at work. In *Understanding Poetry*, which is without doubt the most important single literary handbook in North America, the beginning student is told that although 'truth' is the province of scientific statements, most people most of the time aren't really concerned with truth, and so it is at least consistent with our other behaviour that we continue to be interested in poetry.

Science gives us a certain kind of description of the world – a description which is within its own terms verifiable – and gives us a basis for more effective practical achievement. Science is, as Bertrand Russell has called it, 'power-knowledge'...

But we have seen, and can see in real life every day, how much of our experience eludes the statements science can make; and how merely practical statements or statements that approximate a scientific form satisfy only a part of our interests. One does not have to look farther than the fact that this wide domain of human interests exists to find a justification for poetry. Most people are thoroughly satisfied to admit the value of any activity which satisfies a basic and healthy human interest...

The question of the value of poetry, then, is to be answered by saying that it springs from a basic human impulse and fulfills a basic human interest. To answer the question finally, and not immediately, one would have to answer the question as to the value of those common impulses and interests. But that is a question which lies outside of the present concern. As we enter into a study of poetry it is only necessary to see that poetry is

[1] I. A. Richards, 'Poetry and Beliefs', *Critiques and Essays in Criticism 1920–1948* (New York: Ronald Press Co., 1949), p. 330.

not an isolated and eccentric thing, but springs from the most fundamental interests which human beings have.[1]

Now, Unterecker, Brooks and Warren, and I. A. Richards have a common problem which arises from the fact that all three think that the language used in poetry is defective in some important sense. If the language used in poetry is 'pseudo-statement', or if 'no symbol has a meaning', or if the value of poetry lies just in the fact that it changes the way we feel (a cold shower? a good meal?), then the primary legitimate activity of the critic is not interpretation, but to do the sorts of experiments psychologists do. Poems, on these accounts, are primarily sensory stimuli, hortatory ejaculations, and comfortable gestures.

Is it possible to avoid the problems that beset Unterecker, Brooks and Warren or I. A. Richards? A beginning can be made by looking at the verifiability criterion. Ayer's formulation of the criterion did at least two jobs. First, it told us which sentences expressed true or false propositions; and second, it provided a criterion which distinguished between meaningful utterances and 'emotive' language. I doubt that many reputable philosophers would want to quibble with the force of Ayer's remarks about the use of true and false. Suppose I say that 'there is a gremlin in my watch', but it turns out that I have no evidence for this, and what is more important, there is no evidence that I will allow against the claim. Is there any point to my assertion that the statement is true? Someone who believed certain sorts of Idealist doctrines might claim that 'Reality is one', but there is absolutely nothing that would count as confirmation. Furthermore, there is no imaginable way we could dispute the claim. What could we find out about the world that would make any difference one way or the other? Whatever the value of Ayer's particular formulation of this argument about 'true' and 'false', it is clear that the general direction of his remarks *is* correct.

However, his further claim that only true or false statements were meaningful seems much less useful. Ayer's book was polemical, and like most polemics, tended to oversimplify certain important issues that were only peripheral to the principal issue. Ayer over-simplifies the notion of meaning; the commonly-held belief that he claimed all sentences which did not express true or false

---

[1] Cleanth Brooks and Robert Penn Warren, *Understanding Poetry* (New York: Henry Holt & Co., 1957), p. lv.

propositions or *a priori* truths, are meaningless, is not clearly a misreading of *Language, Truth and Logic*. That Ayer was mistaken in holding that 'meaning' was related to 'true' and 'false' in the way that has been outlined above is reflected in one sort of criticism of the verifiability criterion. On Ayer's account of *a priori* statements the criterion was clearly not *a priori*. If it were to be true or false, then it should be verifiable. But clearly it is not the sort of thing that is verifiable. Ayer was not claiming that no one used the word 'true' of statements like 'Reality is one'. He said they did, but they shouldn't. Suppose this criticism goes through. Then on its own account (1) the criterion is neither true nor false, and (2) the criterion is meaningless. Of the two, the second is the more damaging criticism. For, in reply to one, a verificationalist might offer a number of satisfactory descriptions of the principle which would make his point, and which would not deny that the critic was right in saying the criterion was neither true nor false. Here is one example:

the empiricist criterion of meaning, like the result of any other explication, represents a linguistic proposal which itself is neither true nor false, but for which adequacy is claimed in two respects: First in the sense that the explication provides a reasonably close analysis of the commonly accepted meaning of the explicandum – and this claim implies an empirical assertion; and secondly in the sense that the explication achieves a 'rational reconstruction' of the explicandum, i.e., that it provides, together perhaps with other explications, a general conceptual framework which permits a consistent and precise restatement and theoretical systematization of the contexts in which the explicandum is used – and this claim implies at least an assertion of a logical character.

Though a proposal in form, the empiricist criterion of meaning is therefore far from being an arbitrary definition; it is subject to revision if a violation of the requirements of adequacy, or even a way of satisfying those requirements more fully, should be discovered. Indeed, it is to be hoped that before long some of the open problems encountered in the analysis of cognitive significance will be clarified and that then our last version of the empiricist meaning criterion will be replaced by another, more adequate one.[1]

Hempel has answered the first criticism by showing that we are quite prepared to take seriously the sort of proposal he thinks the

[1] C. G. Hempel, 'Problems and changes in the empiricist criterion of meaning', from E. Nagel and R. B. Brandt, *Meaning and Knowledge – Systematic Readings in Epistemology* (New York: Harcourt, Brace & World, Inc., 1965), p. 27.

criterion is. But that he has done so shows the inadequacy of the bifurcation of language into either true or false statements, or emotive utterances. For it is clear that Ayer and Hempel are engaged in an important intellectual activity, and that the statements they make have intellectual or cognitive impact. What has replaced the simple split between language that is true or false and emotive language is a willingness to pay attention to how language is used. In this respect at least, Wittgenstein's analogy between language and a tool box is central to the spirit of contemporary English linguistic philosophy. One important effect of Wittgenstein's work has been to shift attention away from the model of scientific language, and even to reduce in importance the role of true or false sentences in language. Of course, this could not be carried out as a radical programme. (One can imagine a language that included no performatives, or no literature. But a language without true or false sentences would be incredibly impoverished.) Much of our legal system is based on the activity of promising; and promising is a linguistic activity. But the sentences we use in promising are not, as Austin showed, true or false. This sort of point could be made about a great deal of our language. So that it is possible at this point to see that our attempt to find out about 'meaning' and 'symbol' in literature is for the most part an attempt to see how language is used in poetry, and how language is used in criticism, and the relationship between the two.

We have seen that Richards's acceptance of the verifiability criterion led him to the conclusion that statements in literature were not verifiable, and therefore pseudo-statements; and that the notion of a pseudo-statement was a consequence of the identification of meaningful statements with true or false statements. But there is another criticism possible of Richards. Plato claimed that poets were liars, meaning that the sentences they produced were false. At least a *prima facie* case can be made for this view. Here is what Ayer has to say on the subject:

The view that the metaphysician is to be reckoned among the poets appears to rest on the assumption that both talk nonsense. But this assumption is false. In the vast majority of cases the sentences which are produced by poets do have literal meaning. The difference between the man who uses language scientifically and the man who uses it emotively is not that the one produces sentences which are incapable of arousing emotion, and the other sentences which have no sense, but that the one is primarily concerned with the expression of true propositions, the other with the creation of a work of art. Thus, if a work of science contains true and important propositions, its value as a work of science will hardly be diminished by the fact that they are inelegantly expressed. And similarly, a work of art is not necessarily the worse for the fact that all the propositions comprising it are literally false. But to say that many literary works are largely composed of falsehoods, is not to say that they are composed of pseudo-propositions. It is, in fact, very rare for a literary artist to produce sentences which have no literal meaning.[1]

Adjudicating this dispute between Ayer and Richards will prove instructive. But the only question that will be looked at is whether or not poets say things that are false. Ayer's justification of the poets' lack of respect for truth, namely that they are interested in art, will be ignored. But I will give reasons for ignoring considerations about works of art in this context. Many discussions of literature begin by examining the relationship between literature and the other arts on the one hand, and literature and 'truth' or 'meaningfulness' on the other. These two problems may well be distinct, but it has proved unusually difficult to separate them. Most philosophers, if they have discussed the problems of truth or meaningfulness in literature at all, have been concerned with this problem from the standpoint of aesthetics and have tended to see the problem as a part of the larger problem of the relationship between 'art' and 'meaning'. I am not sure that one necessarily has to approach the question of meaningfulness or truth in literature from this angle; and, in fact, it may even be the case that a discussion in terms of 'meaning' and its relationship to 'art' may introduce a number of unnecessary complications in an already complex issue.

An important reason for this is the term 'art' itself. First, 'art' is applied to a number of related kinds of human endeavour, but of these only literature is primarily linguistic. It is at once obvious that non-linguistic works of art, if they have meaning at all, must be significant in a very different manner than linguistic structures. A theory of 'artistic' truth, since it is a theory about how all 'art' signifies, cannot be sensitive to this difference. This alone is enough reason to try to examine the problem of signification in literature without recourse to a theory about signification in art.

[1] Ayer, *Language, Truth and Logic*, p. 44.

Second, when we consider the intention of 'art', we cannot fail to notice the tremendous diversity of activities which are included. There is little that a novel, a painting, a musical composition, and a piece of pottery have in common, but we call them 'art', and make statements which are intended to be descriptive of all of them. It is generally assumed that what makes these objects part of a definitely delineated class of things is that they can produce in a beholder an aesthetic pleasure. Hospers's *Meaning and Truth in the Arts* is typical of this attitude; the book begins with the statement that 'the starting point of all philosophy of art is the fact of aesthetic experience'. Hospers goes on to say that

The esthetic attitude has been variously defined in terms of repose, of detachment or isolation, 'synaestheses', feeling of unreality, or simply pleasure. These conceptions are not necessarily incompatible with one another; each of them seizes upon some aspect or element of a kind of experience which we have – for example in art, appreciation – and defines the esthetic experience in terms of it alone... It is not my purpose here to discuss and compare these conceptions, or to decide among them. It must suffice to say that there is one kind of attitude which is fundamental to all of the experiences described, and without which the use of the 'esthetic' to apply to anything distinctive in our experience must quite disappear. This fundamental attitude consists in the separation of the esthetic experience from the needs and desires of everyday life and from the responses which we customarily make to our environment as practical human beings ...The esthetic attitude can occur only when practical response to our environment is held in suspension...On these occasions we are perceiving something 'not for the sake of action, but for the sake of perceiving'.[1]

Let us assume that Hospers has given an adequate account of what is generally meant by 'aesthetic', and that his definition is adequate for the non-visual arts, although he obviously is thinking primarily in terms of the visual. It is at once obvious, and Hospers is aware of this, that any object can be regarded aesthetically. Furthermore, it is probably true that for almost everyone most aesthetic experience is in no way connected with art. Nor does it seem possible to argue that 'art' may be defined as that which is aesthetic; that is, that it is the aim of art or the artist to cause the perceiver to have an aesthetic experience, since that is true of things other than art. That is, aesthetic appeal of some sort inheres in almost every commodity that appears on the market,

[1] John Hospers, *Meaning and Truth in the Arts* (Chapel Hill: University of North Carolina Press, 1946).

and is as characteristic of a soup-tin as of a Rembrandt. Further-more, many things that are considered art have a purpose, for example, a building designed by Le Corbusier, and are only inci-dentally aesthetically pleasing. Furthermore, it is true of a large number of works of art that their effect is not to suspend our practi-cal desires at all, but rather to direct them. Satire, whether a sketch by Hogarth or an essay by Swift, is not something perceived for the sake of perceiving. The concepts of 'art' and 'aesthetic' since they are used indiscriminately to cover both linguistic and non-linguistic activities, and since they are relatively ill-defined, will not be of much use in arriving at a functional description of literature.

Now, if we put aside all theories about art, and about the aesthe-tic, and yet we still want some sort of theory about literature, where are we to begin? I have already indicated that it is because literature is primarily linguistic that theories about art seem to be of little help. A good theoretical account of literature will take into account the fact that literature is a particular way of using language.

It is clear, however, that in order to do this some more specific attention must be paid to delimiting the sort of language we are dealing with. One perfectly reputable use of the word 'literature' includes works by historians, philosophers, biographers; we some-times call everything that is well-written, literature. But it is clear that statements made in these contexts would be true or false. They are meaningful in the usual way, and so they do not occasion the sort of problems we are discussing. Furthermore, distinctions on the basis of form or genre will not capture the difference that concerns us here. In Pope's poem, which he called an essay on criticism, he says of poets and critics: 'Ten censure wrong for one who writes amiss.' We approve of this sentence because it is exactly the sort of sentence that can be true or false, and we think it true. When Ayer says that most of the sentences in literature are false he obviously has other sorts of works in mind. What he means might best be understood by thinking about a novel.

My father's family name being Pirrip, and my Christian name Philip, my infant tongue could make of both names nothing longer or more explicit than Pip. So, I called myself Pip, and came to be called Pip.

I give Pirrip as my father's family name, on the authority of his tomb-stone and my sister – Mrs. Joe Gargery, who married the blacksmith. As I never saw my father or my mother, and never saw any likeness of either of them (for their days were long before the days of photographs), my first fancies regarding what they were like, were unreasonably derived from their tombstones.[1]

If I were to tell you that my sister's name was Mrs Joe Gargery you could find out whether what was said were true or false. A great deal of literature seems at first to describe people, events, objects, or processes, and to fail to describe them by virtue of a failure of reference. That is, you can't check to see if Pip is saying something true, or something false, not because our records of births and deaths are incomplete, but because Pip doesn't exist. Sentences like these have been argued about by philosophers. Russell's example is 'The present king of France is bald', and Russell claims that the proper way to analyse this sentence is into a conjunction of several assertions, one of which is 'There is a (present) king of France'. If this is an adequate analysis of the proper way to take the sentence then 'The present king of France is bald' is false. The reason Russell wants this to be so is that the sentence is obviously significant, and he wants to argue against the Meinongian claim that it is significant because there exists, exists being used in some special sense, a King of France. Meinong's world of subsistent entities is, of course, very like the Idealists' notion that what the poet does is to create a 'world' that is in some sense real. Whether or not Russell is correct is still an open question, but many philosophers would agree with the criticisms Strawson levels against Russell. Strawson's criticism is based largely on an analysis of language usage and becomes relevant to the problem of a language in literature at this point. About the present king of France, he says:

The fact that the sentence and the expression, respectively, are significant just is the fact that the sentence could be used, in certain circumstances, to say something true or false, that the expression could be used, in certain circumstances, to mention a particular person; and to know their meaning is to know what sort of circumstances these are. So when we utter the sentence without in fact mentioning anybody by the use of the phrase, 'The king of France', the sentence does not cease to be significant; we simply fail to say anything true or false because we simply fail to mention anybody by this particular use of that perfectly significant phrase. It is, if you like, a spurious use of the sentence, and a spurious use of the expression; though we may (or may not) mistakenly think it a genuine use.

[1] Charles Dickens, *Great Expectations* (New York: Holt, Rinehart and Winston Inc., 1964), p. 1.

And such spurious uses are very familiar. Sophisticated romancing, sophisticated fiction, (The unsophisticated kind begins: 'Once upon a time there was...') depend upon them. If I began, 'The king of France is wise', and went on, 'and he lives in a golden castle and has a hundred wives', and so on, a hearer would understand me perfectly well, without supposing either that I was talking about a particular person, or that I was making a false statement to the effect that there existed such a person as my words described. (It is worth adding that where the use of sentences and expressions is overtly fictional, the sense of the word 'about' may change. As Moore said, it is perfectly natural and correct to say that some of the statements in *Pickwick Papers* are *about* Mr. Pickwick. But where the use of sentences and expressions is not overtly fictional, this use of 'about' seems less correct; i.e. it would not in general be correct to say that a statement was about Mr. X or the so-and-so, unless there were such a person or thing. So it is where the romancing is in danger of being taken seriously that we might answer the question, 'Who is he talking about?' with 'He's not talking about anybody'; but, in saying this, we are not saying that what he is saying is either false or nonsense.[1]

For reasons partly rhetorical I will call these expressions, when they occur in literature, referentially-truncated uses, instead of spurious uses. (Strawson, by the way, now prefers to call them secondary uses.) However, the class of expressions I so designate is not quite co-extensive with Strawson's. A rule of thumb which by and large demarcates those sentences in literature which are referentially truncated is to notice that such referentially-truncated expressions are the sorts of things which we interpret. That is, in reading a poem, we often find that despite the fact that we *know* what all the words mean and how the grammar works, we still do not know what the play, the novel, the poem, the stanza or the line of poetry means. We are asking a question about the point of telling us about this fictional situation, object, process, event, etc. Now it is clear that if we *understand* what all the words mean, and how the grammar works, in a bit of history or philosophy, and it still needs interpretation, then there is something wrong with it. But that a poem needs interpretation is the normal course of events. Consider what has been said elsewhere in this book about the poem 'Leda and the Swan', where a poem which is first of all a description of the mythical event of the rape of Leda is taken to be about a whole variety of meta-historical questions. Furthermore,

1 P. F. Strawson, 'On Referring', *Mind*, LIX (1950), 320–44.

it is often the case that the explication of a poem is expressed in sentences that are verifiable. A poem, novel or play can be about almost anything. And there is no obvious restriction on the kinds of things that can be said by the poet, and thus no objection to doing our best to explicate literary works in sentences that are true or false. Now, it is clear that when a critic says that this is what a poem 'means', the sentences he utters are not synonymous with nor entailed by the sentences in the poem. What the relationship is will be discussed later.

To this point we have been contrasting literature like Pope's 'Essay on Criticism' with poems like 'Leda and the Swan'. Pope's poem contains sentences that are verifiable, and Yeats's poem contains sentences that are peculiar in that if we try to verify them they turn out to be about non-existent entities. Often, however, we find statements that in ordinary language are true or false, but just by virtue of being in a literary work become referentially neutral. Novels often contain accurate descriptions of cities, or inaccurate descriptions. Poets often write about events that actually happened, for example, Pope's 'Rape of the Lock' or Yeats's 'Among School Children', and they change the events a little, or a lot, or not at all, in accordance with what they want to get said. And in cases of this sort we just do not care to go beyond the fiction to see whether the description of the real event or real object is accurate. That is, in these cases, the particular utterances are there to be interpreted and so the question of truth or falsity does not arise. Instead, the sentences in novels, or plays, or most poems function in a manner similar to the directions that are sometimes included with unassembled machinery. We are asked to think about an object, event or process, so that we might see that certain sorts of relationships hold, or that the world is really like this imaginary facsimile of it, or that behaviour of a certain sort has unwelcome consequences. The list could go on. But by and large the sentences which comprise the work of literature just tell us about the event or process or object. The sophisticated reader of literature recognises that these sentences make no claims about the world – they just say 'think about this' – and whether or not (and it sometimes goes either way) 'this' is in the world, is not an issue. But, if the 'poet never affirmeth', what he doesn't affirm is the truth or falsity of his sentences. He says 'think about this' and we don't worry whether or not 'this' is an actual state of affairs, but he doesn't stop there. For in saying 'think about this' he is saying 'think about this and you will see what I mean'.

Let me review what has been said to this point. The sentences in most literary works are not true or false; they simply focus our attention on objects, events, processes, or persons. Usually, these are imaginary, but this is not always the case. We can, with just a little trouble, take the care necessary to insure that we do not talk as if 'imaginary' is just another adjective, like 'green' or 'tall'. Crazy Jane doesn't exist, or subsist, in some special world, and no such claim is involved in referring to her. Since this is the work done by the sentences in literature, we are not surprised to discover that the interpretation of a poem is not synonymous with, or entailed by, the sentences comprising the poem. The critic's job is to discover the import of the icon, not to re-phrase the poet's sentences. At this point we can see clearly not only why Richards goes wrong, but how Unterecker goes wrong. If the analysis I have given is correct, then literary symbols are not words, but what I have called icons, and to ask what a symbol means is not to ask, for example, what 'moon' means, as if the dictionary was somehow overthrown, irrelevant, to how words are used in poems – but to ask what is the import of this imaginary object, the moon, described in this way and in relationship to these other objects. But in the confused passage from Unterecker that I quoted earlier it is at least very likely that one problem he has is that he thinks he is talking about words. This is a very elementary mistake, and one that is rarely, if ever, actually made when someone does criticism. Yet it is common whenever a discussion reaches any degree of abstraction.

What has been claimed is that the sentences or sentence surrogates in poems, novels or plays differ from ordinary sentences in that they do not refer in the normal way. So Ayer is mistaken in claiming that most of the sentences uttered in poems, novels or plays are false. But we are not forced to call them pseudo-statements as Richards does. The poet does not pretend to make claims about the world; he tells us a story. This description holds not just for obvious stories, such as nineteenth-century novels, but for poems like Blake's 'The Sick Rose' or Yeats's 'Among School Children'. The story does not have to be complete in Aristotle's sense of the imitation of a complete action, nor does it have to focus around personality or character. Blake tells us a story about a rose, and we understand that he is not talking about a real rose, but only an imaginary rose. When we talk of interpreting a poem or a novel we are talking about interpreting a story, and we are not, except by extension, talking about interpreting, or discovering the meaning of, words or sentences. Because the stories that poets tell us are often not like what we most often think of as stories,[1] a new term, 'icon', has been introduced. This term has some currency in critical theory, since it was used in the title of W. K. Wimsatt Jr and M. C. Beardsley's fine book, *The Verbal Icon*. Wimsatt and Beardsley got the term from C. S. Pierce, but by and large ignored the consequences of Pierce's view of signification for the problems of critical theory.

The description of the critic's work as the interpretation of an icon rather than a group of sentences, in no way reduces the importance of a poet's language. For we must realise that it is only through the poet's language that we can discover the icon we are to interpret. Since the language of literature is referentially truncated, that is, since we are dealing with an imaginary object, event or process, we have only as much event, object or process as the poet gives us. There are no 'facts' about the icon that can be discovered in the world. It is for this reason that the rejoinder 'But it's not in the poem' or 'There's no evidence for that interpretation in the poem' seem to be the most powerful sort of rejoinder to interpretations we think wrong. We don't care what sort of thing someone does before they interpret the poem – an ouija board is fine, if it helps – but the interpretation, however discovered, is good only in so far as it is an interpretation of the 'icon', of this set of imaginary events. There are always at least two jobs that a critic or reader must do. We must first get clear what the icon is (what happens in *Hamlet*?) and only then is it possible to discover what the import of the icon is. When we talk about what a poem means most of our attention is focused on the second job, but doing the second job is only possible when we have done the first.

I have been talking as though there were no theoretical problems involved in the notion of interpreting a story, or discovering the meaning of an event, of locating the import of an object. In practice, there is no problem; these are activities that form a part of our everyday life, and in which we are continually engaged. But there

[1] That is, all of what we call 'stories' are icons. But some icons would not normally be called 'stories'.

is a theoretical difficulty, and the remarks that follow address themselves to that difficulty.

C. S. Pierce used the term 'icon' in an analysis of signification that asserted that there were, in general, three kinds of sign, and thus, three kinds of signification. According to Pierce, one thing could be a sign of another merely by virtue of a convention. A traffic light is a good example of a non-linguistic sign of the merely conventional or arbitrary type. Why does a round red light mean stop? Why don't we use square blue lights? Many words function in this way; if and when they are used denotatively. A word like 'wolf' can be used to talk about these animals and not those because we have rules or conventions governing our use of the word. There is no reason why we could not call all wild canines 'sheep' on Monday, and 'goats' on Tuesday, apart from the fact that we would soon become confused, and that eventually this sort of behaviour would make communication impossible. But in saying that some signs are meaningful by virtue of a convention we do not have to presuppose that there ever was a convention convened to decide what words to use to denote what objects.

Pierce's second sort of sign was called an index, and was intended to cover those cases where one thing was a sign of another by virtue of being really affected by that other thing. Examples of this sort of signification are 'Those clouds mean rain' or 'That tic means he is nervous'.

Pierce's third sort of sign was called an icon, and following Pierce, some philosophers have talked of 'iconic signification'.[1] A sign is an icon if it signifies by virtue of a real quality of its own. A good example of a non-linguistic icon is a map. Although some elements in a map, for example, the names printed on them, or the dots used to represent cities, are conventional, for the most part, a map signifies the geography mapped by virtue of its (that is, the map's) proportions. The map and the area mapped are isomorphic, and by virtue of the map's proportions we are able to read off the proportions of the geographical area. In order for one thing to serve as an icon for another, someone must take them to have at least one property in common. In order for someone to successfully get someone else to take one thing as an icon for another, that someone else must recognise something in common between the two objects. We do not usually teach someone what a map or diagram

[1] Henle, Alston.

60

means; we teach them how to read the map or diagram. Once someone knows how to read maps or diagrams, that is, once they have learned what sorts of properties are to be transferred, they no longer need to be in possession of all, or even most, of the facts about the object iconised, to see how the icon works. We can read a map of an area that we don't know, and we can reject a map that is not properly isomorphic. The 'icons' in poems are, it is my contention, icons in Pierce's sense of iconic. That is, they are imaginary events, objects or processes which are significant by virtue of a property or properties of their own, which property or properties they share with other elements of ordinary experience. It is clear that proportion is not the only property that can be held in common, and thus serve as the basis for iconic signification. Any member of a class can signify a class simply by virtue of whatever it is that makes it a member of a class. Adam can be a symbol of mankind by virtue of being an (imaginary) man. But the poet has to find a way of delimiting or indicating which classes are relevant, and by and large must operate within the normal range of associations that are normally available to his audience. Adam is also a member of the class of ungreen things, and by virtue of being ungreen can be an icon for ungreen things. But a poet who wanted to talk about ungreenness would have to take special pains to get us to notice that Adam was ungreen. The process by which an author specifies how we are to take the icon varies from poem to poem, and becomes more problematic as the icon becomes less complex. Novels are normally easily captured when all we want is some general statement about their 'subject-matter'; the area of experience they resemble is large and usually familiar, so there is little difficulty in getting the general import. The serious work, when the icon is complex, is getting clear on the less general details. Yeats is fond of the short poem, and here the opposite is true. Most of the hard work in extremely short poems lies in seeing what area of experience to relate to the icon:

STATISTICS

'Those Platonists are a curse,' he said,
'God's fire upon the wane,
A diagram hung there instead,
More women born than men.'

(*Collected Poems*, p. 271)

The icon in this poem is a comment by an (imaginary) speaker on 'Those Platonists', and the comment is one that is familiar. What the speaker says is that the 'Platonists' replace the vibrant, fecund world of things by abstractions, mere diagrams. When we take the title of the poem into account however, we begin to see what the point of the poem is. Yeats is showing us that the modern practical love of statistics, the seemingly tough approach to experience that is characteristic of the social sciences, of modern politics, and of newspaper speculation, is just as abstract as the Platonic belief in a world of supra-sensible forms. How easy it is to misread poems of this sort may be illustrated by a comment of Unterecker's. After saying that the three poems which follow the poem 'Symbols' are about the place of symbols in modern times, Unterecker offers a reading of statistics.

'Statistics' continues the attack against the literalists. (Modern man, not Yeats, is of course the 'he' of the first line. Yeats, like the Platonists, found his symbolic diagrams necessary connecting links between the physical and the ideal world.) And 'Three Movements' brings those literalists, here represented as naturalists, gasping on the strand that had been revealed by the receding wave of 'The Nineteenth Century and After'.[1]

Unterecker cannot come to grips with the poem because he does not understand that the poem is not a report on Yeats's beliefs, but a bit of imaginary experience, an 'icon', to be interpreted. The things he says about the 'he' of the first line are especially disturbing since the device is so common in Yeats's short poems. Essentially, the device is an attempt to create a *persona* in a brief compass. Because the *persona* is usually passionate, but at the same time only one-dimensional, he is usually referred to in the third person. 'Tom the Lunatic' or 'Crazy Jane', or any of the speakers who are described only as saying this or that, are not well-developed characters. By avoiding the device of the first person *persona* Yeats assures only limited interest in the *persona*, and a concentration on the one or two important features of the *persona*. But Unterecker does not recognise the device, and therefore misunderstands the poem.

This failure to see that a poem is a bit of imaginary experience which is to be interpreted, rather than a collection of statements about the world, is made even more often when Yeats uses a first-person *persona*. A brief look at a fine early poem, and some comments on the poem, should demonstrate how this happens.

1 Unterecker, *Reader's Guide to William Butler Yeats*, p. 209.

THE COLD HEAVEN

Suddenly I saw the cold and rook-delighting heaven
That seemed as though ice burned and was but the more ice,
And thereupon imagination and heart were driven
So wild that every casual thought of that and this
Vanished, and left but memories, that should be out of season
With the hot blood of youth, of love crossed long ago;
And I took all the blame out of all sense and reason,
Until I cried and trembled and rocked to and fro,
Riddled with light. Ah! when the ghost begins to quicken,
Confusion of the death-bed over, is it sent
Out naked on the roads, as the books say, and stricken
By the injustice of the skies for punishment?

(*Collected Poems*, p. 140)

In the poem the *persona* has a vision of heaven in which it appears
as the union of opposites (fire and ice), yet as perfectly pure
('was but the more ice'). The total effect of the description is to
create a heaven which is pure, cold and distant. Furthermore, it is
a 'rook-delighting heaven' which, when compared to the impure,
contradictory life of man in the world, can only serve to make the
speaker aware of his imperfection. The heaven of the poem functions in the same manner as all ideals. For if ideals, the belief in
heavenly perfection, spur us on to great deeds, they must also, of
necessity, constantly serve as a reminder of how we have fallen
short of perfection. So the heaven in the poem functions first of all
as an inspiration or goal for the speaker, banishing all the casual
thoughts of ordinary living (lines three and four), and introducing
in him a kind of idealism that is proper to young men, but which
can only make him unhappy in his current situation (lines five and
six).

Any form of idealism, any desire for an ideal or perfect state,
must make our necessarily imperfect lives seem shoddy and poor.
Whether we desire the perfect love, or heaven, what we have will
seem less valuable, less bearable, just because we can conceive of the
ideal. So the young man's thoughts of love function in much the
same way as the religious man's thoughts of heaven. But the point
is that the desire for the perfect is unreasonable, and judging what
we are in the light of the perfect or ideal is destructive. The
persona of the poem recognises this in retrospect and says that his
vision of the heavens, and his remembering the ideal of love he had

63

as a young man, caused him to take 'all the blame out of all sense and reason,/Until I cried and trembled and rocked to and fro,/ Riddled with light.'

He is 'riddled' by the light of heaven, of the perfect; he is driven almost mad by the idea of perfection. Yeats is here giving an 'icon' for the disturbing and destructive role that idealistic thinking plays in the lives of men. The *persona* is suddenly ashamed of what he is, what all men must be, because he has had one of those visions of perfection that all men are sometimes afflicted with. The sort of masochistic self-torture that the *persona* indulges here is something that we all recognise and face.

In the last three and a half lines of the poem the *persona* asks whether the soul is sent out naked to suffer the injustice of the skies for punishment. Whether or not Yeats believes in an after-life is not an issue, any more than whether or not Shakespeare believed in ghosts is an issue in reading *Hamlet*. Yeats might have been a flaming atheist and still have written the poem. In the same way the question of what 'books' are involved doesn't really mat-ter here either. We are asked to imagine a soul sent out naked after death to wander the road in the kind of cold invoked earlier. And the soul of an imperfect man would be an imperfect soul. And an imperfect soul would be 'stricken' by the skies for exactly the reasons that a man would. The heaven is unjust just because it is perfect, and its perfection would torture a soul even more than the living man because the soul is 'naked' – that is, the soul doesn't even have the protection from idealism, from the desire for perfec-tion, that a living man has. For the living man has his 'clothes', his body and his everyday activities and concerns ('Casual thought of that and this') to distract him from whatever image of perfec-tion may haunt him. Finally, we may notice that the soul's punish-ment is 'for' his desire for perfection. It is a consequence of our desire for the perfect that we are punished, made to feel imperfect. The skies, our ideals, or desires for perfection, punish us only so far as we allow them to. The point in the last three lines is this – Yeats has extended the conflict between what we are and what we want to be to the ghost or spirit of man in order to suggest that this conflict and the pain it causes us are central facts about all men. Whether or not we survive after death is not important, nor is the reader's opinion on this question relevant. What is important about the last image is that it suggests how central and how inevitable and how painful the conflict between the ideal and the actual is for most men, and it suggests it to the atheist and the theist, the spiritualist and the scientist alike.

This is not a complete reading, of course, but it is one that covers the major implications of the poem. 'The Cold Heaven' is not a difficult poem, and only moderately complex; but any 'icon' is very quickly going to achieve a resonance that is impossible in ordinary discourse. To describe all the aspects of even a simple map in normal discursive language is difficult, though not theoretically impossible. The number of true statements that could be uttered about a complex map would defy a computer; and the number of true statements that could be uttered about the relationship between the map and the area mapped, though each immediately obvious from the map, would take forever to utter. So the number of true statements that could be uttered in describing how the imaginary speaker's experience, and his question, relate to human experience, defies normal discursive language. But just as we are anxious to say that this is a map of Europe and not of the moon, so we are anxious to say the sort of thing that has been said about 'The Cold Heaven'. Poems, like maps, are not shoddy ways of doing what propositions do, but are an activity that is cognitive, although logically independent of propositional language.

The failure to bear in mind the complex consequences of the fact that poetry is not a collection of second-rate, but pretty, propositions has effects on the practice of criticism. Ellmann is the best of Yeats's critics, but he often makes this mistake:

In relation to Yeats's artistic problems, 'The Cold Heaven' is the most significant poem in the book and points the way to his later development. The heaven which he now sees in vision is not that which he had imagined in the 'nineties, a pretty heaven of 'embroidered cloths', but a cruel and remorseless one of burning ice; for a staggering instant he beholds himself shorn of all his accomplishments and defenses, with no memory left except that all-important one of love crossed long ago, for which he feels inexplicably compelled to take all the blame. The poem ends in terror:

> Ah! when the ghost begins to quicken,
> Confusion of the death-bed over, is it sent
> Out naked on the roads, as the books say, and stricken
> By the injustice of the skies for punishment?

In comparison with an early poem like 'The Secret Rose', 'The Cold

Heaven' exhibits a great advance in force. The former also ended with a question,

> Surely thine hour has come, thy great wind blows,
> Far-off, most secret, and inviolate Rose?

but the question there is a kind of prayer. In 'The Cold Heaven' the question at the end forces itself out like an exclamation; instead of reluctantly admiring the poet's facility, we are swept into the poem, and find his reaction dramatically possible and meaningful for ourselves.

'We sing amid our uncertainty,' Yeats wrote in *Per Amica Silentia Lunae*. Much uncertainty can be found in 'The Cold Heaven'.

Neither Dante nor the writer of the apocryphal book of Enoch, who probably affected the poem, nor Ruysbroeck, whose statement that the mystic ecstasy 'not this or that' Yeats incorporated in one of the lines, would have used the point of interrogation; they would have used declarative statement. But Yeats' problem was to admit doctrine (the idea of a heaven) and doubt (the divergence from the Christian conception of heaven, and the possibility that heaven may be only a state of mind), and then to transcend them by directing the emphasis away from them to the emotional state of speaker. Through dramatic metaphor Yeats was able to escape a large share of the responsibility for his fictions despite the title of the volume, and at the same time to attain more powerful mode of expression.[1]

Ellmann assumes that the poet is trying to tell us something about heaven; or at least about the question whether or not there is a heaven. Instead of looking at the qualities of the imagined experience, and asking how and where it is like other experiences, he asks whether or not Yeats believes that there is a heaven. But the final question of the poem is not a question about whether or not there is an after-life. It is a rhetorical question which begs that question in order to give us a final image for the destructive qualities of the human ability to conceive of perfection. Heaven, love and the after-life of the soul get into the poem so that question can be asked and no other. Ellmann's scholarship, his attention to sources, and biographical details, could have been useful, but because he makes a theoretical mistake about how poems work, all his energy is wasted. The scholarship turns out to be just spinning the wheels; it doesn't help us to understand the poem.

This sort of mistake is becoming increasingly common. Consider Zwerdling's comment on the poem.

[1] Richard Ellmann, *Yeats, The Man and the Masks* (New York: E. P. Dutton & Co. Inc., 1948), pp. 204–5.

Even the most casual reading of this poem suggests that the 'heaven' of the title has little connection with the familiar Christian conception. Perhaps the closest parallel is Shelley's 'Mont Blanc', which also associates ice and eternity and suggests the ultimate destructiveness of the eternal world. The conception, however, is clearly based on a private 'vision', achieved through no particularly familiar spiritual discipline, and seemingly not induced at all: 'Suddenly I saw...' The validity of this direct vision of the cold heaven, it should be noticed, is not questioned. Yet there is a question at the end of the poem which suggests the incompleteness of the revelation. It is interesting that the end of the poem tenuously brings us back from the private vision to more orthodox thought, for Yeats speculates whether his own vision conforms with 'what the books say'.

'The Cold Heaven' also illustrates how Yeats solves the problem of effectively describing something which is both private and supernatural. We can see the same method used in the vivid evocation of Byzantium, or of the beast in 'The Second Coming'. Yeats lavishes his finest descriptions, his most precise pictures, on material with which he cannot expect the reader to be familiar. The 'cold and rook-delighting heaven/That seemed as though ice burned and was but the more ice' becomes as real as the more traditional descriptions of heaven with which we are presumably familiar. The emotion of the speaker is described with equal care. Yeats suggests the quality of the ecstatic state by ending the descriptive portion of the poem with the ambiguous, telling phrase (emphasized by its placement at the beginning of the line and before a transition), 'riddled with light'. This brings us to a final important point about the poem, that it concentrates less on the nature of the vision than on the heroism of the visionary, a reminder that we are still dealing with a heroic individual whose visionary power is itself more important than what he sees.[1]

Zwerdling also takes the poem to be just another sort of description; he too thinks that because Yeats's poem begins 'Suddenly I saw...' that what the poem is about is the possibility of having experiences of this sort. As an example of practical criticism the treatment of this poem in Yeats's scholarship is dismaying. I have found the poem treated by six of Yeats's critics. All six attempts to handle the poem are vitiated by the same sorts of mistakes we have seen in Ellmann and Zwerdling.[2] However, Unterecker's treatment of this poem warrants lengthier consideration.

---

[1] Alex Zwerdling, *Yeats and the Heroic Ideal* (New York: New York University Press, 1965), pp. 160–1.
[2] Raymond Cowell, *W. B. Yeats* (London: Evans Brothers, 1969); T. R. Henn, in *An Honoured Guest*, eds. D. Donoghue and J. R. Mulryne (London: Edward

Yet in spite of so much praise there is also evaluation and careful thought. 'The Cold Heaven', the most difficult of these poems, is complicated by intricate speculations about the afterlife which, in Yeats' subsequent work, grow increasingly important. To 'understand' the poem, one must keep firmly in mind Yeats' treatment of his poetic material, particularly symbolic images and scenes (frequently founded on visions or reported visions). The poet uses the image or the symbolic scene, Yeats felt, by carefully studying it for possible 'meanings', possible philosophical parallels, and possible correlations to other significant images or scenes. 'Meaning' does not exist for Yeats in sets of abstract propositions ('scientific laws') carefully extracted from an observed physical world, but rather directly in things themselves. Birds, for instance, suggest to him a whole host of felt values: speed, lightness, freedom, flight, quickness of intellect; they link to artist – since their language is song, to the afterlife – since the medium which they inhabit is thin air; they fly against symbolic sun and moon, nest in the symbolic tree, and hatch symbolic eggs. On the other hand, Yeats was not particularly interested in scientific birdwatching: the physical principles of flight, theories on the mechanics of bird song, calculations as to why ducks float all left him cold.

'The Cold Heaven' draws, therefore on a visionary scene and all the felt relationships – no matter how irrational – Yeats can attach to it. The poem itself, he told Maud Gonne, began with his efforts to describe the feelings brought on by the cold, detached beauty of a winter sky. Starting at 'the rook-delighting heaven', he sees it transformed into a pattern of burning, expanding ice. The burning ice itself ties the two seemingly antithetical subjects of the rest of the poem into a felt unity: burning passions of youth balance against the freezing naked soul of a dead old man which, 'naked on the roads', is stricken by those cold burning skies for punishment. Though Yeats allows us to make up our own minds what that soul is punished for, the poem seems to offer two possibilities: his failure to bring his passions to fruition in love (the punishment, consequently, being that that naked soul will be burned by cold skies), or his recklessly taking the blame for the failure of love – a failure which he was not responsible for (the punishment for which, anticipated in advance, he already experiences: 'riddled by light' – shot through with light and insight – he already sees in vision the anguish the cold skies will ultimately force on his soul). Yet within the framework of the poem both answers are the right one and neither is right. For the poet is also made skeptical by light (he is 'riddled by light' – its shining conundrums plague him). Confused as a man on a death-bed, he ends his poem with a question.[1]

Arnold, 1965); B. Rajan, *W. B. Yeats; a critical introduction* (London: Hutchinson & Co., 1965); Peter Ure, *Yeats* (London: Oliver & Boyd Ltd., 1963); T. R. Whitaker, *Swan and Shadow* (London: Oxford University Press, 1966).
[1] Unterecker, *Reader's Guide to William Butler Yeats*, pp. 127–8.

Unterecker starts well, in that he has discarded his earlier claim that literary symbols are words, and he is now talking about a bird rather than 'bird'. But we can see the same mistake that has been discussed earlier, in that Unterecker thinks that the afterlife is not a symbol, or part of the icon, but that Yeats is really concerned to say something about the afterlife. The poem, he says, 'is complicated by intricate speculations about the afterlife which, in Yeats' subsequent work, grow increasingly important'. This is one source of confusion. But Unterecker feels that he has not really straightened out the poem for the readers he is guiding so he affixes a paragraph of more general comment to his explication.

Yeats offers us the experience of a shattering illumination, the memories it evokes, and – in the question that at first seems unrelated to the rest of the poem – a possible consequence of either the memories or his interpretation of them. The 'meaning' we draw from the poem, can therefore be as trivial ('He remembers how much he used to be in love with Maud Gonne'.) or as rich (speculations about the ethical structure of the universe) as we choose to make it. Each poem, in itself a symbol compounded from symbols, is a reservoir of possibilities.[1]

It is not that Unterecker is confused about how to take the poem, or that he makes mistakes, that is dismaying about this passage – rather it is the expansion of doubt and confusion into a theoretical principle.

The practical consequences of the sort of theoretical considerations that have been offered can be reasonably summarised by the precept that the first question to be asked when dealing with a poem is not 'Did this happen?' or 'Is this true?' or 'Does the poet really believe what he says?', but 'Why did this (idea, event, object or process) occur at this point in the poem?' The question for the critic is not 'Is this so?' but 'Why is it so in the poem?'

The theory also provides some interesting information about the critical vocabulary. By critical vocabulary I mean those words that are intended to answer to our needs for a conceptual framework rather than the words we used to award praise or accord blame. The words I will talk about are (1) image, symbol, structure and icon; (2) metaphor and simile; and (3) symbolism and allegory.

The technical vocabulary of the critic is unlike that of the scientist in that it consists of words that are an accepted part of everyday conversation. This is not surprising, since literature, and the

[1] *Ibid.*, p. 128.

discussion of literature, are so closely connected with everyday life. We need a word that will capture both what happened to Hamlet, and what happened to the man we like down the street, and if we tried to stipulate another word to do the job that 'tragedy' does in criticism, but which was to be purely a technical word, we would quickly find either that we couldn't make the word stick, that no one would use it, or that if it were used, it would quickly be used in contexts outside of discussions of literature. Words used in ordinary discourse have to do a lot of work, and the work they do is of a different kind from the work done by technical terms in a highly organised and theoretical field. In order to do the ordinary jobs that occur outside a theoretical discipline a certain amount of flexibility is required. The flexibility of language that is necessary and useful in ordinary discourse is a disadvantage in physics, but not necessarily in literary criticism. For it is only by preserving the ordinary everyday uses of these words that the critic can do the sorts of jobs that are required of him. But what has often proved disastrous is to assume that it is possible for the critic to use language in the way a physicist does. Any attempt to use a word like 'tragedy' rigorously either limits out certain normal uses of the word or produces some gross distortions in the description of things that don't really fall under the new rubric, but did under the old, and which are mis-described so as to seem to fit the new definition. The first sort of mistake is made by Aristotelians, the second sort by Northrop Frye and his disciples. One step beyond the attempt to create a technical vocabulary is the constant reification of concepts that results in absurd talk about 'the comic' or 'the tragic' or 'the novel'. However, to avoid the kinds of definitions necessary to physics or chemistry is not simply to give up in despair. What is necessary is that instead of trying to create an inflexible vocabulary made up of words which are used only by virtue of the strictest sort of convention within the discipline, we pay attention to the less systematic way we actually use our critical language.

A case in point is the use of 'metaphor' and 'simile'. A great deal of theoretical energy is spent trying to clarify the use of these words. The reason for this seems to be that it is commonly held that works of literature are in some sense metaphors, and so if we get to the bottom of what we are doing when we use metaphors, we shall know some things about literature. Yet the word is rarely employed when anyone does practical criticism. Asking why is isn't used often in criticism will be a revealing exercise. First of all, we shall notice that there are remarkably few metaphors in literature. It is not that they do not often occur, but that they occur just as often in other sorts of language as well. So we have noticed that 'metaphor' is not a term especially connected with literature, and that it is a term we use to describe a grammatical form, which is why it is usually discussed with 'simile'. Now, distinctions between grammatical forms are not within the central area of interest for the literary critic; although they are sometimes important to us, they rarely occupy our attention in the way they occupy the attention of the grammarian or philosopher. Consider this poem by Yeats:

THE WITCH

Toil and grow rich,
What's that but to lie
With a foul witch
And after, drained dry,
To be brought
To the chamber where
Lies one long sought
With despair?

(*Collected Poems*, p. 135)

If we wanted to decide whether or not the single sentence of the poem is a metaphor or simile we would have to decide some rather special grammatical questions about the way certain sorts of sentences function, and in particular, what sort of transformations we would get from the phrase. 'What's that but'. This is an interesting problem for a grammarian, or even a certain sort of philosopher, but for the student of literature it is of peripheral interest. We want to know how to 'take' the poem; and in most cases, as in this case, asking whether the sentence that gives us the 'icon' is a simile or metaphor is not relevant. Similies and metaphors are sometimes used by poets in the writing of poems, but they form only a minority of those sentences. Furthermore, the analysis of grammar is only peripheral to criticism. A short digression may clarify the issue. A number of philosophers have attempted to explain metaphor in terms of iconic signification, in much the same way iconic signification has been used to describe the way a poem signifies in the past few pages. But there is this difference: they try to analyse what a sentence employing a metaphor means, and say of a sentence like 'John is a pig' that the sentence means 'Consider the general characteristics of a pig, and you will have an icon for John'. Now, if you are sympathetic to what has been said, about iconic signification in general, then you are probably sympathetic to this analysis of metaphor. But that this analysis of metaphor is suspect in a way that our analysis of literature isn't, seems clear. For it is hard to imagine how one sentence can be said to mean what the other sentence means, on either a grammatical or philosophical account of sentence synonymy, entailment, etc. The fact that iconic signification seems to be involved in both the interpretation of a poem and the understanding of metaphor serves as an explanation of why 'metaphor' has seemed so important to literary theorists. The further reflection that metaphor is a grammatical form has explained why the term is not central to practical criticism. For an icon can be given to us through a metaphor, or without metaphor. Doing criticism is not doing a job of translation; not producing sentences synonymous to the sentences in the poem, but rather it is explicating the icon. So the question of the grammatical form of the sentences that give us the icons is secondary in criticism.

The terms that are important are terms that we use to isolate significant details of the icon, that is, symbol, image and structure. These are the functional words when criticism is actually being done, because they involve both in criticism and in ordinary language, either an object or event, or some feature of an object or event, or some relationship between the elements of an event, or details of an object, that can be taken to be significant. Whether we use one of these three words rather than another is a function of a number of considerations. It is clear that to talk about structure is usually to talk about pattern within the whole icon, and that to talk of an image or symbol is to isolate part of the icon. But a repeated image or symbol can be a structural device, and an important image or symbol may turn out to have a structure. At this point, we are wise to let events go the way they go, and not try to be rigorous in our classifications. Restraint should also be exercised in differentiating between a symbol and an image. There doesn't seem to be any clear principled grounds on which we can differentiate all cases of symbols from all cases of images; although there are often though not even usually, good *ad hoc* reasons. Creatures are never called images, and always symbols, although someone's thought of an animal may be an image. 'Image' is rarely used of a central bit of the icon, but this doesn't mean that we are necessarily dismayed when it is so used. Just how far we should go in trying to differentiate the 'terms' is a moot question, but one closely tied to how we actually use the words now. What is important is that we notice that in our present use of critical language, '*metaphor*' and '*simile*' are used of a grammatical form, and '*image*', '*symbol*' and '*structure*' of the icon. The first line of 'The Cold Heaven' is neither a metaphor nor a simile. ('Suddenly I saw the cold...') and the second line is a simile ('That seemed as though ice burned and was but the more ice'). The language of poetry, whether metaphorical or not, functions by giving us a description of an imaginary event or object, which events or objects are symbols or images by virtue of appearing in poems, and being taken as such by an audience.

It is clear that something can function as an icon for something else only because the person who takes the icon as significant has noticed at least one feature in common between the icon and what the icon signifies. It is only by convention and regularity of interest that we know how to begin to locate the import of the icon, only because we have certain beliefs and conventions in common that if someone talks of a bull we are more likely to think about virility than four-footedness. The larger the role of convention in a specific literary work, the more likely we are to call the work an allegory. *Piers Plowman, Pilgrim's Progress*, or *The Faerie Queen* are the works most often cited in discussions of allegory in English literature, and in them we find one device in particular that is most often cited when they are described as allegories. In all these works, a character or a geographical object, or a man-made object, stands for some ethical quality, and usually that quality is one that we have been interested in sufficiently to have a single word available that captures the quality. The personification of the seven deadly sins in *Piers Plowman* is one example we might give. It is theoretically possible that this sort of technique might be pushed to the point where the object given in the poem was not an iconic symbol at all, but a conventional symbol, and that the convention would provide the only way of understanding the symbol, as is the case with words like 'wolf' or signs like red traffic lights. However, to do this would simply be to give up the special advantages that accrue to someone telling a story. One might as well use discursive language. In the works that we describe as allegory, conventional devices play a more prominent role than they do in other sorts of literature; but the major tool in allegories is iconic signification. No sensible writer would use a serene, benevolent man as an allegorical device to signify jealousy; Langland's seven deadly sins are magnificent examples of the sins they stand for. The distaste for allegory that was characteristic of the artistic milieu that Yeats inhabited in the late nineteenth and early twentieth century rejected allegory on the grounds that it was simply conventional. The doctrines about symbolism that were current saw symbolism as a natural language, and allegory as simply a conventional language. The language of symbolism was the only way that the higher realities or spiritual realities could be discovered. As we shall see, this was a point of doctrine that Yeats accepted in the early years of his career as a poet, and which, to a limited extent, was retained throughout his life. But within the talk of symbolism as the natural intimation of a higher spiritual reality Yeats and his contemporaries had begun to see the sorts of things that have been discussed as iconic signification. They had begun to understand that the poet, or novelist, or dramatist, had tools which allowed them to get at common experience without propositional language, by a symbol that stood outside the hard and fast conventions of ordinary language or allegorical art. In 1898 Yeats wrote in an essay entitled 'Symbolism in Poetry':

The other day, when I sat for my portrait to a German Symbolist in Paris, whose talk was all of his love for Symbolism and his hatred for allegory, his definitions were the same as William Blake's, of whom he knew nothing. William Blake has written, 'Vision or Imagination' – meaning symbolism by these words – 'is a representation of what actually exists, really or unchangeably. Fable or Allegory is formed by the daughters of Memory.' The German insisted with many determined gestures, that Symbolism said things which could not be said so perfectly in any other way, and needed but a right instinct for its understanding; While Allegory said things which could be said as well, or better, in another way, and needed a right knowledge for its understanding. The one gave dumb things voices, and bodiless things bodies; while the other read a meaning – which had never lacked its voice or its body – into something heard or seen, and loved less for the meaning than for its own sake. The only symbols he cared for were the shapes and motions of the body; ears hidden by the hair, to make one think of a mind busy with inner voices; and a head so bent that back and neck made the one curve, as in Blake's 'Vision of

Bloodthirstiness' to call up an emotion of bodily strength; and he would not put even a lily, or a rose, or a poppy into a picture to express purity, or love, or sleep, because he thought such emblems were allegorical, and had their meaning by a traditional and not by a natural right. I said that the rose, and the lily, and the poppy were so married, by their colour and their odour, and their use, to love and purity and sleep, or to other symbols of love and purity and sleep, and had been so long a part of the imagination of the world, that a symbolist might use them to help out his meaning without becoming an allegorist. I think I quoted the lily in the hand of the angel in Rossetti's 'Annunciation' and the lily in the jar in his 'Childhood of Mary Virgin' and thought they made the more important symbols, the women's bodies, and the angels' bodies, and the clear morning light, take that place, in the great procession of Christian symbols, where they can alone have all their meaning and all their beauty.

It is hard to say where Allegory and Symbolism melt into one another, but it is not hard to say where either comes to perfection; and though one may doubt whether Allegory or Symbolism is the greater in the horns of Michael Angelo's 'Moses', one need not doubt that its symbolism has helped to awaken the modern imagination; while Tintoretto's 'Origin of the Milky Way' which is Allegory without any Symbolism, is, apart from its fine painting, but a moment's amusement for our fancy. A hundred generations might write out what seemed the meaning of the one, and they would write different meanings, for no symbol tells all its meaning to any generation; but when you have said, 'That woman there is Juno, and the milk out of her breast is making the Milky Way,' you have told the meanings of the other, and the fine painting, which has added so much irrelevant beauty, has not told it better.[1]

It is clear that in many respects Yeats's early position on symbolism is radically different from what has been offered an independent account. For one thing, Yeats specifies the particular subjects which symbolism is to treat; like most Symbolists at this time he thought that symbolism was particularly concerned with the supernatural. Still, it seems to me that it can fairly be said that Yeats's idea of symbolism is basically what has been described in the preceding paragraphs. He seems to have felt that allegory was arbitrary, simply an intellectual fancy, while a symbol was a natural or inevitable sign.

Symbolism said things which could not be said so perfectly in any other way, and needed but a right instinct for its understanding; while allegory

[1] W. B. Yeats, *The Collected Works of W. B. Yeats* (Stratford-on-Avon: 8 vols., Shakespeare Head Press, 1908), vol. 6, pp. 176-9.

said things which could be said as well, or better in another way, and needed a right knowledge for its understanding.[1]

That is, symbols signify iconically. However, Yeats enlarges upon this definition of symbolism in two directions. The first direction is toward the area of myth or archetype. We have defined a symbol as an event, process, or object which signifies another event, process, or object by virtue of a real quality of its own. A myth or archetype is, in Yeats's view, a fictional story which, by virtue of its isomorphism with a universal or near-universal human experience, signifies that experience in an immediate, sensuous and concrete manner. It is created as an exemplum of the universal human experience, and it may be counted on to recall that experience in an immediate manner, in all who are told or read the story. Further, although the stories may vary slightly in different cultures, all cultures have some version of most or all myths which reflect important aspects of the human condition. In the poem, 'Her Vision in the Wood' (*Collected Poems*, pp. 312–13), Yeats sets forth this part of his view on symbolism.

> Dry timber under that rich foliage,
> At wine-dark midnight in the sacred wood,
> Too old for a man's love I stood in rage
> Imagining men. Imagining that I could
> A greater with a lesser pain assuage
> Or but to find if withered vein ran blood,
> I tore my body that its wine might cover
> Whatever could recall the lip of lover.
>
> And after that I held my fingers up,
> Stared at the wine-dark nail, or dark that ran
> Down every withered finger from the top;
> But the dark changed to red, and torches shone,
> And deafening music shook the leaves; a troop
> Shouldered a litter with a wounded man,
> Or smote upon the string and to the sound
> Sang of the beast that gave the fatal wound.
>
> All stately women moving to a song
> With loosened hair or foreheads grief-distraught,
> It seemed a Quattrocento painter's throng,
> A thoughtless image of Mantegna's thought –

[1] Yeats, *Essays and Introductions*, pp. 146–7.

Why should they think that are for ever young?
Till suddenly in grief's contagion caught,
I stared upon his blood-bedabbled breast
And sang my malediction with the rest.

That thing all blood and mire, that beast-torn wreck,
Half turned and fixed a glazing eye on mine,
And, though love's bitter-sweet had all come back,
Those bodies from a picture or a coin
Nor saw my body fall nor heard it shriek,
Nor knew, drunken with singing as with wine,
That they had brought no fabulous symbol there
But my heart's victim and its torturer.

This is an exceptionally fine poem, as well as one which gives us
a good deal of information about Yeats's ideas about symbolism at
this stage of his development. It is strange, therefore, to discover
that it has not been much noticed. As far as I know, the only critics
who have discussed it at any length are Ellmann and Unterecker.
Unterecker's comment is:

'Her Vision in the Wood', the first of the three 'old' poems can best be
understood if one bears in mind the last stanza's assertion that the visionary troop had in their invocation to the slain body of Adonis conjured
up in the secret wood 'no fabulous symbol' but rather both the lady herself and her 'heart's victim'. They had unintentionally called her to the
sacred spot to be a witness to the symbolic death of torn Adonis; and she,
by the symbolic wound she has given herself, is able to participate in the
ritual. But the Adonis proves to be her own lover. As she, 'Too old for a
man's love,' wounded by her own nails and so like the visionary lover
'blood-bedabbled', stares into the drying 'glazing eye' of 'That thing all
blood and mire, that beast-torn wreck,' 'Love's bitter-sweet' floods back
over both their bodies. Each wounded yet loved by the other, each made
impotent – she by the 'dry timber' of age and he by the boar's wound –
the ancient lovers are nevertheless momentarily revitalized by the blood
which flows down their loins. (Yeats is careful in lines 8 and 9 that there
can be no doubt about the place in which the lady wounds herself.) But the
moment of interpenetrating eyes is all they have, The Adonis-lover dies.
She falls, shrieking, to earth.[1]

The poem clearly is a record of a self-induced hallucination.
Why Unterecker endows the 'visionary troops' with an existence
independent of the old woman's tortured imagination I do not

[1] Unterecker, *Reader's Guide to W. B. Yeats*, p. 238.

know. Nor does Unterecker provide much in the way of explication; instead he offers to explain what might be called, for lack of a better word, the plot of the poem. For instance, instead of trying to understand the last lines, Unterecker invents another detail: 'The visionary troop had...conjured up in the sunset wood... both the lady herself and her heart's victim.'

Ellmann is aware that the vision is a vision. But he concludes that the poem contrasts the richness of immediate experience with the pale abstractions of symbols.

His portrayal of the Adonis legend is even more remarkable. The heroine of 'Her Vision in the Wood' has a sudden vision of the God's being slain by a boar: (quotes the entire poem)

The speaker, full of grief at her impotent old age, loses herself among the troop of women who mourn Adonis and sing maledictions upon the boar. But she differs from them in that her grief is not held in control by the stately processional. Her vision goes beyond theirs; the dead man looks at her with his 'glazing eye', and she shrieks and falls, recognizing that this is not the fabulous, symbolic god in whose death she might feel a genuine but detached grief, like that of an actor in a tragic play, but her own lover who is both torturer and victim as love itself is both bitter and sweet. This knowledge comes to her not as a similitude but as sudden direct recognition. Pageants in Yeats have a way of turning into realities. The symbol strikes to the heart; while 'those bodies from a picture or a coin' of the ageless, repetitive chorus pass on unmoved, caught up in the legend which they re-enact in fitting, legendary style, immediate experience overwhelms her.[1]

I agree with Ellmann that the poem deals with the relationship between the Adonis myth and the experience of the woman 'too old for a man's love'. But, as will be seen, the poem is not intended to reveal the poverty of myth, but rather to explore the way the myth parallels the experience of the woman. Adonis is, after all, a fertility god, and the myth explores his loss of fertility just as Yeats's poem explores the woman's loss of fertility.

The crux of the poem is in the last two lines. In the second to last line Yeats says the symbol is 'no fabulous symbol', meaning not that it is not a symbol, but that the symbol is in no way esoteric. In fact, Yeats has his visionary say that the symbol is her 'heart's victim'; that is, it is a reflection of her experience. The same impulse which has caused her to rend 'whatever could recall the

---

[1] Ellmann, *The Identity of Yeats*, pp. 172–3.

lip of lover' has created her vision of the suffering Adonis. The myth is a function of human experience, and by reflecting that experience, is victimised by it. Adonis suffers as humanity suffers. But before the old woman has had the vision she only imperfectly understands her experience. Through the myth she is able to understand her relationship with her lover, and the relationship between the love of her youth and her old age. Through the myth she can now fully recall love's bitter-sweet along with the horrible emotions of her old age. The sexual passion she tried unsuccessfully to 'imagine' by ripping her body, the longing she tried to 'assuage', is satisfied by the myth. Love's bitter-sweet had 'all come back'. The result is to deepen her understanding.

The Adonis myth thus fulfils Yeate's condition for a symbol in that it is an icon for her loss of fertility, and in that she is able to recognise it as such. By increasing her understanding, it is her heart's torturer; and this relationship is the obverse to the relationship of victim and creator. Thus the last line states that Adonis's suffering in the myth is her creation; a creation which casts Adonis in the role of victim, but because Adonis's victimisation is an accurate and revealing reflection or icon of her own plight, his suffering casts him in the role of her torturer as well. The telescoping of the process of life, the ability to feel at once the pain of old age and the bitter-sweet of love, is a torment. Ellmann's statement that it is 'her own lover who is both torturer and victim as love itself is both bitter and sweet' does not make sense of the final lines.

There are two additional elements in the poem which deserve comment. First it should be noted that the chorus and the Adonis figure are not described as consciously motivated characters. They are simply the 'thoughtless' image of visionary thought. Because she has not yet recognised the true nature of the spectacle the old woman becomes momentarily angry. 'Why should they think that are forever young?' Yeats has used her point of view in his narrative, and to assume that he means us completely to accept her reaction to the vision is to misread the poem. He has created a picture of hysteria, and the vision is induced by self-immolation. It is her 'vision', and to miss the fact that it is a vision, a self-induced trance, is to mis-read the poem.

Secondly, it is important to notice that her vision corresponds to the vision of others. It is a 'thoughtless image of Mantegna's thought,' meaning that it is a projection, without consciousness of its own, which might equally be her vision or Mantegna's. Yeats continues to try to assure the reader of the communal nature of her vision; the vision is equally 'a Quattrocento painter's throng' or 'bodies from a picture or a coin'. The symbol or icon is a natural, not a conventional, sign. It is by virtue of the fact that it is natural and not arbitrary that it is understood, and because it is natural it tends to recur, to suggest itself time and time again, as the necessary image of the destruction of fertility.

III

So far, Yeats's notion of symbolism is in no way extraordinary. The poem just discussed is an intelligent and moving presentation of a view which a great many people would share. But Yeats introduced other considerations which serve to differentiate his theory of the nature of symbolism in literature from the simply naturalistic view.

The ideas on symbolism that Yeats puts forward in 'Her Vision in the Wood', reflect only a small part of his thought on this subject. Anyone who believes, as Yeats certainly did, that reality is not exhausted by our perceptual apparatus, that the world which we see is a function of another reality, and that the one reality stands in a definable relationship to the other, might claim that, in the sense defined in Section II of this chapter, these realities were 'symbols' for each other. That is, a Platonist might claim that a chair was an icon for the idea 'chair', etc. But, it is not usually possible to find this kind of relationship between the noumenal and phenomenal in Yeats's poetry and prose. He can, and does, avail himself of Platonic notions in occasional poems, in poems where he is not primarily concerned with stating his philosophical position or expanding his myth. The poem 'Before the world was made' provides a typical example of this kind of casual use of a philosophical position which Yeats does not himself agree with. Explaining the female desire to appear beautiful as an attempt to discover a face which existed 'Before the world was made', is an ingenious adaptation of Platonic ideas. However, Yeats cannot claim this relationship to be the basis of literary symbolism if he is to be consistent and if his myth is to be unified. For in terms of nineteenth-century German philosophy there is no place for ontologically distinct ideas. Reality is divided, not between ideas and copies as in the Platonic and neo-Platonic theories but between mind and its reflection in the phenomenal. If there were something other than mind and its characteristic projection, then this something was unknowable. That is, in Kantian terms, the phenomenal world was the product, jointly, of the *Ding-an-sich* (thing-in-itself) and the forms and categories of the intellect. But one could know only the relationship between the mind with its forms and categories, and the phenomenal. The relationship between the noumenal and phenomenal remained unknowable. In neo-Kantian philosophy, of course, there were no things-in-themselves.

If one were to hold this view, and at the same time wish to assert that through symbols one was able to discover more about reality than is revealed in the phenomenal, the theory of symbolism which resulted would of necessity be very different from the Platonic or Berkeleyan. This is, as we shall see, Yeats's position. But it is a position which he shared with other English poets, most noticeably Coleridge and Blake. It is a position which substitutes the idea of creation for the idea of imitation. It fastens on the notion that the phenomenal is created by the human mind in accordance with the structure of the mind, and claims that the poet, when he functions as poet or creator, makes a new phenomenal configuration which reveals the structure of the human mind in a new guise. So Coleridge, in his *Biographia Literaria,* when looking for the first principle of both being and knowledge, says:

THESIS V

Such a principle cannot be any thing or object. Each thing is what is is in consequence of some other thing. An infinite, independent thing is no less a contradiction than an infinite circle or a sideless triangle. Besides a thing is that which is capable of being an object of which itself is not the sole percipient. But an object is inconceivable without a subject as its antithesis. *Omne perceptum percipientem supponit.*

But neither can the principle be found in a subject as a subject, contradistinguished from an object: for *unicuique percipienti aliquid objicitur perceptum.* It is to be found therefore neither in object nor subject taken separately, and consequently, as no other third is conceivable, it must be found in that which is neither subject nor object exclusively, but which is the identity of both.

THESIS VI

This principle, and so characterized, manifests itself in the SUM or I AM, which I shall hereafter indiscriminately express by the words spirit, self and self-consciousness. In this, and in this alone, object and subject, being and knowing, are identical, each involving and supposing the other. In other words, it is a subject which becomes a subject by the act of constructing itself objectively to itself; but which never is an object except for itself, and only so far as by the very same act it becomes a subject. It may be described therefore as a perpetual self-duplication of one and the same power into object and subject, which pre-suppose each other, and can exist only as antitheses.

SCHOLIUM. If a man be asked how he *knows* that he is, he can only answer, *sum quia sum*. But if (the absoluteness of this certainly having been admitted) he be again asked how he, the individual person, came to be, then in relation to the ground of his existence, not to the ground of his knowledge of that existence, he might reply, *sum quia deus est*, or still more philosophically, *sum quia in deo sum*.

But if we elevate our conception to the absolute self, the great eternal I AM, then the principle of being, and of knowledge, of idea, and of reality, the ground of existence, and the ground of the knowledge of existence, are absolutely identical. *Sum quia sum*; I am, because I affirm myself to be; I affirm myself to be, because I am.[1]

It is Coleridge's intention to deduce from this a theory of the imagination. Only because Coleridge has received a letter (which he reprints in the body of his book) from a friend most concerned that he will confuse his readers with metaphysics, are we spared a lengthy discussion of the exact steps by which Coleridge deduces his theory of the imagination from his metaphysics. But we do get a statement of Coleridge's theory of the imagination.

The imagination then I consider either as primary, or secondary. The primary imagination I hold to be the living power and prime agent of all human perception, and as a repetition in the finite mind of the eternal act of creation in the infinite I AM. The secondary I consider as an echo of the former, co-existing with the conscious will, yet still as identical with the primary in the kind of its agency, and differing only in degree, and in the mode of its operation. It dissolves, dissipates, in order to re-create; or where this process is rendered impossible, yet still, at all events, it struggles to idealize and to unify. It is essentially *vital*, even as all objects (as objects) are essentially fixed and dead.[2]

This notion of the imagination is one of the central features of the romantic movement. It meant that the poet's attention tended to shift away from the world to his own personality, and that this

[1] Samuel Taylor Coleridge, *Biographia Literaria* (London: J. M. Dent & Sons Ltd., 1962), pp. 150-1.
[2] *Ibid.*, p. 167.

personality was considered to be the ground of reality. The work of literature, the symbol, was not an imitation of the world, or an imitation of ontologically separate and distinct forms. Instead, it was a new creation formed by the imagination, and as a symbol, it stood in relation to the mind which created it. What was displayed was not an exterior reality, but a reality that came into being by virtue of being thought, and that revealed a new possibility for the human mind. Yeats's mature view of the imagination and of symbolism conforms in many respects to Coleridge's.

Yeats's early formulation of symbolism which occurs in the essay 'Magic' was transformed into a theory of the imagination like that of Coleridge or Blake. The nature of Yeats's theory of the imagination will be the subject of the next chapter. I shall try to show how Yeats's theory of the imagination and especially the role played by symbols in the theory, provide a key to Yeats's ideas about history, philosophy and art, and the phenomenal world itself.

4

Art, history and the phenomenal world

In Coleridge's theory of the imagination there occurs almost at once a radical dichotomy, a schism, between the primary and secondary imagination. But it is still a fact, for Coleridge, that the ordinary phenomenal world is a creation of the human mind. Ignoring the transcendental subject (in Coleridge's version of idealism, the great I AM), it is possible to say of Coleridge's theory that the imaginative act involved in perceiving the world is the same imaginative act as is involved in the creation of a work of art. The dichotomy occurs because Coleridge introduces into his analysis of the primary imagination the notion of the Absolute Self. That is, he claims that the normal imaginative act (what most of us would call perception) of the individual, repeats the imaginative act of the Absolute Self. If Coleridge had been less influenced by his reading of the neo-Kantians, and more influenced by Kant, he could simply have said that the world we perceive is inter-subjectively real though transcendentally ideal. That is, Kant had claimed that although 'things-in-themselves' were unknowable, because we all share the same conceptual apparatus (we all wear blue spectacles, as it were), we share a world that is real in that it is inter-subjective (that is, we can check with each other). To say this is to say something like 'the primary imagination I hold to be the living power and prime agent of all human perception, and as a repetition in the finite mind of the eternal act of creation in the infinite I AM'. But in shifting to a position more properly characterised as neo-Kantian, Coleridge creates a grave difficulty. For in introducing the 'infinite I AM' Coleridge ignored the radical innovation that lay behind the whole enterprise, and which was the original source of his attraction to Kant's theories. For if what we perceive is identical with what is the eternal creation of the I AM, then why not simply say, with Berkeley, that what we perceive is guaranteed by God? Coleridge's theories have rightly been regarded as an attempt to create a superstructure which would provide a place for the creative role of human consciousness and so provide an escape from the passive and mechanistic theories of mind of Hartley and Locke. But is there any point, once we have the guarantee provided by the great I AM, in trying to find out what the inter-subjective world is like by finding out what our minds are like? If we are interested in what we perceive, we can attend to it directly. Coleridge's idealism has turned into a simple-minded realism. Just how thoroughly confused Coleridge was about this point can be further illustrated from this strange comment on Kant in Chapter IX of the *Biographia Literaria*.

In spite therefore of his own declarations, I could never believe it was possible for him to have meant no more by his Noumenon, or Thing in Itself, than his mere words express; or that in his own conception he confined the whole plastic power to the forms of the intellect, leaving for the external cause, for the *materiale* of our sensations, a matter without form, which is doubtless inconceivable.

Coleridge has thoroughly misunderstood Kant. He has failed to grasp the purpose of the enterprise, which was just to get rid of the sort of problem the empiricists, including Berkeley, found whenever they had to deal with perception as an interpretation of something given prior to sensation. Kant may not have been radical enough in his rejection of the traditional model (one continual criticism of Kant, made by the neo-Kantians and others, has been that, given his theory, he had no right to talk about noumena at all) but Kant certainly cannot be charged with claiming that noumena were matter without form. What he said was that things in themselves were unknowable. The problem is that he then goes on to say that they are the cause of sensations; and given that they are unknowable a critic can ask how he came to know that they cause sensation. There are a number of alternatives open to anyone confronted by a gap between sense data and the external world. One move, Kant's, was to deny that the problem was properly stated, and so to collapse the problem. The traditional empiricist move was to seek for a way to guarantee the validity of sense impressions. Coleridge rejects, in the *Biographia Literaria*, all such attempts as confused attempts to create a mechanistic theory that will account for mind (cf. especially his comments on Berkeley). Yet his theories themselves partake of the faults he finds in others. It is difficult to see any significant difference between his theory of perception (the primary imagination) and his talk of the infinite I AM, and Berkeley's theory of perception, and his talk of God.

But despite what he says about the primary imagination, Coleridge's central interest is the nature of the relationship between mind and perception; he does not really want to guarantee a reality independent of perceiving minds. So, since he has removed the usefulness, from this point of view, of examining what happens in ordinary experience, he shifts his attention to extraordinary experience.

The secondary (imagination) I consider as an echo of the former, co-existing with the conscious will, yet still as identical with the primary in the kind of its agency, and differing only in degree, and in the mode of its operation. It dissolves, dissipates, in order to re-create; or where this process is rendered impossible, yet still, at all events, it struggles to idealize and to unify. It is essentially *vital*, even as all objects (as objects) are essentially fixed and dead.

This paragraph represents Coleridge's thought at its worst: that it has received so much attention has been disastrous both for romantic poetry and for those who have sought to make sense of the romantic movement and romantic poetry, including that of Coleridge in his more characteristic mood. For the whole drift of the romantic movement was to regard normal perception on the Kantian model, to see that what Locke portrayed as simply a passive activity was in fact active and creative. What is at the core of the romantic movement is a rejection of 'objects (as objects)' – the notion that there is a 'fixed' or 'dead' exterior reality which the mind simply copies to itself. Coleridge's definition of the imagination invites us to regard objects not perceived by the secondary imagination as ' dead,' and to regard normal perception or imagination on a Lockean model.

It is generally recognised that Western Europe underwent a sea change at the end of the eighteenth century. Central to the developments of the period was the shift from an empiricist to an idealist theory of perception. What happened was not that everyone read and understood Kant, but that ideas that were becoming widespread found their philosophical locus in his work. Because Coleridge was interested in philosophy, it is his treatment of these ideas in prose that has been taken to be the central statement of romantic epistemology, and his definition of the imagination in the *Biographia Literaria* has become a sort of sacred text. I shall argue that the definition is not consistent with the rest of Coleridge's avowed position, nor with the beliefs of the other major romantic poets. In

order to see how misleading Coleridge's definition of the imagination is, it will be necessary to shift our attention from what is
primarily philosophical discourse to the more generalised way that
philosophical ideas normally function in poetry.

Probably the most instructive single issue will be raised by
examining the difference between Wordsworth's rejection of Hart-
leyan associationalism and Coleridge's. In order to get at what I take
to be Wordsworth's views of this issue I shall quote at some length
from Geoffrey Durrant's two books on Wordsworth.[1] Professor
Durrant discusses fully 'I wandered lonely as a cloud' and 'The
Reverie of Poor Susan'. He shows how, in 'I wandered lonely as a
cloud' Wordsworth is intent on providing an analysis of the art of
perceiving imaginatively, while in 'The Reverie of Poor Susan' he
is providing an analysis of perceiving passively. The argument is
lengthy and I am telescoping two distinct discussions, so I have
taken some liberties in order to reduce the argument to manageable
proportions.

'I wandered lonely as a cloud' is only superficially about the daffodils
which Wordsworth remembers so vividly. What it offers us in fact is an
account of the experience of poetic creation. The poem opens with the poet
wandering in a state of loneliness and passivity. When he says that 'he
wandered lonely as a cloud' he reminds us of those moods when we are
aimless, undirected, and not fully related to the world around us. This sense
of disconnectedness from experience is strenthened by the description of
the clouds which 'float on high'. The mood of detachment, or rather of
indifference and passivity, is suddenly broken in upon by the appearance
of the daffodils:

> When all at once I saw a crowd,
> A host, of golden daffodils.

These very lines show the poetic process itself at work. At first the daffodils are seen as 'a crowd'; but with a sudden shift of attention and a sudden energy of mind the poet slightly re-arranges the pattern they form in
his mind, and sees them as 'a host'. In other words the shapelessness, as of
a crowd, which the daffodils at first seemed to exhibit, is turned into a
pattern, though not a rigid one – the order of an army like the host of
angels in *Paradise Lost* rather than the drill order of the barrack-square.
The poet's mind is already at work ordering the experience that flows into
it, giving it coherence and vividness. The vividness appears immediately
in the heightening of the colour of the daffodils from yellow to 'golden'.

---

[1] Geoffrey Durrant, *William Wordsworth* (Cambridge: Cambridge University
Press, 1969), and *Wordsworth and the Great System* (C.U.P., 1970).

This process, by which the objects seen in the landscape are invested with brightness and coherence by the poet's own mind, is described in the rest of the poem.

(*William Wordsworth*, p. 20)

Professor Durrant provides a close analysis of the poem, in which image after image yields to his treatment of the poem as a record of the order and unity discovered in the scene. But he claims that for Wordsworth the order and unity that is being discovered is a function of a nature that is firmly 'out there'.

Daffodils grow best in the shade and where there is water, and so the flowers are not accidentally at this particular point in space and time. The curve they describe along the lake is the curve of necessity, and it is immediately related by Wordsworth's active intelligence to the very curve of the heavens:

> Continuous as the stars that shine
> And twinkle on the milky way,
> They stretched in never-ending line
> Along the margin of a bay:
> Ten thousand saw I at a glance,
> Tossing their heads in sprightly dance.

In these lines Wordsworth shows the daffodils as part of a universal order, as growing where they do because of the natural law which dictates their existence. Just as the stars in the Milky Way are fixed in their courses, and show a beauty which arises from necessity, so the daffodils are triumphantly themselves in their own particular place and time. There is a poignancy here because in all creation man seems to be the only creature that is capable of feeling not at home, of 'wandering lonely as a cloud'; and, unlike the cloud, being aware of his loneliness and his lack of a settled habitation. The joy exhibited by both the 'dancing' flowers and the stars that 'twinkle' is attributed to them by the poet, as he well understands. This joy is the counterpart of the loneliness and passivity experienced by the poet until his mind was awakened to a new life by the daffodils themselves. Even while this thought is being advanced, the poet's mind is actively imposing a further pattern upon the daffodils. They are described as 'fluttering and dancing in the breeze'; so there is a leap of the mind from seeing the movements of the daffodils as a mere disorganized 'fluttering' to a perception that it is a kind of dance, a harmonious movement in which a pattern may be discerned. In this the flowers resemble the stars, in whose movements men from Newton's time onwards – and Wordsworth was educated in Cambridge to a deep respect for Newton – had increasingly learned to discover a comprehensible and even delightful pattern.

(*Ibid.*, pp. 21–2)

Professor Durrant finds in the breeze that blows through the daffodils a symbol for the harmony between nature and the minds of
men.

The breeze is important to Wordsworth, not only as an essential element in the poem in which rhythmic patterns of water, and the rhythmic
dance of the flowers, form so large a part of the pleasure, but also because,
for Wordsworth, a breeze or wind is a common symbol of the creative
activity of the poet. The breeze that blows on the lake and sets the waves
and daffodils dancing is the natural equivalent of the breeze of poetic
'glee' which is now blowing through the poet's mind. So Wordsworth
declares:

> The waves beside them danced; but they
> Out-did the sparkling waves in glee:
> A poet could not but be gay,
> In such a jocund company:

The poet is gay because his mind is once more active, making order in a
world which seemed so short a time ago disorderly and pointless. Where he
was lonely, he is now in 'a jocund company'. It should be noted, however,
that Wordsworth does not say that nobody could fail to be gay in such a
situation. He speaks here of 'a poet'. The poet, although he is essentially
like other men – 'a man speaking to men' – has, according to Wordsworth,
'a greater organic sensibility', and has usually 'thought long and deeply'.
It is such a man, and such a man only, who finds himself in a state of
creative joy when placed in such a situation.   (*Ibid.*, p. 23)

Professor Durrant goes on to say that the last stanza tells us that
the power of imagination, once gained, is a defence against the
anomie of the poet's original mood – 'the delight in creative perception recurs when the poet finds himself in need of it – when he is once
more, ''in vacant or in pensive mood'', as he was in his loneliness at
the beginning of the poem'. The argument, then, consists in re-
iterating the fact that this is a poem about the 'imagination' in that
it is a poem which deals with the way we react to the world. But it
is not a poem which can be properly said to be about an epistemological question. For Wordsworth the world is firmly 'out there'
– epistemological questions about the adequacy of our perception
of the external world never arise.

We gain a strong sense of the actuality and immediacy of the daffodils, so
that it is natural, when we think casually of the poem, to give it in our
minds the title 'Daffodils'. And...this is an essential part of the poem's
success. In the dialogue between nature and the perceiving mind, both

voices must be heard. The polarity between subject and object must be sustained if the true wonder of the commerce between the mind and the world that we 'half create and half perceive' is to be communicated. This polarity between the 'real' world and the subjective mind is too often lost in romantic poetry. The pervasive, ever-present sense of nature as external, objective and real distinguishes Wordsworth's poetry from that of most of his imitators, and gives to the ordering and harmonizing tendencies of his mind something of a heroic quality. It is easy to unify what has no unity or order of its own, but Wordsworth's great achievement was to harmonize without falsifying, at any point, his strong sense of what was actually *there*. This he does with such success in this poem that at times we forget that it is a poem 'of the Imagination', and are tempted to look on it as fragment of autobiography or as a brilliant flower-piece.

(*Wordsworth and the Great System*, p. 134)

Professor Durrant's remarks about 'I wandered lonely as a cloud' seem to me correct. For Wordsworth's poetry is at its best just when we have a strong sense of what is given in normal perception. What is important to notice is that Wordsworth operates within the framework of a common world, and that he is able to do this just because he does not ask epistemological question. Time, space, cause and effect – none of this is of interest to Wordsworth at his best. Wordsworth's concern with the imagination is a practical and psychological concern not a philosophical one.[1] What brings this home most effectively is Professor Durrant's juxtaposition of 'I wandered lonely as a cloud' with 'The Reverie of Poor Susan'.

In 'The Reverie of Poor Susan', which he composed in 1797 and published in 1800, Wordsworth describes the effect upon a country girl who is living in the city of the song of a thrush heard at a street corner. This poem was deliberately placed by Wordsworth next to 'I wandered lonely as a cloud', with the comment that it showed the same capacity of the mind to respond to 'a simple impression'. The difference here is that 'poor Susan' is not a poet, and she is therefore at the mercy of the laws of association, which call up memories which she is unable to organize or control, and which she cannot recall at will. When the thrush sings, Susan remembers her home in the country, and sees a mountain, 'a vision of trees' and a river flowing through the city of London. She remembers also her childhood in the country and the happiness of the home that she loves. But unlike the poet of 'I wandered lonely as a cloud' she remains passive, and can only remain helpless as the vision vanishes for ever:

[1] No value judgment is intended, or necessary. Shakespeare is not philosophical in the sense in which Wordsworth is not philosophical.

> She looks, and her heart is in heaven: but they fade,
> The mist and the river, the hill and the shade:
> The stream will not flow, and the hill will not rise,
> And the colours have all passed away from her eyes!

The distinction between these two experiences was for Wordsworth an important one. He had in his early days fallen under the influence of the theory of memory and of knowledge propounded by Hartley, who held that the operation of the mind was essentially mechanical and automatic. If this was true, there was no room for the creative activity of the poetic imagination. 'I wandered lonely as a cloud' not only describes this act of creative power; it also asserts its validity. The contrast between the poet who can give permanent life to his experience, and the 'poor Susans' of this world, who depend upon the fitful coming and going of the fancy as the laws of memory dictate, is illustrated by these two poems which Wordsworth placed side by side, and linked together with his note on the workings of the imagination.

It must not be thought that Wordsworth sets poets and ordinary men and women apart; on the contrary, the poet is 'a man speaking to men', and all men have within them the capacity for poetry, or at least for the brightness and unity of perception which may be called the poetic vision. He insists in *The Prelude* that the 'poetic spirit' exists in all men from childhood, though in most men it is overlaid by habit:

> Such, verily, is the first
> Poetic spirit of our human life,
> By uniform control of after years,
> In most, abated or suppressed; in some
> Pre-eminent till death.   (II, 260–4)

'Poor Susan', who lives in the city, can catch only a passing glimpse of the radiance of her childhood. She is one of those in whom the 'poetic spirit' has been 'abated or suppressed'. Wordsworth, however, insists that all men may recover the use of the poetic faculty within them, however, much it has been overlaid by habit:

> 'tis thine,
> The prime and vital principle is thine
> In the recesses of thy nature...
>   (*The Prelude*, XIV, 214–16)
>   (*William Wordsworth*, pp. 26–7)

Hartley's theory is one which raises both psychological and philosophical issues which are intricately connected. Professor Durrant shows clearly that Wordsworth's interest was primarily in the psychological issues raised. That is, Wordsworth is interested in contrasting the rather mechanical way that poor Susan thinks, with the more exciting and rewarding way the poet thinks. He is not interested in stating the epistemological problem; he is primarily interested in the practical and moral character of thought and perception. Wordsworth sees that some people think mechanically and are in the grip of their immediate surroundings, and that others are able to think more profoundly and to find complicated relationships between the areas of their experience. He sees, moreover, that people can learn to make more of their experiences. He is aware of the importance of cultivating this sort of consciousness. So the whole force of his poetry is thrown into the job of cultivating that consciousness and speculating about its workings. His is a practical and ethical response. Wordsworth's concern with practical, ethical and psychological questions does not make his poetry less valuable than Coleridge's. For Wordsworth realises that the reason people read poetry is not primarily because they are interested in philosophical questions, but because they are interested in how to live. It is just because he knows this that 'Tintern Abbey' is his finest short poem dealing with the psychology of perception. Here we see that close observation of perceptual experience leads directly to the ethical concerns that have traditionally occupied a central place in Western culture. And we may safely contrast Wordsworth's success here, and in *The Prelude*, with Coleridge's pleasant dream in 'Kubla Khan', and his despair in 'Dejection: An Ode'. It is only in *The Ancient Mariner* that Coleridge succeeds in writing poetry that is of the order of Wordsworth's best work, and one negative reason that may be given for his success on this occasion is that in that poem he has escaped from his philosophical obsessions.

To say that Wordsworth's poems are meaningful on a practical rather than philosophical level, however, does not mean that we cannot be enlightened by examining the poems in the light of contemporary philosophical developments. Placing his poetry against the background of the epistemological questions is exactly the sort of task that we characterise as intellectual history. And it is probably true that it is only when speculation about epistemological questions takes an idealist turn that poems like 'I wandered lonely as a cloud' or 'Tintern Abbey' can be written. But what will cause confusion is to try to relate what Wordsworth does in these poems to Coleridge's definition of the imagination. For what is central to the Wordsworth poem is just that the act of mind involved in seeing the daffodils is a kind of normal perception. A poet is 'a man speaking to men', and his ability to say something new and valuable to us depends solely on his ability to do better than most what everyone does. Furthermore, there is no point in arguing about whether Wordsworth's talk about what we 'half-create and half-perceive' is only compatible with idealism, or whether it is only compatible with a Lockean model, or whether it is compatible with both. Philosophical doctrines are only relevant to Wordsworth's poetry as models, for Wordsworth was thinking about people actually going about in the world and not about the general character of thought. He could simply accept as co-existing a mechanical model for thought, and a vitalist model. Since his was a practical concern, he could simply jump from one model to the other, without having to decide which of the two, since they are *prima facie* incompatible, was right. So he can use the mechanical model to show us what is wrong with the quality of poor Susan's life. The point is that Wordsworth does not follow Coleridge in making normal perception uninteresting, and in insisting that the artist's vision is, in some important respect, different from normal perception.

So we see that Coleridge's famous definition is misleading in two respects. First, it is misleading in that it distorts the philosophical doctrine it represents in that it carries forward the conception of perception which Kant wished to challenge: and second, it is misleading in that it postulates a gap between normal perception and the perception of the poet, a postulate that is demonstrably not shared by the greatest of the romantic poets, Yeats, Wordsworth, and Keats.

When Coleridge turns his attention to a rebuttal of Hartley's Associationism he presents arguments that are, if no more cogent than what he says in the definition of imagination, at least consistent with the main thrust of the romantic movement. In Chapters v and vi of the *Biographia Literaria* he is interested in showing that a mechanical associationist account is confused; in Chapter vii Coleridge argues that Hartley's theory is open to all the objections that one could raise against any dualistic system. (Coleridge obviously has all the anti-Cartesian arguments in mind.) But in this chapter Coleridge raises as more important even than the difficulties, the fact that such a theory is incompatible with freedom of the will, and that it makes nonsense of the notions of praise or blame, and with the existence of God. I now want to put in evidence two well-known passages from Chapter VII of the *Biographia Literaria*. I suggest that Yeats took it that they formed the real centre of Coleridge's notion of the imagination, and that they are a more useful indication of what Coleridge thought than the better known and famous definition.

The soul becomes a mere *ens logicum*; for as a real separable being, it would be more worthless and ludicrous than the grimalkins in the cat-harpsichord described in the Spectator. For these did form a part of the process; but in Hartley's scheme the soul is present only to be pinched or stroked, while the very squeals or purring are produced by an agency wholly independent and alien. It involves all the difficulties, all the incomprehensibility (if it be not indeed, ὡς ἐμοὶ δοκεῖ, the absurdity) of intercommunion between substances, that have no one property in common, without any of the convenient consequences that bribed the judgement to the admission of the dualistic hypothesis. Accordingly, this *caput mortuum* of the Hartleian process has been rejected by his followers, and the consciousness considered as a result, as a tune, the common product of the breeze and the harp: tho' this again is the mere remotion of one absurdity to make way for another equally preposterous. For what is harmony but a mode of relation, the very *esse* of which *is percipi/* an *ens rationale*, which presupposes the power that by perceiving creates it/ The razor's edge becomes a saw to the armed vision; and the delicious melodies of Purcell or Cimarose might be disjointed stammerings to a hearer whose partition of time should be a thousand times subtler than ours. But this obstacle too let us imagine ourselves to have surmounted, and 'at one bound high overleap all bound!' Yet according to this hypothesis, the disquisition to which I am at present soliciting the reader's attention may be as truly said to be written by Saint Paul's church as by me: for it is the mere motion of my muscles and nerves; and these again are set in motion from external causes equally passive, which external causes stand themselves in interdependent connection with every thing that exists or has existed. Thus the whole universe co-operates to produce the minutest stroke of every letter, save only that I myself, and I alone, have nothing to do with it, but merely the causeless and effectless beholding of it when it is done. Yet scarcely can it be called a beholding; for it is neither an act nor an effect; but an impossible creation of a *something-nothing* out of its very contrary! It is the mere quicksilver plating behind a looking-glass; and in this alone consists the poor worthless I! The sum total of my moral and intellectual intercourse dissolved into its elements is reduced to extension, motion, degrees of velocity and those diminished copies of configurative motion which form what we call notions, and notions of notions. Of such philosophy well might Butler say

> The metaphysics but a puppet motion
> That goes with screws, the notion of a notion,
> The copy of a copy and lame draught
> Unnaturally taken from a thought;
> That counterfeits all pantomimic tricks,
> And turns the eyes like an old crucifix;
> That counterchanges whatsoe'er it calls
> B' another name, and makes it true or false,
> Turns truth to falsehood, falsehood into truth,
> By virtue of the Babylonian's tooth.
>
> 'Miscellaneous Thoughts'

The inventor of the watch did not in reality invent it; he only look'd on, while the blind causes, the only true artists, were unfolding themselves. So must it have been too with my friend Allston, when he sketched his picture of the dead man revived by the bones of the prophet Elijah. So must have been with Mr. Southey and Lord Byron, when the one fancied himself composing his *Roderick*, and the other his *Childe Harold*. The same must hold good of all systems of philosophy; of all arts, governments, wars by sea and by land; in short, of all things that ever have been or that ever will be produced. For according to this system it is not the affections and passions that are at work, in as far as they are *sensations* or *thoughts*. We only *fancy* that we act from national resolves, or prudent motives, or from impulses of anger, love or generosity. In all these cases the real agent is a *something-nothing-everything*, which does all of which we know, and knows nothing of all that itself does.

The second passage is:

In every voluntary movement we first counteract gravitation, in order to avail ourselves of it. It must exist, that there may be a something to be counteracted, and which by its reaction aids the force that is exerted to resist it. Let us consider what we do when we leap. We first resist the gravitating power by an act purely voluntary, and then by another act, voluntary in part, we yield to it in order to light on the spot which we had previously proposed to ourselves. Now let a man watch his mind while he is composing; or, to take a still more common case, while he is trying to recollect a name; and he will find the process completely analogous. Most of my readers will have observed a small water-insect on the surface of rivulets which throws a cinque-spotted shadow fringed with prismatic colours on the sunny bottom of the brook; and will have noticed how the little animal wins its way up against the stream, by alternate pulses of active and passive motion, now resisting the current, and now yielding to it in order to gather strength and a momentary fulcrum for a further propulsion. This is no unapt emblem of the mind's self-experience in the act of thinking. There are evidently two powers at work which relatively to each other are active and passive; and this is not possible without an intermediate faculty in all its degrees and determinations the *imagination*. But in common language, and especially on the subject of poetry, we appropriate the name to a superior degree of the faculty, joined to a superior voluntary control over it.

Essentially the first of these passages represents a defence of the traditional concepts of Western society against the consequences of a scientific metaphysics, and the second is simply an analogy which Coleridge uses to indicate the nature of the experience of thinking. The conclusion of the negative side of Coleridge's argument makes clear that romanticism, and the romantic interest in the epistemological and metaphysical speculation of idealism, is essentially an attempt to defend traditional concepts of human action against the unpalatable conclusions we would be driven to if we accepted the philosophical tenets that the scientific revolution was based upon.

These two passages are worth examination not just because they are characteristic of Coleridge in a way in which the famous definition is not, but because they led directly to two poems in which Yeats deals directly with many of the same questions, in terms of the images provided by Coleridge's prose. The more complex of the poems is 'The Statues'. The relevance of the first passage from Chapter VII of the *Biographia Literaria* to the poem is, I think, obvious. But because 'The Statues' is an extremely difficult poem, I would rather collect together all the passages that will be helpful in interpreting before beginning detailed examination of the poem.

The reason why the passage from Coleridge first suggests itself as useful is that it employs two images in dealing with the issues – the mirror and grimalkin – that Yeats uses in 'The Statues'. Just how central Yeats thought the image of the mirror was is illustrated by two passages which were quoted in Chapter I, and which I will quote once again.

The Romantic movement seems related to the idealist philosophy; the naturalistic movement, *Stendhal's mirror dawdling down a lane*, to Locke's mechanical philosophy, as simultaneous correspondential dreams are related, not merely where there is some traceable influence but through their whole substance, and I remember that monks in the Thebaid, or was it by the Mareotic Sea, claimed 'to keep the ramparts', meaning perhaps that all men whose thoughts skimmed the 'unconscious', God-abetting, affected others according to their state, that what some feel others think, what some think others do. When I speak of idealist philosophy I think more of Kant than of Berkeley, who was idealist and realist alike, more of Hegel and his successors than of Kant, and when I speak of the romantic movement I think more of Manfred, more of Shelley's Prometheus, more of Jean Valjean, than of those traditional figures, Browning's Pope, the fakir-like pedlar in *The Excursion*.

And

When Stendhal described a masterpiece as a 'mirror dawdling down a lane' he expresses the mechanical philosophy of the French eighteenth century. Gradually literature conformed to his ideal; Balzac became old-fashioned; romanticism grew theatrical in its strain to hold the public; till, by the end of the nineteenth century, the principal characters in the most famous books were the passive analysts of events, or had been brutalised into the likeness of mechanical objects.

Yeats's use of the image of the mirror, however, was not simply as an adequate image for the nature of empirical epistemology. In the paragraphs quoted earlier Coleridge uses the image in an attempt to characterise what was wrong with that epistemology, as Yeats does in 'The Statues'. Furthermore, in his prose Yeats acknowledged Coleridge's image in a passage that attempts to show how many of the works that are considered central to twentieth-century literature are written from an epistemological position that is essentially empiricist.

The romantic movement with its turbulent heroism, its self-assertion, is over, superseded by a new naturalism that leaves man helpless before the contents of his own mind. One thinks of Joyce's *Anna Livia Plurabelle*, Pound's *Cantos*, works of an heroic sincerity, the man, his active faculties in suspense, one finger beating time to a bell sounding and echoing in the depths of his own mind; of Proust who, still fascinated by Stendhal's fixed framework, seems about to close his eyes and gaze upon the pattern under his lids. This new art which has arisen in different countries simultaneously seems related... to that form of the new realist philosophy which thinks that the secondary and primary qualities alike are independent of consciousness; that an object can at the same moment have contradictory qualities. This philosophy seems about to follow the analogy of an art that has more rapidly completed itself, and after deciding that a penny is bright and dark, oblong and round, hot and cold, dumb and ringing in its own right, to think of the calculations it incites, our distaste or pleasure at its sight, the decision that made us pitch it, our preference for head or

tail, as independent of a consciousness that has shrunk back, grown intermittent and accidental, into the looking glass. *Some Indian Buddhists would
have thought so had they pitched pennies instead of dice.*

If you ask me why I do not accept a doctrine so respectable and convenient, its cruder forms so obviously resurrected to get science down from
Berkeley's roasting-spit, I can but answer like Zarathustra, 'Am I a
barrel of memories that I should give you my reasons?' Somewhere among
those memories something compels me to reject whatever – to borrow a
metaphor of Coleridge's – drives mind into the quicksilver. And why
should I, whose ancestors never shared the anarchic subjectivity of the
nineteenth century, accept its recoil; why should men's heads ache that
never drank? I admit there are, especially in America, such signs of pro-
phetic afflatus about this new movement in philosophy, so much conso-
nant with the political and social movements of the time, or so readily
transformable into a desire to fall back or sink in on some thing or being,
that it may be the morning cock-crow of our Hellenistic Age.[1]

This quotation juxtaposes the mirror image and Buddha in the
same manner as does the third stanza of the poem. Yeats's vision of
the modern era, of the period from the decline of Rome to the
present, sets before us the image of a fat dreaming Buddha, and
insists that as long as mankind thinks of itself as simply the record
reality, as Coleridge's quicksilver behind the mirror, each of us will
remain a mirror in a circus funhouse, an empty reflection of our
brother's emptiness. The contrast is that between the Romantic,
the man who seeks to clarify and measure the world, to know reality
by seeking its source in the forms and categories of the intellect,
and the Buddhist belief, controlling both West and East, both
before and after the temporary recrudesence of the subjective man
during the Renaissance, that reality is what is out there beyond the
mind, and that 'mirror on mirror is all the show'. With these
passages in mind I turn to 'The Statues'.

THE STATUES

Pythagoras planned it. Why did the people stare?
His numbers, though they moved or seemed to move
In marble or in bronze, lacked character.
But boys and girls, pale from the imagined love
Of solitary beds, knew what they were,
That passion could bring character enough,
And pressed at midnight in some public place
Live lips upon a plummet-measured face.

[1] Yeats, *Essays and Introductions*, pp. 405–7.

No! Greater than Pythagoras, for the men
That with a mallet or a chisel modelled these
Calculations that look but casual flesh, put down
All Asiatic vague immensities,
And not the banks of oars that swam upon
The many-headed foam at Salamis.
Europe put off that foam when Phidias
Gave women dreams and dreams their looking-glass.

One image crossed the many-headed, sat
Under the tropic shade, grew round and slow,
No Hamlet thin from eating flies, a fat
Dreamer of the Middle Ages. Empty eyeballs knew
That knowledge increases unreality, that
Mirror on mirror mirrored is all the show.
When gong and conch declare the hour to bless
Grimalkin crawls to Buddha's emptiness.

When Pearse summoned Cuchulain to his side,
What stalked through the Post Office? What intellect,
What calculation, number, measurement, replied?
We Irish, born into that ancient sect
But thrown upon this filthy modern tide
And by its formless spawning fury wrecked,
Climb to our proper dark, that we may trace
The lineaments of a plummet-measured face.

(*Collected Poems*, pp. 375–6)

One book that had made a great impression upon Yeats was Whitehead's *Science and the Modern World* (cf. Chapter 6). Whitehead discusses at some length Pythagoras's position in the history of Western thought. What he claims is that Pythagoras was the first to have discovered the importance of generality in thought. For Whitehead, Pythagoras is a sort of patron saint of thought, because he was the first man to break though into the abstract world of concepts, especially mathematical concepts. For Whitehead the intellectual history of man begins when man is able to find the abstract tools that give him a perspective outside time and accident. One way that Whitehead makes his point is to illustrated the advantage of mathematical concepts over the classificatory science and logic of Aristotle. Whitehead claims that Pythagoras is the source of what is best in the Western intellectual tradition just because his sort of thinking allows us to connect the utmost generality of thought with the utmost particularity. Compared to the possibilities embodied in this sort of thinking – Whitehead claims that modern physics is conceptually close to Pythagoras – the system of Aristotle is an unhappy half-way house. It is in his role as the founder of Western thought that Pythagoras appears in this poem, rather than as a member of the mystical tradition. But we must notice that what Pythagoras 'plans' is a work of art. In the statues which Yeats imagines Pythagoras creating is embodied a passionate love of correct proportion, an abstract notion of human form, which will direct and educate the passion of Greek society. His numbers are embodied in marble or bronze. But although they are so abstract that they cannot be mistaken for an imitation of actual people (they 'lack character'), what they are is recognised at once by the boys and girls of Greece, who are striving toward the same vision of the human form. The boys and girls of Greece are pale from the effort of finding 'imagined' love; Pythagoras simply presents to them those numbers which are already in their minds. Their reaction to Pythagoras's numbers is one of knowledge or recognition. His numbers have clarified their own thought for them, so that all that remains is for them to acknowledge their dreams in his numbers, and make public and communal what had first been private, fragmentary, and illusory.

In order to understand fully what Yeats is saying we must remember that for Kant, and for many mathematicians since Kant, mathematical truths are examples of synthetic *a priori* judgments.[1] That is, Kant did not just say that mathematical truths were independent of experience of the world, but that although they were independent of experience of the world (i.e. *a priori*), they were constitutive of any experience of the world. We can use mathematical concepts to comprehend our experience, because mathematical concepts are an important part of our form of thought. We think the world mathematically: our numbers are synthetic as well as *a priori*. So Yeats says that Pythagoras 'planned' rather than described, that the boys and girls 'imagined' rather than they searched.[2] The proportions that become a public standard of human

---

[1] Apparently this is now a minority view, but it is still held by a number of mathematicians and philosophers of mathematics.

[2] If mathematical concepts were analytic, then we could say only that we described the world in the terms of a closed system whose truths were true *a priori*. But that mathematical description would be only a description, and not an act of the imagination.

excellence are not simply 'there' in the world, but are there because our consciousness requires that they be there.

We can see what Yeats means on a more practical level if we
begin to think about how standards of beauty actually work. Everyone knows that faces are lopsided: the distortions that result if we
cover up one side of a face are an entertaining reminder of this fact.
But we do not respond to the irregularities of the physiognomies of
the actual people we meet, but impose a regularity that is not
simply there. We all use a plumment, we all measure. When the
artist or sculptor creates an image of the human body it is the
regularities of form which he portrays: we would not know what
to do with a picture that tried to be formless. Of course, it is true
that whenever a new style of art comes along there are those who
cannot see the formal relations in that art, and so say that what is
produced is ugly. But once a style is understood it is understood in
terms of formal relationships, and once these relationships are
understood, the charge that the new painting is ugly or formless
disappears. 'Beauty' is a convention about what sorts of formal
relationships we approve.

There is one more question about this stanza that should be
considered. We are told that the boys and girls of Greece knew
what Pythagoras's 'numbers' were, and so knew that passion
could bring character enough. What Yeats means is something like
this. Once we acknowledge the communal nature of thought, and
the universality of our conceptual scheme, we are freed from the
modern striving after originality and difference. The 'theatrical'
search for people who are different, who are 'characters', is based
upon a profound misrepresentation of the nature of human activity.
Paradoxically the striving to be different or original is normally
thought of as a romantic notion, and once again we can see how
Coleridge's definition of the imagination encourages this. But if we
turn our attention to the major documents of the romantic poets
– to Wordsworth's *Prelude*, or the Preface to the *Lyrical Ballads*,
to Keats's letters or the 'Ode on a Grecian Urn', we can see that the
central attempt of the romantic movement was to write about the
common human imagination. The need to be different springs
from the Empiricist habit of counting and the Aristoteilan notions
of categorising, and not from the romantic notion of imagination.
The Romantics believed in a passionate commitment to the common human imagination which freed them from our modern feeling

of insecurity; a feeling that springs from the sense of being merely an object to be thought about, to be counted and described. For the humanist, to be fully human was originality enough, and passion and intellect together were all that were necessary to become human. One salutary effect of taking Yeats seriously is to release us from the psychological pressure of the modern belief that to be valuable one has to be different.

One major difference between Kant and Whitehead on the one hand, and the neo-Platonists and the majority of the neo-Kantians on the other, can best be described as the difference between transcendental speculation and descriptive metaphysics. Kant and Whitehead were intellectuals in the sense that they were primarily interested in describing the nature of thought. But for both of them what they were doing was an attempt to formulate the nature of normal human activity, rather than to suggest, as do the neo-Platonists, a way to escape normal human activity. Yeats is interested in the role that intellect plays in determining our experience, and not in an escape from that experience. So for him art becomes the supreme example of intellect in that it combines the utmost generality of thought with the utmost peculiarity of experience. Phidias is a greater intellect than Pythagoras because he can direct the full scope of his thought, his numbers, to the minute particulars of mankind.

> No! Greater than Pythagoras, for the men
> That with a mallet or a chisel modelled these
> Calculations that look but casual flesh, put down
> All Asiatic vague immensities,
> And not the banks of oars that swam upon
> The many-headed foam at Salamis.
> Europe put off that foam when Phidias
> Gave women dreams and dreams their looking-glass.

Civilisation is the process whereby men create a world of definite form; it is the Apollonian desire for measurement embodied in the totality of what men do. And history is the record of civilisation. It is the Greek ability to measure, and to take the general into the particular that created the greatness of Greece. The ability of Asia to tolerate multiplicity, to be satisfied with dim perspectives, and to delight in disorder, becomes a symbol for all that is not civilised, for all that must be rejected. The foam is simply froth, the uncharacterisable bubbling of minds that do not know themselves, of something less and more than human, and therefore monstrous. It is the *Principium Individuatum*, the Apollonian element in Greek life, the ability to form images, to create form, to separate one object from another, which defeats Asia.

> Europe put off that foam when Phidias
> Gave women dreams and dreams their looking-glass.

There is a remarkable similarity between these two lines, and the concluding lines of 'Her Vision in the Woods'. Both poems stress the reflexive nature of the symbol. In the one case, the symbol, being an accurate reflection of the woman's plight, both reveals her fate (is her heart's torturer) and suffers through her because it is created as a symbol of her fate (her heart's victim). In 'The Statues' Greek sculpture gives women dreams in that it clarifies the ideal for each woman and functions as a looking-glass for that ideal, in so far as the ideal is communal. That is, in that the dream is prior to the realisation, the actual statue is a *reflection* of human aspiration, of the possibility of form. Just as at one level the statue creates the dream, the pre-conscious form, at another more primitive level it is a reflection of the communal pre-conscious form. Thus Yeats can claim that the statues reflect the dreams of Greek civilisation, even while creating them.

The third stanza makes use of a number of particular pieces of information, and one symbol which is, I think, almost private to Yeats. I think it best to clear up these difficulties before trying to explicate the stanza. Yeats knew that Greek art was imported into Asia by Alexander and he believed it led to those images of Buddha developed by Andhara sculpture; and that this development reached its height at the time that the middle Ages were most fully immersed in the 'fabulous formless darkness' of Christianity, in the first few hundred years after the destruction of Rome. Yeats's attitude to Buddhism is ambiguous; he borrows from it and often seems to approve of many of its tenets. But at the same time his reading of Nietzsche had left him with a permanent distaste for the abnegation of personality involved in Buddhism.

Further, Yeats believed that the Renaissance represented an attempt to forge unity of being out of the chaos of the multiform Middle Ages. But the Renaissance did not represent as high a level of achievement as did Greece; it was the last gasp of the historical cycle which began with Christ and which was making its weary way towards its close in the bloody and senseless conflicts of the twentieth century.

In the third stanza the image that crosses the many-headed, going from Greece to Asia, is the *exemplum* of the process, in Asia and in Europe, by which the subjective impulse to locate reality through understanding the role of the human mind, was destroyed. The image of Buddha is contrasted with Hamlet, who represents the Renaissance attempt to reformulate the principles of Greek civilisation, but who is only able to discover the buzzing multiplicity of the abstractions already defeating the Renaissance Ideal. The use of flies as a symbol for the denatured abstractions of the end of an era occurs in the poem 'The Crazed Moon', as well as in 'The Statues'. However, it is the peculiar use of mirrors in this stanza which provides the key to Yeats's meaning. Yeats and Coleridge both reject the mirror as an adequate symbol for the operation of the human mind (in stanza two Yeats talks of the statue as a mirror which reflects the mind of Phidias and the Greeks). The reason for this rejection was that the implicit epistemology of accepting the metaphor left the mind no role other than that of a passive acceptance of a reality independent of it. As Coleridge says, and Yeats re-iterates, the mind is just the quicksilver at the back of the mirror, a *something-nothing* that merely reflects the normal process of events. The point of Coleridge's metaphor was that human activity, on this model, is meaningless. Our minds are merely a kind of epi-phenomena, outside the nexus of events, and functioning solely as an imbecile reflection of those events.

The soul becomes a mere *ens logicum*; for as a real separable being, it would be more worthless and ludicrous than the grimalkins in the cat-harpsi-chord described in the Spectator. For these did form a part of the process; but in Hartley's scheme the soul is present only to be pinched or stroked while the very squeals or purring are produced by an agency wholly independent and alien.

And

Thus the whole universe co-operates to produce the minutest stroke of every letter, save only that I myself, and I alone, have nothing to do with it, but merely the causeless and effectless beholding of it when it is done. Yet scarcely can it be called a beholding; for it is neither an act nor an effect; but an impossible creation of a something-nothing out of its very contrary! It is the mere quick-silver plating behind a looking-glass; and in this alone consists the poor worthless I!

In the passage in which Yeats picks up on Coleridge's image he describes the modern version of this sort of theory.

The romantic movement with its turbulent heroism, its self-assertion, is over, superseded by a new naturalism that leaves man helpless before the contents of his own mind. One thinks of Joyce's *Anna Livia Plurabelle*, Pound's *Cantos*, works of an heroic sincerity, the man, his active faculties in suspense, one finger beating time a bell sounding and echoing in the depths of his own mind; of Proust who, still fascinated by Stendahl's fixed framework, seems about to close his eyes and gaze upon the pattern under his lids. This new art which has arisen in different countries simultaneously seems related . . . to that form of the new realist philosophy which thinks that the secondary and primary qualities alike are independent of consciousness; that an object can at the same moment have contradictory qualities. This philosophy seems about to follow the analogy of an art that has more rapidly completed itself, and after deciding that a penny is bright and dark, oblong and round, hot and cold, dumb and and ringing in its own right, to think of the calculations it incites, our distaste or pleasure at its sight, the decision that made us pitch it, our preference for head or tail, as independent of a consciousness that has shrunk back, grown intermittent and accidental, into the looking glass. *Some Indian Buddhists would have thought so had they pitched pennies instead of dice.*

The empty eyeballs of the Buddha are a continuation of this image. We are given a vision of a society in which all minds are united in the belief that everything that happens is independent of minds. Since each of us is, according to this analysis, simply a reflection of what is independent of us, as a group we are empty. For we can only reflect our own emptiness to our neighbour, and receive back that emptiness from the emptiness of our mirror-neighbour. 'Mirror on mirror mirrored is all the show.' We are the empty reflections of each other's emptiness. Finally we are reduced to the grimalkins of Coleridge's cat-harpsichord. We accept ourselves as simply part of the mechanism, we no longer try to pretend that we can act of our own free will. Once we have accepted this, we crawl to Buddha's emptiness, we delight in the formless immensities of unregulated experience, and worship at the feet of an idol that does not require that we accept our human responsibilities.

Yeats chose Hamlet to represent the failure of the Renaissance to stem the influx of Asia because of conclusions he had reached about Shakespeare's art many years earlier.

The Greeks, a certain scholar has told me, considered that myths are the activities of the Daimons, and that the Daimons shape our characters and our lives. I have often had the fancy that there is some one myth for every man, which, if we but know it, would make us understand all he did and thought. Shakespeare's myth, it may be, describes a wise man who was blind from very wisdom, and an empty man who thrust him from his place, and saw all that could be seen from very emptiness. It is in the story of Hamlet, who saw too great issues everywhere to play the trivial game of life, and of Fortinbras, who came from fighting battles about 'a little patch of ground' so poor that one of his captains would not give 'six ducats' to 'farm it', and who was yet acclaimed by Hamlet and by all as the only be-fitting king.[1]

The poem then, claims that the victory at Salamis was short-lived, and that from the decline of Rome to the present Europe and European subjectivity and measurement, have been swallowed by the mindless objectivity of Asia.

In the fourth stanza Yeats suggests that the Irish may create another Salamis, and re-fashion the course of history, if they too can examine the nature of the Irish mind, if they too can create the necessary symbol, out of the dark pre-phenomenal human imagination. The Irish will have to climb to their 'proper dark', find their right image in the pre-conscious tendency of the Irish mind. That it is the mind which must be surveyed, that it is the nature of the mind which determines both art and history, is evident from Yeats's insistence that the Irish must find their 'proper dark'. History and art are not a function of the phenomenal, nor are the ideas of men a function of some exterior reality. Like the Greek boys and girls who gave history its impetus at midnight, like Pythagoras who first precisely formulated the Greek world and Greek art, the Irish must 'plan' reality, must create their symbols, that they 'may trace the lineaments of a plummet-measured face'.

These ideas about the relationship between history and art, and their genesis in certain qualities of the human mind, which Yeats contemplates in 'The Statues', are noticeably present in many of Yeats's poems. Of these the finest are 'Long-Legged Fly' and 'Under Ben Bulben'. The same quality of the mind that was denoted in 'The Statues' by 'measurement' is here embodied in the refrain:

LONG-LEGGED FLY

That civilisation may not sink,
Its great battle lost,

1 Yeats, *Essays and Introductions*, pp. 107–8.

Quiet the dog, tether the pony
To a distant post;
Our Master Caesar is in the tent
Where the maps are spread,
His eyes fixed upon nothing,
A hand under his head.
Like a long-legged fly upon the stream
His mind moves upon silence.

That the topless towers be burnt
And men recall that face,
Move most gently if move you must
In this lonely place.
She thinks, part woman, three parts a child,
That nobody looks; her feet
Practise a tinker shuffle
Picked up on a street.
Like a long-legged fly upon the stream
Her mind moves upon silence.

That girls at puberty may find
The first Adam in their thought,
Shut the door of the Pope's chapel,
Keep those children out.
There on that scaffolding reclines
Michael Angelo.
With no more sound than the mice make
His hand moves to and fro.
Like a long-legged fly upon the stream.
His mind moves upon silence.

(*Collected Poems*, pp. 381–2)

The first stanza attributes the Roman talent for war to the same force that Yeats found behind the Greek victory at Salamis – the ability to create, and to measure reality. The third stanza describes the process of artistic symbolisation, and the ability of the symbol to create the same impulse in others that gave birth to it in the artist. In the second stanza Yeats even suggests that Helen's beauty is her own symbolisation. She creates her beauty, it is a function of intellect, in the same way as are Caesar's battles and Michael Angelo's Adam. Yeats's view of the act of creation shows us, not God moving on the face of the water, but the human mind. It is a man who is the creator, who creates out of himself, from his

107

own mind. And instead of the Old Testament's flamboyant creation, or even Milton's epic strain, we have the quiet precision of a
fly delicately balancing on the surface tension of the stream.

It seems clear to me that Coleridge's metaphor of the insect using
the surface tension of the stream is the precise source of the image
in the refrain, but the poem is perfectly clear without any reference
to the source.

These same ideas may be observed in 'Under Ben Bulben'.
While there is not room for a full scale explanation of this poem,
I would like to deal with the four stanzas which provide its vital
centre.

II

Many times man lives and dies
Between his two eternities,
That of race and that of soul,
And ancient Ireland knew it all.
Whether man die in his bed
Or the rifle knocks him dead,
A brief parting from those dear
Is the worst man has to fear
Though grave-diggers' toil is long,
Sharp their spades, their muscles strong,
They but thrust their buried men
Back in the human mind again.

III

You that Mitchel's prayer have heard,
'Send war in our time, O Lord!'
Know that when all words are said
And a man is fighting mad,
Something drops from eyes long blind,
He completes his partial mind,
For an instance stands at ease,
Laughs aloud, his heart at peace.
Even the wisest man grows tense
With some sort of violence
Before he can accomplish fate,
Know his work or choose his mate.

IV

Poet and sculptor, do the work,
Nor let the modish painter shirk
What his great forefathers did,

> Bring the soul of man to God,
> Make him fill the cradles right.
>
> Measurement began our might:
> Forms a stark Egyptian thought,
> Forms that gentler Phidias wrought.
> Michael Angelo left a proof
> On the Sistine Chapel roof,
> Where but half-awakened Adam
> Can disturb globe-trotting Madam
> Till her bowels are in heat,
> Proof that there's a purpose set
> Before the secret working mind:
> Profane perfection of mankind.
>
> *(Collected Poems,* pp. 398–9)

The first stanza reiterates the conclusion of 'News for the Delphic Oracle'. There is no reality other than the reality fashioned by the human mind. The transcendent world, the heaven where, according to more traditional views gravediggers send the souls of buried men, is here the human mind, the Absolute Self.

The second stanza informs us that this Absolute Self is not transcendent or ineffable. On the contrary, every man, faced with important decisions, can 'complete his partial mind'. Yeats's condition of holiness does not consist in a right relationship with the universe, or with a transcendent God. It consists in knowing yourself as a man, understanding your relationship with mankind, and in fulfilling, or rather in creating in yourself, the role of man.

In the first stanza of Section IV the artist's task is defined as bringing 'the soul of man to God', the result of this being that this will make 'him', who I take to be generic man, 'fill the cradles right'.

But in terms of what I have called Yeats's myth, and in terms of what has been said about the earlier sections of the poem, God seems out of place. That is, if Yeats holds the views ascribed to him, he could not have an ordinary theistic conception of God. I think it important to note that, in the stanza which follows, Yeats provides a gloss on the cryptic comment in the last two lines of the previous stanza.

> Measurement began our might:
> Forms a stark Egyptian thought,
> Forms that gentler Phidias wrought.

> Michael Angelo left a proof
> On the Sistine Chapel roof,
> Where but half-awakened Adam
> Can disturb globe-trotting Madam
> Till her bowels are in heat,
> Proof that there's a purpose set
> Before the secret working mind:
> Profane perfection of mankind.

Bringing the soul of man to God is equivalent to revealing the purpose set before the working mind – and this purpose is the 'profane perfection of mankind'. Yeats's notion of God is not the ordinary one, but one made up equally of German Idealistic notions and Blake. From German Idealism comes the notion of the Absolute Self, and the Yeatsian concept of the great mind that had been elaborated previously. From Blake comes the tag discussed earlier, 'god only acts or is in existing beings or man'. However, there is another notion of Blake's that is extremely important in reference to these stanzas of 'Under Ben Bulben'. Yeats summarises Blake's notion of God in the following manner.

Dante, like other medieval mystics, symbolized the highest order of created beings by the fixed stars, and God by the darkness beyond them, *The Primum Mobile*. Blake, absorbed in his very different vision, in which God took always a human shape, believed that to think of God under a symbol drawn from the outer world was in itself idolatry, but that to imagine Him as an unpeopled immensity was to think of Him under the one symbol furthest from His essence – it being a creation of the ruining reason, 'generalising' away 'the minute particulars of life'. Instead of seeking God in the deserts of time and space, in exterior immensities, in what he called 'the abstract void', he believed that the further he dropped behind him memory of time and space, reason builded upon sensation, morality founded for the ordering of the world; and the more he was absorbed in emotion; and, above all, in emotion escaped from the impulse of bodily longing and the restraints of bodily reason, in artistic emotion; the nearer did he come to Eden's 'breathing garden', to use his beautiful phrase, and to the unveiled face of God. No worthy symbol of God existed but the inner world, the true humanity, to whose various aspects he gave many names, 'Jerusalem', 'Liberty', 'Eden', 'The Divine Vision', 'The Divine Members', and whose most intimate expression was art and poetry. He always sang of God under this symbol:

> For Mercy, Pity, Peace, and Love
> Is God our Father dear;

> And Mercy, Pity, Peace, and Love
> Is Man, His child and care.
>
> For Mercy has a human heart;
> Pity a human face;
> And Love the human form divine;
> And Peace the human dress.
>
> Then every man, of every clime,
> That prays in his distress,
> Prays to the human form divine –
> Love, Mercy, Pity, Peace.[1]

Not only can we understand Yeats's notion of God more clearly by considering his comment on Blake, but if we read further in this essay we can understand why he did not follow Blake's particular view more closely. Yeats paraphrases Blake in this manner:

Our imaginations are but fragments of the universal imagination, portions of the universal body of God, and as we enlarge our imagination by imaginative sympathy, and transform with the beauty and peace of art the sorrows and joys of the world, we put off the limited mortal man more and more and put on the unlimited 'immortal man'.[2]

and quotes further:

Blake upon the other hand cried scorn upon the whole spectacle of external things, a vision to pass away in a moment, and preached the cultivated life, the internal Church which has no laws but beauty, rapture and labour. 'I know of no other Christianity, and of no other gospel, than the liberty, both of body and mind, to exercise the divine arts of imagination, the real and eternal world of which this vegetable universe is but a faint shadow, and in which we shall live in our eternal or imaginative bodies when these vegetable mortal bodies are no more.'[3]

But for Yeats it was exactly the imaginative creation of the vegetable universe which is valuable. Blake's imagination was eventually to lead us out of the world. It is for this reason that Yeats prefers Michelangelo to Blake: for while Michalangelo leads us to the world of the senses, Blake is only able to 'prepare a rest for the people of God'.

---

[1] Yeats, *Essays and Introductions*, pp. 133–4.   [2] *Ibid.*, p. 138.   [3] *Ibid.*, p. 135.

> Gyres run on;
> When that greater dream had gone
> Calvert and Wilson, Blake and Claude,
> Prepared a rest for the people of God,
> Palmer's phrase, but after that
> Confusion fell upon our thought.

'Under Ben Bulben' is a celebration of the process of symbolisation, of the process whereby the imagination clothes itself in 'casual flesh'. And the command which greets the reader from Yeats's tombstone is a command to his reader to consecrate himself to the celebration.

> *Cast a cold eye*
> *On life, on death,*
> *Horseman, pass by*!

The cold eye is cold with the brightness and gaiety of the eyes of the sages in 'Lapis Lazuli' – cold with the knowledge that all things die, that 'all things fall and are built again, and those that build them again are gay'. There is no final goal in Yeats's system; he is content to celebrate the process as an end in itself. It is the imaginative process, the process of symbolisation in history and art, which is the core of Yeats's myth, and throughout the later poetry we find celebration after celebration of this.

Yeats shares Coleridge's philosophical interests, yet his poetry has more in common with the best of Wordsworth, than with Coleridge. The reason for this is that Yeats's theoretical speculation leads directly to the sort of practical concerns that characterise Wordsworth's poetry. Yeats knew that the poet's imagination was the same as the imagination of the rest of us: that imagination is normal perception when we are prepared to pay attention to the powers of perceiving, and when we are prepared to give our whole mind to it. His commitment to this position is the epistemological equivalent to Wordsworth's claim that the poet is a 'man speaking to men', and it allows us to inhabit a shared world of common experience, instead of the 'romantic' dream of new worlds produced by the secondary imagination. Because he believed we share a common world Yeats, like Wordsworth, can examine the source of our moral and emotional experience in our perception of the world, and can present our experience of the world, and the world itself, with the solidity that Professor Durrant finds in

Wordsworth, and finds lacking in much of what is normally spoken of as romantic poetry. Both Yeats and Wordsworth are great poets, because they are able to talk, as men speaking to men, of the central aspects of human experience. Both are romantic poets in that they characteristically explore the relationship between our perception of the world, and our actions in it.

II

Yeats found the key to all human experience in what has been described variously as the 'imagination' or the power of symbolisation. We have seen that for him this process provides a theory of history, a theory of perception, and a theory of art. His theory of perception, and the relationship between perception and art, is more technical than the relationship between history and art. In order to approach the topic clearly it is necessary to view the subject matter of Chapter 1 from a slightly different angle.

To a discussion of modern art in *A Vision* which is very similar to the one I quoted earlier when talking about the mirror image in 'The Statues', Yeats appends the following footnote:

Mr. Wyndham Lewis, whose criticism sounds true to a man of my generation, attacks this art in *Time and Western Man*. If we reject, he argues, the forms and categories of the intellect there is nothing left but sensation, 'eternal flux'. Yet all such rejections stop at the conscious mind, for as Dean Swift says in a meditation on a woman who paints a dying face,

> Matter as wise as logicians say
> Cannot without a form subsist;
> And form, say I as well as they,
> Must fail, if matter brings no grist.[1]

Yeats's reasons for setting Wyndham Lewis's criticism alongside Swift's little poem provide an instructive introduction to Yeats's ideas on the subject. First, Yeats uses the expression 'forms and categories of the intellect' to describe Lewis's view because he believes that Lewis is a Kantian.

I have read *Time and Western Man* with gratitude, the last chapters again and again. It has given, what I could not, a coherent voice to my hatred. You are wrong to think Lewis attacks the conclusions of men like Alexander and Russell because he thinks them 'uncertain'. He thinks them false. To admit uncertainty into philosophy, necessary uncertainty, would seem

[1] Yeats, *A Vision*, p. 4.

to him to wrong the sovereignty of intellect, or worse, to accept the hypo-critical humility of the scientific propagandists which is, he declares, their 'cloak for dogma.' He is a Kantian, with some mixture of older thought, Catholic or Greek, and has the vast Kantian argument behind him, the most powerful in philosophy. He considers that both 'space and time are mere appearances', whereas his opponents think that time is real though space is a construction of the mind.[1]

But why if he thinks Lewis is a Kantian, does he then quote Swift's quatrain, which is, after all, a very simple rhyming of the usual Platonic notions of form and matter? The answer seems to be that Yeats did not simply take the poem as Swift intended it. Yeats had evidently given it a good deal of thought and as a re-sult, the poem had an added significance for him. But before ex-amining Yeats's other comments on Swift's lines, I would like to recapitulate some of the primary tenets of the Kantian position. According to Kant form is a quality of the mind, an order which the mind imposes upon the phenomenal world. Space and time, al-though they are empirically real, are transcendentally ideal; that is they are not qualities of noumena, but are the tools of aesthetic intuition which are common to all minds. They are not trans-cendentally real, but since they are common to all minds, they are empirically real. The imagination can do strange things, can conceive of an elephant which is pink, or has as many legs as a cen-tipede, but it cannot avoid space and time. It is impossible to con-ceive of a non-spatial elephant. The scientific notions of cause and effect, etcetera, are also rules of the mind. They do not bear any relationship to the noumenal reality. Thus it is that Kant is led to claim that *percepts without concepts are blind* – that is, we cannot have experience (perceptions) without imposing the forms of space and time and the categories which govern relationships within space and time. And as a corollary, *concepts without percepts are empty* – they are only mental constructs which despite Plato, have no independent reality.

This is probably one of the best-known of the Kantian slogans, almost the Kantian equivalent to the slogan from Berkeley that '*esse est percepi*'. When Yeats says in a letter to T. Sturge Moore:

There are four lines of Swift that I find good guides, if one substitutes 'percept' for 'matter', and 'intellect' for 'form' – though that it is to modernise, not to improve:

[1] *Yeats–Moore Correspondence*, pp. 122–3.

> Matter as wise logicians say
> Cannot without a form subsist;
> And form, say I as well as they,
> Must fail, if matter brings no grist...[1]

we can see why he has juxtaposed what seemed two discordant philosophical positions. Substituting in the original poem, we get:

> Percept as wise logicians say
> Cannot without an intellect subsist
> And intellect, I say as well as they
> Must fail, if Percept bring no grist.

And since he uses intellect here as almost synonymous with concept, as that which is capable of conception, he means that percepts without concepts are blind, concepts without percepts are empty.

The Kantian slogan, or Yeats's use of Swift's quotation as a restatement of that slogan, describes his theory, as applied to both art and the phenomenal world. Either of these formulations of Kant might serve as an epigram for the poem 'Byzantium'. (*Collected Poems*, pp. 280–1).

It is often remarked that Byzantium is Yeats's city of the imagination, his Golgonooza. But for Yeats the imagination was what Coleridge termed the 'primary' imagination, and not the 'secondary' imagination which was for Coleridge the private preserve of the poet. In effect, Byzantium is the city of the mind, it is a world shared by all individual minds. The mosaic world of Byzantium is the world which governs percepts, and the mosaic-like patterns are the concepts which the mind imposes on experience. The emperor is the intellect, the ruler of the city of concept, intellect or form.

> The unpurged images of day recede;
> The Emperor's drunken soldiery are abed;
> Night resonance recedes, night-walkers' song
> After great cathedral gong...

The mind is seen as withdrawing completely from experience. The 'drunken soldiery', the senses, are abed, and we are in a world of intellect, empty of perception, in a world of pure form. The image of the senses as the soldiers of the intellect is well-chosen, and the absence of even 'night resonance' serves to indicate a state

---

[1] *Yeats–Moore Correspondence*, p. 147.

beyond sleep, a state of pure intellectuality which is, as we shall see, a kind of death.

> A starlit or a moonlit dome disdains
> All that man is,
> All mere complexities,
> The fury and the mire of human veins.

This serves to reiterate that Byzantium's experience, once the senses have been put to sleep, is the opposite of normal experience. The references to starlight and moonlight indicate the extremes of human experience, extremes where experience is not possible to human beings because of their inhuman purity (cf. *A Vision*). The dome is probably a reference to Shelley's dome, and is characterised by the adjectives 'starlit' or 'moonlit'. But Shelley's dome was 'a dome of many-coloured glass' which 'stains the white radiance of eternity'. Yeats sees the dome as the symbol of that which is out of life, thus reversing the role of the dome. The purity of the dome is seen as disdaining or rejecting human experience. Now, the word 'disdain' is a crux – there is considerable evidence that Yeats meant 'distains'.[1] The problem is complicated by the fact that Yeats's handwriting is nearly always illegible, and that the primary sources are cold comfort to both sides. However, although I cannot prove that the word should be 'distains', a remark of Yeats has led me to believe that, if he did not actually mean to write 'distains', he intended 'disdains' to function in the context of this poem, in much the same way as 'distains' would. Continuing his discussion of Swift's quatrain he says:

Swift's form and matter are concepts and matter in the sense that, if our analysis goes far enough, we cannot imagine even the vaguest film of tint or shade without such mental concepts as 'space' and 'before and after', and so on, *or the concepts without the film.*[2]

Yeats seems to think of the relationship between concepts and the phenomenal world in terms of the relationship between the unstained and stained slides used in the biological sciences. And this imaginative interpretation of the problem is very much like the consistent reversal of Shelly's dome symbolism in the poem.

---

[1] See G. Melchiori, *The Whole Mystery of Art* (London: Routledge & Kegan Paul, 1960), *passim*.

[2] *Yeats–Moore Correspondence*, p. 143.

In both cases the phenomenal is seen as a kind of film which over-whelms and enriches an ephemeral schema.

One of Yeats's favourite methods of composition is to set up an opposition between two extreme views, and mediate between them; or at least indicate one extreme and, by thinking about it, move to a more complex and viable position. Whether the word is 'disdains' or 'distains', Yeats is here indicating an extreme position, one which either oversimplifies human experience (distains) or one that refuses to acknowledge certain aspects of human experience (disdains). Of course these positions are similar. The second stanza continues the presentation of the extreme position:

> Before me floats an image, man or shade,
> Shade more than man, more image than a shade...

'Image' here means a pure concept – not even the ghost of a man, but only the idea of a person.

> For Hades' bobbin bound in mummy-cloth
> May unwind the winding path;
> A mouth that has no moisture and no breath
> Breathless mouths may summon...

Yeats's notion of the winding and unwinding of human lives along the gyres of experience is well-documented. However, what is noticeable about this passage is not the continuation of experience, but the absence of experience. I take 'unwind' to be literally what is involved. Ariadne's thread is not re-wound but unravelled, straightened out. Once again, Yeats indicates his revulsion from that which is out of human experience. He has talked about the possibility of an end to the cyclical scheme of things at least once before.

> When thoughts that a fool
> Has wound upon a spool
> Are but loose thread, are but loose thread;
>
> When cradle and spool are past
> And I mere shade at last
> Coagulate of stuff
> Transparent like the wind...
>
> from 'The Fool by the Roadside'
> (*Collected Poems*, p. 247)

The passage is charged with ironic comment. The references to 'Hades' bobbin bound in mummy-cloth' and 'breathless mouths'

build up a tension within the verse which is released in the supre-
mely ironic closing lines of the stanza

> I hail the superhuman;
> I call it death-in-life and life-in-death.

The echo of Coleridge's *Rime of the Ancient Mariner* is quite
deliberate. Yeats knew Coleridge's critical work well, and the
suggestion that life-in-death, death-in-life was the result of too
much imagination in 'Byzantium' instead of too little as in *The
Ancient Mariner*, is explicable in view of their different historical
perspectives. Yeats has been exposed to the pre-Raphaelites and the
Celtic Twilight, and his aim is to avoid the medieval never-never
land of degenerate romanticism. The struggle here is to avoid the
twilight zone, to fight back to reality.

In the first two stanzas Yeats sets up one extreme, a world of
pure form. The third stanza represents a radical shift in mood, and
in direction. As is usual in his poetry, Yeats's style is elliptical
and compressed, and the relationship between the first four lines of
the third stanza and the rest of the poem is not immediately apparent.

> Miracle, bird or golden handiwork,
> More miracle than bird or handiwork,
> Planted on the star-lit golden bough,
> Can like the cocks of Hades crow...

The tone here becomes exultant, tense. After the vague and
unsubstantial spirit of the last verse the golden bird, planted on the
golden bough, and crowing, represents both a return to a substantial, almost physical, reality, and to a return to normality.
Furthermore the golden bird is compared with the cocks of Hades
which Yeats knew to be the heralds of rebirth from his reading of
Eugenie Strong's *Apotheosis and Afterlife*. Our attention has shifted
from the dome far overhead, to the spirits which float before us, to
a golden bird, which we shall learn later, is pictured in a floor mosaic beneath our feet. Furthermore the fact that the golden bird is
crowing re-introduces sound into the disturbing silence created by
the absence of night-resonance and Keatsian 'unheard melodies' of
the 'breathless mouths'. And where previously the centre of our
attention was occupied by a superhuman form which was outside
human experience, and antithetical to it, the golden bird is vitally
connected with human experience and in fact sings of the flux of

temporal events, of the rebirth in time. These four lines are reminiscent of the final stanza of 'Sailing to Byzantium' in that once again the immortal work of art that is imbedded in the artifact leads us back to human experience and sings, although immortal, of mortality and of 'what is past, or passing, or to come'. Thus we have dialectical opposites in the poem. We have seen Byzantium as in some way instrumental in giving direction and movement to human life and perception, and Byzantium as completely isolated from any kind of real experience. This is a theme which becomes increasingly prominent as Yeats grows older. Comparing his thoughts in this poem with two of the poems discussed earlier reveals a continuity of theme.

> Pythagoras planned it. Why did the people stare?
> His numbers, though they moved or seemed to move
> In marble or in bronze, lacked character.
> But boys and girls, pale from the imagined love
> Of solitary beds, knew what they were,
> That passion could bring character enough.
> And pressed at midnight in some public place
> Live lips upon a plummet-measured face.
>
> (from 'The Statues')

and

> *Forms* a stark Egyptian *thought*,
> Forms that gentler Phidias wrought.
> Michael Angelo left a proof
> On the Sistine Chapel roof,
> Where but half-awakened Adam
> Can disturb globe-trotting Madam
> Till her bowels are in heat,
> Proof that there's a purpose set
> Before the secret working mind:
> Profane perfection of mankind.
>
> (from 'Under Ben Bulben')

Art then, like the golden bird, presents us with the schema which determines the shape of human existence and which directs and controls the temporal process while remaining out of time itself. But what this direction is has only been hinted at. In this poem, and especially in the last four lines of this stanza and in the fourth stanza, Yeats returns to exorcise fully the vision of Byzantium, as discrete from and antithetical to human experience.

> Or, by the moon embittered, scorn aloud
> In glory of changeless metal
> Common bird or petal
> And all complexities of mire or blood.[1]

This is a recapitulation of the first two stanzas. The strong 'or' placed strategically at the beginning of the second line indicates the fact that the two possibilities are mutually exclusive. The following two stanzas set out the two Byzantiums, and Yeats indicates his preference for the latter.

> At midnight on the Emperor's pavement flit
> Flames that no faggot feeds, nor steel has lit,
> Nor storm disturbs, flames begotten of flame,
> Where blood-begotten spirits come
> And all complexities of fury leave,
> Dying into a dance,
> An agony of trance,
> An agony of flame that cannot singe a sleeve.

The bird, firmly planted, disappears before another of those phantasmagorias. The time is midnight, and the evidence of the senses is absent. The mind is invaded by flames which have no real existence, which 'flit' above the Emperor's pavement. They are flames which bear no relationship to anything (flames begotten of flames) and are unaffected by the real world ('nor storm disturbs').

This is the holy city to which 'blood-begotten spirits come' and are purged of their sensuality, become pure spirits; in short, a Christian heaven. But Yeats was anti-Christian, and his attack on the notion of the generation of the soul is best documented in 'Veronica's Napkin', (*Collected Poems*, p. 270) which I quote in its entirety.

> The Heavenly Circuit; Berenice's Hair;
> Tent-pole of Eden; the tent's drapery;
> Symbolical glory of the earth and air!
> The Father and His angelic hierarchy
> That made the magnitude and glory there
> Stood in the circuit of a needle's eye.

---

[1] In the first stanza the expression 'a starlit or a moonlit dome' turns out to have a more than casual meaning. Starlight turns out to represent an intellectual passion to discover relationships – an allusion to Pythagoras's theories; and moonlight to represent the flux of temporal events.

> Some found a different pole, and where it stood
> A pattern on a napkin dipped in blood.

This astonishing little poem is a companion-piece to 'Byzantium'. Yeats states that he wrote both poems on a theme befitting an old man, and in order to 'warm' himself back into life. The poem makes use of the male–female antinomy of which Yeats was so fond; and translates the tree of knowledge into the largest phallic symbol possible. The first two lines alone should have guaranteed the poem a certain amount of critical attention and a great deal of applause. However, where the poem has not been ignored it has received poor treatment.

This poem contrasts two kinds of religion, of art, or of thought, the first based on transcendence of life, the second on participation in it. Veronica's napkin, wiped on Christ's face and carrying his image, represented the second, while the constellations represent the first.[1]

This is, I think, an exact reversal of Yeats's meaning. The first stanza represents Yeats's belief that the noumenal world of idea and *daimon* reveals itself in the physical world. That is, if Yeats keeps to the old mind–body dualism, he does so by making the two such close parallels that for all intents and purposes they become one. For both Kant and Yeats, souls were noumenal objects, outside space and time. Hence, Yeats gets the angelic hierarchy into a needle's eye. And for both men the noumenal world constantly revealed itself in the physical world.

> All the stream that's roaring by
> Came out of a needle's eye;
> Things unborn, things that are gone,
> From a needle's eye still goad it on.
>
> 'A Needle's Eye' (*Collected Poems*, p. 333)

Opposed to the perception of the close inter-relationship of the physical and spiritual, mind and matter, intellect and form, we have the Christian notion of the birth of the soul out of the death of the body, and the Platonic notion of the idea as above the physical.

> Some found a different pole and where it stood
> A pattern on a napkin dipped in blood.

This is exactly the process which is taking place in the fourth stanza of 'Byzantium'.

[1] Ellmann, *Identity of Yeats*, p. 266.

Where blood-begotten spirits come
And all complexities of fury leave,
Dying into a dance,
An agony of trance,
An agony of flame that cannot singe a sleeve.

Now Yeats was well aware that this is not a description of heaven, but a description of hell that is reminiscent of Dante, and of the description of hell-fire in Joyce's *Portrait of the Artist as a Young Man.* The stanza's lurid images constitute a rejection of the Christian–Platonic notion which is made all the more effective by the description of its antithesis in the last stanza.

Astraddle on the dolphin's mire and blood,
Spirit after spirit! The smithies break the flood,
The golden smithies of the Emperor!
Marbles of the dancing floor
Break bitter furies of complexity,
Those images that yet
Fresh images beget,
That dolphin-torn, that gong-tormented sea.

Just as the first stanza of 'Veronica's Napkin' presented a duality of mind and body, spirit and sense, which approached unity, the first lines of this stanza present us with the same unity. The spirits approach Byzantium astraddle the mire and blood of the sensual, physical world. And in this stanza the 'mire and blood' is not rejected but organised. The golden smithies of the Emperor are the tools, that is the concepts, which the intellect uses to organise experience, to break the flood. Now smithies are not smiths, they are the actual forges of the Emperor. And what these forges are is made clear in the following few lines. They are works of art, the Byzantine floor mosaics which provide a kind of schematisation of reality. And over the schematisation flows a massed and disorganised sea of sense-impressions which are ordered by the pattern on the dancing floor.

Marbles of the dancing floor
Break bitter furies of complexity

And the chaos is ordered for a second, grasped conceptually but in its full, phenomenological glory, as sea and image, dancing wave and marble pattern, spread out to encompass life itself – and knowledge returns the reader to the world of phenomena.

> Those images that yet
> Fresh images beget,
> That dolphin-torn, that gong-tormented sea.

This is the final epiphany, life at its height torn by the dolphins of sense perception, and tormented by the ever-active form-imposing mind.

III

Earlier it was claimed that Romanticism tended to separate art and life, to claim that the world of the imagination was separate from our normal reality. Just the opposite is true of Yeats's version of the imagination. For the role of art is to order our perceptions of the world. It is through art that we are able to create and order our universe.

> Marbles of the dancing floor
> Break bitter furies of complexity

It is the concept of a mind which creates and imposes form on the phenomenal, on history, which Yeats makes his first principle. And the primary example of the ability of the mind to create and impose form is art. The role of art is continually reiterated in the poetry; 'The Statues', 'Under Ben Bulben', 'The Long-Legged Fly', 'Her Vision in the Wood', and 'Byzantium' are all attempts to define the role of art in our perception of the world, and to insist that art is only important when it acts in and through the phenomenal.

The repetitive nature of the process, stressed in 'The Statues' and 'Under Ben Bulben', as well as in 'Byzantium', finds its expression in the symbol of the dance. The interweaving of patterns, which is what a dance is, occurs in 'Byzantium' and in the poem immediately before 'Byzantium' in the *Collected Poems*, 'Mohini Chatterjee'. The notion that 'men dance on deathless feet', recurs in both 'Under Ben Bulben' and in 'News for the Delphic Oracle'. In fact the copulation of the nymphs and satyrs of this poem, as they move in time to the music which falls from Pan's cavern, is in many respects a recapitulation of the final stanza of 'Byzantium'.

All human labour, of art, of science, of history, becomes a function of the human mind. Even the intransigent world, the phenomenal world of physical objects, becomes primarily a revelation of the human intellect. Yeats has denied the 'tyranny of fact' which so disturbed him, to choose instead a vision of the individual intellect as the creator, justification, and guarantor of all things.

> *Like a long-legged fly upon the stream*
> *His mind moves upon silence.*

5

Freedom and necessity

The previous chapters have discussed what a number of poems in the canon say about the relationship between mind and experience. Most of these poems reflected a kind of optimism about this relationship, but this optimism was not expressed in terms of a purpose or goal. 'Lapis Lazuli' is probably the best example of Yeats's optimism in that it presents directly his vision of transcendental emptiness, of the absence of any supernatural sanction for human activity, and at the same time presents an uncompromising vision of the absence of progress in history, while still finding human activity meaningful. It is not a poem which would comfort any 'progressive', since there is no earthly goal, no Marxist or even social democrat's paradise. Nor would it please a religious man, since heavenly goals are absent too. Still, it is an optimistic poem, and this optimism is the optimism of the palette and fiddle bow, of poets that are always gay. In the poems discussed earlier, poems like 'Byzantium', which explore the relationship between mind and history, and discover the middle term of this relationship in art, Yeats has discovered a way of thinking about the world which locates all value in the act of mind, and which characteristically discovers the paradigm act of mind in art. What is applauded in 'Lapis Lazuli' is not form, but the act of mind involved in forming, not art, but the ability to make art.

> On their own feet they came, or on shipboard,
> Camel-back, horse-back, ass-back, mule-back,
> Old civilisations put to the sword.
> Then they and their wisdom went to rack:
> No handiwork of Callimachus,
> Who handled marble as if it were bronze,
> Made draperies that seemed to rise
> When sea-wind swept the corner, stands;
> His long lamp-chimney shaped like the stem
> Of a slender palm, stood but a day;
> All things fall and are built again,
> And those that build them again are gay.
>
> (*Collected Poems*, pp. 338–9)

The central human activity is to find and create order and purpose, to make art, and so determine, in a temporary and limited fashion, human history. To be distracted from this task by the search for goals, purposes, or even human happiness, is to ignore what is central to the human condition. The actor must act, must find the role of creator, and hold tight to it. They 'If worthy their prominent part in the play, / Do not break up their lines to weep.' The artist's function is to take the lead in the creation of value, in the discovering of civilisation, despite his understanding of the limits that are placed upon him; despite the fact, and I shall return to this later, that the work of the human intellect, whether art or not, can only stand 'but a day'. How far this is from aestheticism must be noticed. Art is not the opposite of life, not form as opposed to content, nor is there any gap between contemplation and action. In fact art is the very possibility of content, of action, of life itself. To talk of art in this context is not just to talk of these forms, these genres, but to use the word in a manner that encompasses most of what the anthropologist tries to capture with 'artifact', and the historian with 'ideas'.

It is Yeats's belief in the power of mind, in the act of mind, that I tried to indicate when I spoke earlier of his optimism. But 'Lapis Lazuli' has often seemed to its readers not an optimistic evaluation of human potentiality, but cold uncompassionate doctrine. Professor A. G. Stock has written with understanding about these issues. The quotation below is lengthy, but understanding it, both in what it gets right, and what it chooses not to discuss, should prove illuminating. About 'The Gyres' and 'Lapis Lazuli' Professor Stock says

Now, everything leads him to the acceptance of necessity on so vast a scale that necessity itself becomes a kind of faeryland. In *Lapis Lazuli*, a piece of Chinese carved stone sets his thoughts moving. Here is art, like Rocky Face aware of human suffering and still rejoicing, and all around him are people so panic-stricken because their world is ending that art says nothing to them. The aggressive crudity of the verse in the first lines expresses his impatience... [quotes first stanza]

To many English readers these still appear cold-blooded poems. 'We that look on but laugh in tragic joy' is hard to swallow for those who do not count themselves lookers-on, and one may ask whether gaiety is the full response to tragedy. Yeats, however, cared intensely for civilization; but he had already seen its end epitomized in Ireland where his English readers had perhaps seen nothing, and the sheer scale of events could not increase their significance for him. The terror of realization had been put finally in *Nineteen Hundred and Nineteen*:

> He who can read the signs, nor sink unmanned...
> Has but one comfort left: all triumph would
> But break upon his ghostly solitude.

These later poems are written from the far side of a crisis, and

> Things thought too long can be no longer thought;
> For beauty dies of beauty, worth of worth

is a brief synopsis of *Ancestral Houses*.

His political standpoint was neither Communism, Fascism nor Democracy, for he did not see civilization embodied in any of these. It could be found only in an inherited traditional order, accepted in the blood so that acceptance was a part of one's freedom; and it was dying and could only grow again slowly out of centuries of chaos. But since unlike the Marxists he thought of souls, not systems, as the eternal verities, to be on the losing side was neither a crime nor a meaningless calamity. Civilization cannot be reborn except from creative joy, and to maintain faith in the gaiety and glory of life through dark times is to prepare a cradle for its nativity.

Nevertheless there is a certain hardness: the spirit of Yeats' poetry is not compassionate. Neither is it cold, but the warmth of his feeling was for no abstract multitudes but for Ireland, and for men and women he had loved for the greatness he found in them. When he thought of them in *Beautiful Lofty Things* and *The Municipal Gallery Revisited*, his verse was full of poignant regret for the irrecoverable. 'Civilization' was then embodied in

> O'Leary's noble head;...
> Maud Gonne at Howth station waiting for a train,
> Pallas Athene in that straight back and arrogant head;
> All the Olympians; a thing never known again.

It was

> Kevin O'Higgins' countenance that wears
> A gentle questioning look that cannot hide
> A soul incapable of remorse or rest;

and

> John Synge himself, that rooted man,
> 'Forgetting human words,' a grave deep face

and most of all it was Lady Gregory:

> But where is the brush that could show anything
> Of all that pride and that humility?
> And I am in despair that time may bring
> Approved patterns of women or of men
> But not that selfsame excellence again.

With these portraits round him, pride in the life of which he had been part overcame detachment, and he forgot to stand outside of time:

> You that would judge me, do not judge alone
> This book or that, come to this hallowed place
> Where my friend's portraits hang and look thereon;
> Think where man's glory most begins and ends,
> And say my glory was I had such friends.

In such personal, particularized generosity of feeling no modern poet stands anywhere near Yeats. It is different from the compassion for common suffering humanity that our modern sensibility fosters.'[1]

Professor Stock indicates a kind of opposition between what she thinks is Yeats's lack of sympathy for 'common suffering humanity' and his particular power when he writes of individual people – his 'particularized generosity of feeling'. But she does not just contrast public callousness and private generosity; in juxtaposing poems like 'Lapis Lazuli' and 'The Municipal Gallery Revisited', and insisting that Yeats's generosity in the latter poem rises out of something other than an allegiance to the cause of 'common suffering humanity', she suggests a line of investigation that may be fruitful.

Our modern sensibility, our allegiance to 'common suffering humanity', is based upon widely held beliefs which have in common the fact that they all accept one sort of determinism or another. Marxism, Freudian psychology, the social sciences, and progressive liberal opinion are modern in that they all argue from the supposition that every event has a cause, and that events in the lives of men are no less events than the fall of Newton's apple. Now, it is impossible to deny the force of this claim; it is the central doctrine of social science, and to many to deny it is simply to be irrational. But in one particular area at least, it seems to contradict all that is central in our experience. The traditional concepts of human action, the concept of man as a moral being, seem to make

[1] A. G. Stock, *W. B. Yeats: His Poetry and Thought* (Cambridge: Cambridge University Press, 1964), pp. 223–6.

sense only if man is not simply a bundle of phenomena. The concepts of morality, value, praise and blame seem to depend upon a concept of human action as not just free from constraint, but free from psychological or any other sort of necessity. Yeats's philosophical defence against modern determinist thought was Kant's analysis of the role of freedom of the will in the antinomies (see Chapter I). Kant argued that it was possible always to view human action either as phenomena or as free choice, just because it was possible to view mankind either noumenally or phenomenally. For some time Kant's approach has been consigned to the dustbin that philosophers label Metaphysics[1] but in recent years at least one important contemporary philosopher has held a view like Kant's. I will attempt to summarise what P. F. Strawson says in his article 'Freedom and Resentment'. Strawson's essential point is that as long as we regard someone as a person, as long as we are in a human relationship with someone, we are obliged to use the language of freedom. The concepts appropriate to such a relationship are concepts that assume freedom of the will, even when they are negative. That is, it is possible to remain in a human relationship with someone even while you blame him for his actions, possible to remain in a human relationship with someone even if you punish him (e.g. no determinism is entailed by our having a penal system). But when the vocabulary of the social sciences is invoked you cease to deal with persons, and deal with phenomena. Moral categories are now irrelevant, as are indeed most of the traditional categories we use to discuss human action. In a sense, Strawson has posed the problem in a wider context, for of course all philosophers (indeed everyone who has thought about the problem) have known that there was a *prima facie* case for assuming that freedom and determinism are incompatible. So all Strawson has done is show what the consequences of choosing one view or the other would be in terms of questions that go beyond the scope of the philosophy of mind, the philosophy of science, or moral philosophy. He has demonstrated how the consequences of opting for one view or the other will influence even the trivial events of our daily lives. But, having shown how much hinges on our choice between the two conceptual schemes, Strawson does not take sides. He says, in

---

[1] Much of the discussion that was current was about whether or not the concept of choice was incompatible with the notion of cause and effect. It is this sort of speculation that has dominated.

effect, that we have two conceptual schemes for dealing with the world. There are times when one is appropriate – and times when the other is appropriate. In effect, he is opting for an ordinary-language-analysis that parallels Kant's Third Antinomy. Now, these issues arise again and again in Yeats's prose; and they occur always in a language of extravagant imagery compounded equally of spiritualism and Kantian idealism. In Chapter 1 I attempted to be clear, in so far as it is possible, about some representative bits of Yeats's prose that deal with these issues. One reason why Yeats's language in *A Vision* or in 'The Seven Propositions', is so peculiar is precisely that he is unsure of himself. He was never sure what he finally wanted to say about many of these issues; but they were, he knew, too important to ignore. What is remarkable is that these issues occupied his attention at a level of sophistication that was not reflected in philosophical writing then current in the English-speaking world, and that he had the sense to reserve them for *A Vision* and keep them out of his poetry. But he was clear on one thing; that it was important to utilise both conceptual schemes, that his poetry would only be able to reflect the whole of human life if both conceptual schemes were present.

'I found myself upon the third antinomy of Immanuel Kant, thesis: freedom; antithesis: necessity: but I restate it. Every action of man declares the soul's ultimate, particular freedom, and the soul's disappearance in God; declares that reality is a congeries of beings and a single being; nor is this antinomy an appearance imposed upon us by the form of thought but life itself which turns, now here, now there, a whirling and a bitterness. *A Vision*, p. 52

Yeats's Kantianism gave him an advantage in that he had a theoretical sophistication that made it possible for him to resist deciding to accept as the whole answer either a determinist or anti-determinist view. He did not respond to the intellectual tensions between the two positions by drifting into an anti-determinist view. But he was aware that the only way adequately to characterise the direction of modern thought was as an acceptance of a mechanistic determinist view. Let us now consider what is entailed in making a choice for one view or the other.

If we believe in free will, our response to some individual acts will be to evaluate them, and to approve or disapprove of the individual who performs them. If, on the other hand, we take a determinist view, then our reaction to any individual act will be to explain it, and to explain and control the individual who performs it. The radical difference between the two approaches to human behaviour is central to the changes that have occurred in the way our society treats its members, and the way each individual in society reacts to the other individuals. The liberal reforms of Western society have been based on a compassion that sees the individual as the product of social forces, and a compassion that explains human differences, especially large differences, as being caused by prior events. We speak of people who are 'afflicted' with very different opinions as 'neurotic', 'psychotic', etc. The questions raised by the social sciences, and by the determinist view of man are very large, and to regard them as simply political questions would obviously be mistaken. But that they have come to play an important role, a central role, in the infrastructures of political ideologies in this century seems undeniable. In the most general terms, it is correct to say that the political left argues from a determinist position, while the political right argues from a belief in freedom of the will.[1] The politicising of the question of free will in itself explains why Yeats is so often described as a right-wing poet, or accused of being a Fascist. His 'lack of compassion' is simply his refusal to accept the popular determinist of this century and his 'aristorcratic' predilections are simply the positive aspects of this refusal. But, in order to conduct a rational discussion of these questions it is necessary to put aside political labels. It is not just an accident of history that important social reforms have been achieved by those who accept determinism, but there are other grounds for dispensing social justice. Similarly, it is not just an accident of history that those who have been prepared to argue against determinism have often been prepared to defend the cruelties of the system in the name of freedom. The belief in determinist doctrines can lead to compassion for the victims of history, or it can lead to the creation of more victims in the attempt to realise what is considered to be the determined progress of history (for example, the forced collectivisation of Soviet agriculture). A belief

---

[1] The relationship between the political and philosophical issues is made extremely complicated by the confusions that surround all the philosophical attempts to come to terms with the issues raised in discussion of free will, the difficulty in deciding what 'left' and 'right' means in politics and the peculiar practical problems that arise when someone is committed to political action as well as to a belief in determinism.

in freedom of the will can excuse reactionary and vicious politics, or lead to the sort of radical thought that Yeats admired in Swift and Burke. Although we cannot simply read off from the one issue of freedom and determinism a complete philosophy of life and a complete political stance, we must still be prepared to recognise that a decision on that question will have consequences in almost every area of our thought. The problem poses itself every time we think about human actions. When we think about our friends we can either use the vocabulary of, for example, Freud, or the vocabulary of responsibility – praise and blame. Of course, these vocabularies are mutually exclusive. Normally, we recognise that if we use the vocabulary of psychological determinism we strip the object of our discourse of its status as a person, and when we think and talk of those we are close to we use the vocabulary of praise and blame. But it is generally true of our age that we have been increasingly aware of the possibilities of explanation and control that are offered by the vocabularies of psychological and sociological determinism. As we are more and more tempted by the notion of psychological-sociological determinism, it becomes more and more difficult to think of men as heroic or evil, and more and more possible to think of them as victims. On the purely personal level it becomes more difficult to admire anyone who is known personally, and easier to see that person as a subject for analysis. The favourite parlour game of university intellectuals is to insult one another with insults masquerading as diagnosis. Some people even pay to have it done to them. In a society which increasingly feels the power of a determinist analysis of human action it is increasingly difficult to write poetry about heroic individuals, and increasingly difficult to write poetry about men in the mass without adopting an attitude of compassion to those who can only be described as the victims of history. Yeats does both. Stock's comment on Yeats's 'particularized generosity of feeling', and her uneasiness with 'Lapis Lazuli' suggest that Yeats's originality, his *non serviam*, is directed against the popular determinism of the age.

But it would be incorrect to suggest that he was able to replace it with a single-minded or simple-minded belief in 'Freedom of the will'. Let me begin by suggesting what I think an adequate summary of Yeats's position is. Yeats begins with an understanding of the complexities of the issues that he has learned from Kant. He does not have anything new or original to say about the problem when the problem is considered as a philosophical issue. But he is at least aware of the complexities involved in the issue as philosophy, and he avoids because of that knowledge, any simple or foolish consistency. The philosophical issue comes alive at a number of points; in how you think about the people that you know, in how you think about history, in how you think about art, in how you think about politics. Yeats wants to think about these things in terms of the freedom of the will, but he always is aware of the power of the argument for determinism. He finds it easy to ignore the determinist position when he thinks about the people he actually knows, and more and more difficult to ignore determinism when he deals with people 'en masse' or when he thinks about history. But what remains constant in his treatment of these issues is the pressure created by the fact that his opinions are held tentatively, that he is not just intellectually but emotionally unsure of his grounds. This does not mean, however, that I find the poems to be balanced performances. Rather my conviction that he is intellectually unsure of his ground is in part a response to the tone of the poems – poems which are often the most assertive in the canon. In 'A Prayer For My Daughter' Yeats wishes that she might find the 'radical innocence' that springs from an uncomplicated sense of her own worth

> May she become a flourishing hidden tree
> That all her thoughts may like the linnet be,
> And have no business but dispensing round
> Their magnanimities of sound,
> Nor but in merriment begin a chase,
> Nor but in merriment a quarrel.
> O may she live like some green laurel
> Rooted in one dear perpetual place.

The 'magnanimity' that is the centre of aristocratic behaviour can only spring from a mind that is sure of its own freedom, sure of its own power

> Considering that, all hatred driven hence,
> The soul recovers radical innocence
> And learns at last that it is self-delighting,
> Self-appeasing, self-affrighting,
> And that its own sweet will is Heaven's will;
> She can, though every face should scowl
> And every windy quarter howl
> Or every bellows burst, be happy still.

The personal poetry is assertive just in that it is an attempt to create a society built on 'radical innocence' because that is not natural to an age that sees itself as determined. In discovering, that is, creating in his poetry, the freedom and greatness of his friends, Yeats discovers his own freedom, his own greatness of soul. The magnanimity of his personal poetry is achieved by an effort of will, an effort that Yeats makes for himself through his friends. Let us begin by examining 'The Municipal Gallery Revisited' (*Collected Poems*, pp. 368–70).

I

Around me the images of thirty years:
An ambush; pilgrims at the water-side;
Casement upon trial, half hidden by the bars,
Guarded; Griffith staring in hysterical pride;
Kevin O'Higgins' countenance that wears
A gentle questioning look that cannot hide
A soul incapable of remorse or rest;
A revolutionary soldier kneeling to be blessed;

II

An Abbot or Archbishop with an upraised hand
Blessing the Tricolour. 'This is not', I say,
'The dead Ireland of my youth, but an Ireland
The poets have imagined, terrible and gay.'
Before a woman's portrait suddenly I stand,
Beautiful and gentle in her Venetian way.
I met her all but fifty years ago
For twenty minutes in some studio.

III

Heart-smitten with emotion I sink down,
My heart recovering with covered eyes;
Wherever I had looked I had looked upon
My permanent or impermanent images:
Augusta Gregory's son; her sister's son,
Hugh Lane, 'onlie begetter' of all these;
Hazel Lavery living and dying, that tale
As though some ballad-singer had sung it all;

IV

Mancini's portrait of Augusta Gregory,
'Greatest since Rembrandt,' according to John Synge;
A great ebullient portrait certainly;

But where is the brush that could show anything
Of all that pride and that humility?
And I am in despair that time may bring
Approved patterns of women or of men
But not that selfsame excellence again.

V

My mediaeval knees lack health until they bend,
But in that woman, in that household where
Honour had lived so long, all lacking found.
Childless I thought, 'My children may find here
Deep-rooted things,' but never foresaw its end,
And now that end has come I have not wept;
No fox can foul the lair the badger swept –

VI

(An image out of Spenser and the common tongue).
John Synge, I and Augusta Gregory, thought
All that we did, all that we said or sang
Must come from contact with the soil, from that
Contact everything Antaeus-like grew strong.
We three alone in modern times had brought
Everything down to that sole test again,
Dream of the noble and the beggar-man.

VII

And here's John Synge himself, that rooted man,
'Forgetting human words,' a grave deep face.
You that would judge me, do not judge alone
This book or that, come to this hallowed place
Where my friends' portraits hang and look thereon;
Ireland's history in their lineaments trace;
Think where man's glory most begins and ends,
And say my glory was I had such friends.

Throughout the later poetry art is seen as the conceptual prime;
as the supreme example of our 'self-begotten' freedom from necessity. The word 'image' continually focuses our attention on the
freedom of thought from the merely determined, in that what is an
'image' is an epistemological construct that exists on an ontologically distinct level from what is actual. One of the difficulties
with 'The Municipal Gallery Revisited' is that the poem incorpor-
ates the full range of Yeats's thought on the relationship between
'thought' and actuality, the full scope of the ideas discussed in

'Byzantium' and 'The Statues', in a cavalier manner. In ten lines
Yeats indicates how we are to think of the relationship between
Irish thought, Irish art, and his own personal thought

> 'This is not,' I say,
> 'The dead Ireland of my youth, but an Ireland
> The poets have imagined, terrible and gay.'
> Before a woman's portrait suddenly I stand,
> Beautiful and gentle in her Venetian way.
> I met her all but fifty years ago
> For twenty minutes in some studio.

> III
> Heart-smitten with emotion I sink down,
> My heart recovering with covered eyes;
> Wherever I had looked I had looked upon
> My permanent or impermanent images...

'The Municipal Gallery Revisited' is an answer to the question of
the relationship between art and life asked first as a public question,
and finally as a personal question. For Yeats is insisting that the
high, hard, and difficult images that art creates have created what
Ireland has become. And he insists further that the public images
of the artist, the intentional ideals of Ireland's best minds and hearts,
have become his ideals, his 'images'.

The poem deals in the process whereby the individual compels
himself to live in a certain way, and imprints his imagination, his
vision of his own life, on his circumstances. This is possible only if
we can create for ourselves the 'radical innocence' that Yeats wishes
his daughter to recover. The most adequate available symbol for
freedom of the will is the most important example of that freedom –
art. So we can now understand the compliment paid to Hazel
Lavery when Yeats says:

> Hazel Lavery living and dying, that tale
> As though some ballad-singer had sung it all...

A fiction has a consistency that is not causal, a fiction has a meaning. Events can only be explained. It is only if we can conceive of
ourselves as free that our lives can be viewed as meaningful structures.

The famous fourth stanza of the poem is structured upon the
comparison of a life lived with purpose and meaning and a work of

art. For in talking of 'approved patterns of women and men' Yeats simply drives home what has been said in the preceeding stanzas (an approved pattern is just what his images are) and builds upon it in order to achieve his extraordinary compliment to Lady Gregory. For neither her portrait, great though it is, nor any other life lived with the same sort of excellence, can replace the completely autonomous individual – nothing can bring 'that *self-same* excellence again'. With determinism go notions of quantitative and mathematical judgments which make inapplicable words like 'selfsame'. But the 'pattern' of Lady Gregory's life is unique, outside of the world of like causes, like effects, as is a great tragedy. For when it is *Hamlet* we wish to contemplate, neither *Oedipus* nor *Othello* is a possible substitute. The uniqueness of greatness is absolute.

The actions of the autonomous individual are actions that have value; and only the actions of a free individual can have value. The paradox here is that what is necessary (i.e. caused) is, in terms of value, mere accident. It is the autonomy of the will that confers value, that 'hallows' human life.

> You that would judge me, do not judge alone
> This book or that, come to this hallowed place
> Where my friends' portraits hang and look thereon;
> Ireland's history in their lineaments trace;
> Think where man's glory most begins and ends,
> And say my glory was I had such friends.

What Yeats has produced is of no more value than is his friends' friendship and approval, since that friendship and approval is freely given. And in their freedom they have become the Ireland that the poets have imagined 'terrible and gay'. For man's glory, his ability to act as an autonomous individual, to create in himself a unique and irreplaceable excellence, can be bestowed by those that possess it. In choosing Yeats for a friend they have acknowledged in him something worthy of their own excellence. Just as those who people the imagination of Ireland have created Ireland's greatness, so their greatness has, by virtue of becoming Yeats's permanent or impermanent images, created Yeats's greatness. 'My glory was I had such friends.'

Yeats does not confuse art and life, but he recognises their connection. The poem is not, as some critics have imagined,[1] about the failure of art, but about the virtues that art has in changing life. In acting as autonomous individuals, Yeats's friends have achieved the status and the efficacy of works of art. They have become the pictures of their own virtue, so that their 'lineaments' are their thought. And by picturing themselves in their lives they have made all that is valuable in Irish history. Their 'own sweet will' is 'heaven's will'.

Throughout the poetry we may notice that Yeats's society is always a small community of autonomous spirits. It is a community based upon a mutual greatness, a mutual glory, that springs from an allegiance to an aristocratic code of conduct that brooks no weakness, no excuses. The conduct of such friends, or more generally, the relationship between them, is not what is now normally thought of as friendship. The poems about persons in the canon either attempt to create a community of autonomous individuals; or assume such a community. Yeats's 'generosity of mind' consists in his ability to proclaim a commitment on the part of his friends to the values that are proper to a community of heroes. The commitment to these values means that he cannot extend to those that he calls friend the sympathy and understanding that goes with a belief in psychological determinism, and the levelling tolerance that accompanies such beliefs.

TO A YOUNG BEAUTY

Dear fellow-artist, why so free
With every sort of company,
With every Jack and Jill?
Choose your companions from the best;
Who draws a bucket with the rest
Soon topples down the hill.

You may, that mirror for a school,
Be passionate, not bountiful
As common beauties may,
Who were not born to keep in trim
With old Ezekiel's cherubim
But those of Beauvarlet.

---

[1] See Raymond Cowell, *W. B. Yeats* (London: Evans Brothers Ltd., 1969), pp. 124–5.

I know what wages beauty gives,
How hard a life her servant lives,
Yet praise the winters gone:
There is not a fool can call me friend,
And I may dine at journey's end
With Landor and with Donne. (*Collected Poems*, p. 157)

To assert that 'there's not a fool can call me friend' seems to our modern sensibility both arrogant and harsh. Furthermore, the demands that Yeats's attitudes make on us seem hardly bearable.

TO A FRIEND WHOSE WORK HAS COME TO NOTHING

Now all the truth is out,
Be secret and take defeat
From any brazen throat,
For how can you compete,
Being honour bred, with one
Who, were it proved he lies,
Were neither shamed in his own
Nor in his neighbours' eyes?
Bred to a harder thing
Than Triumph, turn away
and like a laughing string
Whereon mad fingers play
Amid a place of stone,
Be secret and exult,
Because of all things known
That is most difficult.   (*Collected Poems*, p. 122)

It is this modern distaste for Yeats's traditional humanism (cf. for instance, Bertrand Russell's attack on the Aristotelian notion of magnanimity) that blinds us to what Yeats is about in the second stanza of 'Lapis Lazuli'. To regard people as victims is, ultimately, to dehumanise them, to deny to them the autonomy that Yeats finds central to his humanity, and his friends' humanity. The hysteria of the women of the first stanza of 'Lapis Lazuli' is, in the context in which we have placed the poem, a denigration of the people that are the object of their hysteria. Now, as Professor Stock points out, Yeats's humanity is always 'particularised' – and her word can now serve as a summary of the whole argument of this chapter. What is extraordinary is that in 'Lapis Lazuli' Yeats is able to extend to all men the particularised praise that is normally reserved for individuals.

All perform their tragic play,
There struts Hamlet, there is Lear,
That's Ophelia, that Cordelia;
Yet they, should the last scene be there,
The great stage curtain about to drop,
If worthy their prominent part in the play,
Do not break up their lines to weep.
They know that Hamlet and Lear are gay;
Gaiety transfiguring all that dread.
All men have aimed at, found and lost;
Black out; Heaven blazing into the head:
Tragedy wrought to its uttermost.
Though Hamlet rambles and Lear rages,
And all the drop-scenes drop at once
Upon a hundred thousand stages,
It cannot grow by an inch or an ounce.

We have, on the one hand, the liberal compassion that is based upon the belief in determinism, and that expresses itself as hysteria. This hysteria is peculiar in that it assumes the hopelessness of action at the level of the individual, while maintaining the efficacy of collective action. It parallels the Marxist ability to forget about determinism when engaged in propaganda battles, or the Freudians' ability to forget their theory when faced with personal decisions. But this liberal hysteria is demeaning; it is a treacly combination of self-pity and self-aggrandisement, an easy way of proving yourself serious while acting in the most frivolous manner. It is placed totally by the first line of the second stanza, 'All perform their tragic play'. We saw, in 'The Municipal Gallery Revisited', that the unity and meaningfulness of art was as a measure for what is best in human life. In replacing pity with the respect one accords to the tragedian Yeats here extends his aristocratic courtesy to all men. Furthermore, we can now understand that mere numbers, and mere events, are truly irrelevant. For when all men freely choose their destiny, when all men are recognised as men, and not victims, then we are freed from pity, and can extend an honourable love, an honourable admiration

Though Hamlet rambles and Lear rages,
And all the drop-scenes drop at once
Upon a hundred thousand stages,
It cannot grow by an inch or an ounce.

We might now begin to read 'Lapis Lazuli', but that is a task I shall delay, in order to examine several other great poems that bear directly on these issues. Yeats's public attitudes grow out of his personal attitudes. I do not say this in order to indicate a psychological priority, in a psychological theory, but in order to indicate an intellectual commitment on his part. The sort of respect he accords men *en masse* in 'Lapis Lazuli' springs from the sort of respect it is possible to award a friend. The values he applies to men in general are those he can apply within his own life. The discovery, or rather the creation of these values, among a community of autonomous individuals, is the subject of poem after poem. I propose to discuss only two of the greatest of these poems, 'Hound Voice' and 'In Memory of Major Robert Gregory'.

HOUND VOICE

Because we love bare hills and stunted trees
And were the last to choose the settled ground,
Its boredom of the desk or of the spade, because
So many years, companioned by a hound,
Our voices carry; and though slumber-bound,
Some few half wake and half renew their choice,
Give tongue, proclaim their hidden name – 'Hound Voice.'

The women that I picked spoke sweet and low
And yet gave tongue. 'Hound Voices' were they all.
We picked each other from afar and knew
What hour of terror comes to test the soul,
And in that terror's name obeyed the call,
And understood, what none have understood,
Those images that waken in the blood.

Some day we shall get up before the dawn
And find our ancient hounds before the door,
And wide awake know that the hunt is on;
Stumbling upon the blood-dark track once more,
Then stumbling to the kill beside the shore;
Then cleaning out and bandaging of wounds,
And chants of victory amid the encircling hounds.

(*Collected Poems*, p. 385)

'Hound Voice' is a poem so completely realised, and therefore so unpretentious, that one may know it for years without understanding it. One may, for instance, notice the sonority of those 'Hound

Voices', the archetypal glory of the sound of the hunt, without noticing how carefully the poem is controlled by the homely image of the solitary individual and a dog.

> Because we love bare hills and stunted trees
> And were the last to choose the settled ground,
> Its boredom of the desk or of the spade, because
> So many years companioned by a hound,
> Our voices carry...

Yeats embodies in his friends a heroic conception of self-hood that is, above all else, solitary. For to accept freedom of the will as a regulative principle in life is to accept a responsibility before greatness, and to accept greatness as a responsibility. The grand manner which so annoys so many of Yeats's readers is no more than the perception that the soul's freedom brings responsibilities that cannot be shared. The society that Yeats craves is a society of heroic individuals, of people who have accepted as a duty the responsibility of their lives. It is, therefore, a society of solitary individuals who can admire each other, exhort each other, but never lift the burden of individuality from each other's shoulders. Each of them bears the duty of creating in their own lives the meaning and pattern of all lives. Each of them must find an image of human life, of meaningful existence, despite the terror that goes with loneliness. For only those who are lonely, who have assumed the weight of their own individuality and freedom, can know what terror is. And it is only through that terror that one can fully understand what it is to be totally committed to one's full humanity.

> The women that I picked spoke sweet and low
> And yet gave tongue. 'Hound Voices' were they all.
> We picked each other from afar and knew
> What hour of terror comes to test the soul,
> And in the terror's name obeyed the call,
> And understood, what none have understood,
> Those images that waken in the blood.

The loneliness, the essential isolation between the speaker and the women is made more poignant by the rejection of the more comfortable aspects of the traditional Western beliefs about love. For there is no soul-merging here, no 'halving' of souls, no comfortable shucking of individual identities, only a mutual recognition of individual destinies. They 'pick each other from afar', they know what terror besieges the other, for they feel the same terror, but they remain essentially alone in their individual solitudes.

Finally, we must take note of the nature of the struggle. It is not just a struggle to avoid the cameraderie of a facile society 'the boredom of the desk or of the spade', but a struggle that is waged against the very conditions of life – 'at stroke of midnight God shall win'. But that struggle against nature is natural to man when man is thought of as more than animal, for it is just the struggle to come to terms with the whole of the natural world. So the hunt, and the hound's voice raised to announce the hunt, becomes a symbol at once for victory over the natural world, and the victory of the natural world over us. The images that waken in the blood are natural to humanity, yet they speak of our desire to be more than natural. The hunt is our victory over the natural world, and the final victory of the natural world over us. Thus the dying fall of the last stanza, the chant of victory that is also a dirge.

> Some day we shall get up before the dawn
> And find our ancient hounds before the door,
> And wide awake know that the hunt is on;
> Stumbling upon the blood-dark track once more,
> Then stumbling to the kill beside the shore;
> Then cleaning out and bandaging of wounds,
> And chants of victory amid the encircling hounds.

What is important in many of Yeats's poems about his friends is the sense of victory snatched from fatality, of an accomplishment that is 'of all things not impossible the most difficult'. The attention that is paid to the difficulty of living your own life, and not a life charted by the exigencies of chance, lies behind Yeats's attempt to create a society of friends, and not some simple-minded belief that it is easy to find one's individuality. Our age is gripped by a moral and emotional sloppiness, an inability to face the realities of life combines with a willingness to forgive anything in order that we might be forgiven. Nietzsche called it the 'herd instinct', the instinct that allows us to rub against each other and poke our dirty fingers in our dirty sores, in the name of humanity and pity. The most famous single example of this sort of self-indulgent nonsense in English poetry is Arnold's 'Dover Beach' ('Let us be true to one another' – as if we have nothing better to do), and this tradition of soft romantic forgiveness has occupied a large place in English literature since Arnold (when Auden tells us we have to love one another he is simply re-writing 'Dover Beach') and its exponents often patronise Yeats's harsher demands. For examples, Louis MacNeice says of Yeats's personal poems:

His poems about, or for, the friends whom he admired were something unusual in what he himself called the age of the satirists. T. S. Eliot's Prufrock, published in 1917, heralded the cynicism of a whole post-war decade. The title poem in that volume was a most delicate piece of self-analysis,[1] self-satire, the portrait of an intellectual who finds nothing worth while, who makes not the great but the complete refusal (there is no greatness in it for he does not believe in what he refuses) –

> 'I am no prophet – and here's no great matter.'

The Portrait of a Lady, again, throws a cold, cruel light on the sort of woman whom Yeats regarded as a masterpiece of civilization. Eliot presents these characters in the manner of a modern novelist, showing up their make-believe worlds and leaving them puppets. It is strange to turn to Yeats and find him admiring individual human beings, not questioning their individuality, not stressing their subservience to circumstance –

> And that inquiring man John Synge comes next,
> That dying chose the living world for text
> And never could have rested in the tomb
> But that, long travelling, he had come
> Towards nightfall upon certain set apart
> In a most desolate stony place,
> Towards nightfall upon a race
> Passionate and simple like his heart.

Yeats in his poems treated Synge or Major Robert Gregory in the same way that Shakespeare treated his tragic heroes and heroines; the hero is conceded full individuality, his Marxist conditioning is ignored. This means simplification, means – in Shakespeare and in Yeats – the elimination from the tragic figure of all psychology except some simple trends, it means the explanation of a man not by his daily life but by one or two great moments; thus we get the paradox that in Shakespeare death is so often the great moment of life and Cleopatra's suicide an assertion of the joy of life. This is what Yeats meant when he wrote in his old age that 'Hamlet and Lear are gay'. The characters are simplified into bold symbolical figures; all Synge's significance is for Yeats summed up in the line – 'dying chose the living world for text'.[2]

Of course Yeats knew that it is difficult to achieve individuality; of course he knew that a man can struggle all his life and achieve

---

[1] One wonders whether Eliot thought it was 'self' analysis.
[2] L. MacNeice, *The Poetry of W. B. Yeats* (London: Faber and Faber, 1967), p. 99.

greatness only once, or not at all. Of course he knew the horrors of modern civilisation.

> We, who seven years ago
> Talked of honour and of truth,
> Shriek with pleasure if we show
> The weasel's twist, the weasel's tooth,
>
> from 'Nineteen Hundred and Nineteen'
> (*Collected Poems*, pp. 235–6)

> We are closed in, and the key is turned
> On our uncertainty...
>
> from 'The Stare's Nest by my Window'
> (*Collected Poems*, p. 230)

> Some think it a matter of course that chance
> Should starve good men and bad advance,
> That if their neighbours figured plain,
> As though upon a lighted screen,
> No single story would they find
> Of an unbroken happy mind,
> A finish worthy of the start.[1]
>
> from 'Why Should not Old Men be Mad?'
> (*Collected Poems*, p. 388)

The poems that Yeats writes about his friends do not assume individuality as simply given; do not assume the perfection of the individual will, but record the creation of that individuality. Furthermore, they are rarely primarily about the individuality of others, but rather documents of Yeats's perpetual struggle to discover his own individuality and autonomy. That is, Yeats takes as his subject in these poems, his life and his life in relationship to his friends. But the relationship between him and his friends is fictionalised in order to accord with the theme of the poems; a society of individuals, of autonomous psyches, is for Yeats the acme of personal and social achievement. The poem 'In Memory of Major Robert Gregory' differs from traditional elegies, differs from say 'Lycidas', in that the poetical mode of the poem is what Keats called 'the egotistical or Wordsworthian sublime'. In Yeats's poems

---

[1] To say that it is 'a matter of course that chance...' is a marvellous bit of intellectual gamesmanship. For even in this despondent poem Yeats is not quite prepared to surrender to the negative emotions. The poem concludes with the line 'Know why an old man should be mad'. Having proved his case he has achieved a victory that in itself is a refutation of the argument of the poem.

about his friends he becomes a central character who speaks not out of a humble respect, but out of a mutual greatness. That this assumed greatness is created out of the greatness of his friends, and their greatness is created out of his greatness is the locus of what he means. For the assumption of greatness is the basis of civilisation. Let us begin by examining 'In Memory of Major Robert Gregory'.

IN MEMORY OF MAJOR ROBERT GREGORY

I

Now that we're almost settled in our house
I'll name the friends that cannot sup with us
Beside a fire of turf in th' ancient tower,
And having talked to some late hour
Climb up the narrow winding star to bed:
Discoverers of forgotten truth
Or mere companions of my youth,
All, all are in my thoughts to-night being dead.

II

Always we'd have the new friend meet the old
And we are hurt if either friend seem cold,
And there is salt to lengthen out the smart
In the affections of our heart,
And quarrels are blown up upon that head;
But not a friend that I would bring
This night can set us quarrelling,
For all that come into my mind are dead.

III

Lionel Johnson comes the first to mind,
That loved his learning better than mankind,
Though courteous to the worst; much falling he
Brooded upon sanctity
Till all his Greek and Latin learning seemed
A long blast upon the horn that brought
A little nearer to his thought
A measureless consummation that he dreamed.

IV

And that enquiring man John Synge comes next,
That dying chose the living world for text
And never could have rested in the tomb
But that, long travelling, he had come

Towards nightfall upon certain set apart
In a most desolate stony place,
Towards nightfall upon a race
Passionate and simple like his heart.

V

And then I think of old George Pollexfen,
In muscular youth well known to Mayo men
For horsemanship at meets or at racecourses,
That could have shown how pure-bred horses
And solid men, for all their passion, live
But as the outrageous stars incline
By opposition, square and trine;
Having grown sluggish and contemplative.

VI

They were my close companions many a year,
A portion of my mind and life, as it were,
And now their breathless faces seem to look
Out of some old picture-book;
I am accustomed to their lack of breath,
But not that my dear friend's dear son,
Our Sidney and our perfect man,
Could share in that discourtesy of death.

VII

For all things the delighted eye now sees
Were loved by him: the old storm-broken trees
That cast their shadows upon road and bridge;
The tower set on the stream's edge;
The ford where drinking cattle make a stir
Nightly, and startled by that sound
The water-hen must change her ground;
He might have been your heartiest welcomer.

VIII

When with the Galway foxhounds he would ride
From Castle Taylor to the Roxborough side
Or Esserkelly plain, few kept his pace;
At Mooneen he had leaped a place
So perilous that half the astonished meet
Had shut their eyes; and where was it
He rode a race without a bit?
And yet his mind outran the horses' feet.

IX

We dreamed that a great painter had been born
To cold Clare rock and Galway rock and thorn,
To that stern colour and that delicate line
That are our secret discipline
Wherein the gazing heart doubles her might.
Soldier, scholar, horseman, he,
And yet he had the intensity
To have published all to be a world's delight.

X

What other could so well have counselled us
In all lovely intricacies of a house
As he that practised or that understood
All work in metal or in wood,
In moulded plaster or in carven stone?
Soldier, scholar, horseman, he,
And all he did done perfectly
As though he had but that one trade alone.

XI

Some burn damp faggots, others may consume
The entire combustible world in one small room
As though dried straw, and if we turn about
The bare chimney is gone black out
Because the work had finished in that flare.
Soldier, scholar, horseman, he,
As 'twere all life's epitome.
What made us dream that he could comb grey hair?

XII

I had thought, seeing how bitter is that wind
That shakes the shutter, to have brought to mind
All those that manhood tried, or childhood loved
Or boyish intellect approved,
With some appropriate commentary on each;
Until imagination brought
A fitter welcome; but a thought
Of that late death took all my heart for speech.

(*Collected Poems*, pp. 148–52)

Of the dozen stanzas only four are about Robert Gregory. Synge,
Lionel Johnson, and George Pollexfen each receive their stanza; and

the other five stanzas (I, II, VI, VII, XII) are usually spoken of as the frame of the poem. Why then, does Major Gregory get so little time in his own elegy? We all know that elegies are not spontaneous expressions of grief, or even formalised expressions of grief. Elegies are poems about how to live (and given our mortality, that must include how to die). Milton's poem for a man he hardly knew is more the norm for the elegy than an oddity, in that the emotion is not immediately for King, but for King only as a representative or type of the heroic individual. We might say the same about Yeats's poems about Major Gregory. But there is this difference – despite the famous arguments about Milton's digression in 'Lycidas', the whole force of Milton's poem reaches us through what is said about King. Milton assumes the *persona* of the humble swain, and disappears into the *persona*. The *persona* itself stays hidden throughout most of the poem, only appearing to twitch the 'mantle blue' and end the poem.[1] Now, the *persona* Yeats adopts in the elegy entitled 'In Memory of Major Robert Gregory' is as much a *persona* as Milton's swain, or the shepherd and goatherd that Yeats creates in another poem to speak of Gregory. But Yeats's *persona* remains at the centre of the poem, and becomes thematically as important as Gregory. That is, what is central to the poem is not so much Major Gregory as the changing mood of the *persona*, and the fact that the *persona* informs us from the beginning that the point of his thinking about Gregory is to induce that change of mood in himself.

> Now that we're almost settled in our house
> I'll name the friends that cannot sup with us
> Beside a fire of turf in th' ancient tower,
> And having talked to some late hour
> Climb up the narrow winding stair to bed:

The formal ritualistic elements of the poem are not just elegiac, but personal. That is, the *conventions* appealed to are those of domesticity. We have moved into a new house, the husband says, and so it is right that we talk of ourselves, interpret ourselves for each other, until we create (more properly re-create) for ourselves and for each other our best selves, our individual greatness. When the poem closes Yeats comments that 'I had thought...to have brought

---

[1] This is, of course, an oversimplification. Milton never totally disappears in his poems, in the way, for example, Marvell does. But the *persona* remains unrealised enough and enough unlike Milton, for the switch to the third person narrative in the last verse paragraph to have its extraordinary effect.

to mind/All those that manhood tried, or childhood loved/Or boyish intellect approved'. This is a fair *précis* of what he has done in the poem. There is an appropriateness to this recital that springs from the occasion – their occupation of their new home. Their fears and weaknesses, their self-doubt, are symbolised by the wind which comes to represent everything beyond their control, everything that will resist them.

The movement of the poem is from self-doubt, from an uncertain perception of self, towards the re-creation of an 'image' that is large enough to consecrate their lives together. So when Yeats begins to speak his speech is full of self-doubt, and self-deprecation that is mirrored in what he says about his friends. The poem begins with the self-conscious acknowledgment that this is a conversation which will establish them in their home, and make it possible for them to occupy it properly – it is a conversation which will light the way to their bed. But immediately after saying this Yeats rushes pre-cipitately towards the aggrandisement of himself and his friends. The next line makes an assertion that has not yet been prepared for; his dead friends are 'Discoverers of forgotten truth'. Because it is too quick, because he is still full of his own self-doubt, the next line recoils from what has been said too quickly – 'Or mere com-panions of my youth'. Their greatness and his own are both in doubt, both at risk. All he knows at this point, all that can free him from both his assertiveness and his doubt, is the incontravertible fact of their death – 'All, all are in my thoughts to-night being dead'.

There is no easier way to relieve the tensions created by the pressures of self-imposed standards or any other worry than by the contemplation of mortality. Nor is there a more direct way to discover what is petty in yourself, and what is ignoble. The fact of death, the death of those he loves, enables him to contemplate in a relaxed manner what is central to the sort of friendship he will be discussing. Furthermore it has freed him so that he can see what is foolish, over-subtle, and disreputable about the state of mind that was documented in the first stanza.

> Always we'd have the new friend meet the old
> And we are hurt if either friend seem cold,
> And there is salt to lengthen out the smart
> In the affections of our heart,
> And quarrels are blown up upon that head;

The suggestion of 'Love me, love my dog' is handled in the most delicate manner possible. His own attitude, which is that of the over-anxious friend, the too quickly bruised ego, is seen from a perspective large enough to make possible a human and indulgent attitude towards his own foibles, and a wry self-criticism.

> not a friend that I would bring
> This night can set us quarrelling,
> For all that come into my mind are dead.

It is only when he has achieved this delicate balance that he can begin to see clearly his friends' greatness. We shall see that in these poems Yeats speaks in the mood that is best described by Keats's 'egotistical sublime', that he is able to praise fulsomely only when he has surmounted his doubts about himself. But this egotism has as its principal enemy the weak egotism that strives to value itself primarily through external comparisons. Pity is the easiest salve for weak egotism in that the implied comparison gives the man who feels pity a sense of his own superiority. The need to feel superior is Iago's 'motiveless malignity'; Othello's generosity before Iago tempts him from it is the type of the egotistical sublime. Yeats shows us an attempt to reach the 'egotistical sublime' directly, when he plunges into praise in the fifth line of the poem. But his own self-doubt, his weak egotism, gets in the way. By remembering that his friends are dead he destroys that weak egotism. For how can one worry about one's relative stature when faced with the fact that those you love are dead? Once having conquered that weakness, once having put aside his doubts about himself, he can discover his friends' virtues.

Putting aside, for the moment, the question of what Yeats actually says about his friends, we may notice the new confidence he has in himself when he talks about his dead friends in Stanzas III to VI. This confidence is just his delight in his friends' achievements, in their greatness of soul. He has been able to praise them, and in being magnanimous, in praising them has achieved that magnanimity that does not shrink from a high opinion of itself. They are, he says, a portion of his mind and life. In being sure of their worth he is surer of his own.

Earlier I wrote of the Kantian notions of the noumenal and phenomenal soul; the one free from the law of cause and effect, the other bound to it. We saw how this lay behind Yeats's use of 'image' in 'The Municipal Gallery Revisited', and how a work of art, because it is meaningful and complete, and the antithesis of accident, became a fit symbol for the freedom of the soul, for 'radical innocence'. These strands are all drawn together in Stanza VI.

> now their breathless faces seem to look
> Out of some old picture-book;
> I am accustomed to their lack of breath,
> But not that my dear friend's dear son,
> Our Sidney and our perfect man,
> Could share in that discourtesy of death.

There is, first of all, the transfiguration of accident into art implied by the notion that they have become their own portraits, that stare at him from a picture book. The language of the stanza creates the impression that they have done this themselves; Yeats says that they look out at him (rather than that he looks at them) and the fact that they are 'breathless' almost becomes an action of theirs – it is as if they held their breath and so became their portraits. The stanza is filled with a high arrogance directed against the merely accidental – and against the accident of accidents that is death. For when Yeats says that 'he has grown accustomed to their lack of breath', and when he talks of Gregory sharing 'in that discourtesy of death', he has achieved a freedom like that of the faces in the picture-book, a freedom that allows him to mock at death itself.

Yeats's self-confidence is based on the way he has been able to create a community about him, albeit a community of dead men. For, having established his solidarity with Johnson, Synge, and Pollexfen, a solidarity established by an almost metaphysical transference (a portion of my mind and life, as it were – the colloquial phrase tacked on in the end demands we acquiesce to a claim that, were it not presented so cavalierly, we would wish more clearly explained), Yeats proceeds to establish his relationship with Gregory.

VII

> For all things the delighted eye now sees
> Were loved by him: the old storm-broken trees
> That cast their shadows upon road and bridge;
> The tower set on the stream's edge;
> The ford where drinking cattle make a stir
> Nightly, and startled by that sound
> The water-hen must change her ground;
> He might have been your heartiest welcomer.

One device of the traditional elegy was that the speaker and the hero share the same ground (cf. for example, 'Lycidas'). What is unusual here is not that Yeats uses the scenery that surrounds the tower to create a common context for himself and Gregory, nor even the extraordinary effect of rich midnight that is created out of shadows and animal movements, but the assumption of the voice of the egotistical sublime which allows him to utter the last line of this stanza as both a high compliment to Gregory, and proof of the fact that he himself has achieved the radical innocence that was lacking when he began to speak. For when he turns to his wife to tell her that Robert Gregory might have been her heartiest welcomer he has achieved the self-confidence that he was searching for when he began to talk of his friends, and so he is able to give to their life in their new home the consecration they seek. And having found his own confidence, his own image, he can speak without doubt about Gregory's greatness.

The quality of the rhetoric Yeats creates in the next three stanzas has been often remarked. All I would add to the general account of it is that much of its force comes from the weight of personality that has been created for the speaker. One of the more important devices used to create in us a sense of loss is just that we have felt the weight of the *persona* Yeats has created for himself. When Yeats says

> What other could so well have counselled us
> In all lovely intricacies of a house
> As he

we feel the loss that Yeats feels because we are sure that he is entitled to take the decoration of his house seriously and the compliment escapes being ludicrous only because we are now prepared to take Yeats so very seriously. For what mere mortal could tell us that an artist was great by claiming that that artist might have done a good job of decorating his house?

The eleventh and penultimate stanza creates an image of Gregory and enrols him in the picture-book in a manner parallel to the treatment of Synge, Johnson, and Pollexfen in Stanza VI. In the three earlier stanzas Gregory was celebrated in life as soldier, scholar, horseman, and artist. In this stanza he achieves a permanence that is like art, and like the 'images' of 'The Municipal Gallery Revisited'. He is still 'Soldier, scholar, horseman', but now he is these things 'as 'twere life's epitome.' He becomes himself, throws off the traces of cause and effect, by consuming 'the entire combustible world in one small room'. The image is difficult, as it is in 'Lapis Lazuli'. For the 'black out' that is achieved in both poems is the best way that Yeats has of expressing the ability of men to give expression to their fullest selves even while being destroyed by the world. (The other image that Yeats characteristically uses to talk about this is the swan's leaping into the heavens.) In remaining himself in the face of death, Gregory literally explodes into another dimension, into the autonomous world of the soul.

> if we turn about
> The bare chimney is gone black out
> Because the work had finished in that flare.

Gregory has become an 'epitome'; what in other poems Yeats calls an 'image', or a 'hound voice'. His life has been wrested from the realm of accident into that of meaning. So the last line of the stanza – it is apparent at this point that the poem depends heavily on Yeats's ability to manipulate the individual stanzas toward their last lines – images Yeats shrugging off, with annoyance, the no longer important fact that Robert Gregory died a young man. 'What made us dream that he could comb grey hair?' – What made us think that he would be subject to the merely accidental exigencies of time? How could we be so jejune? For we are in possession, through Yeats, of 'all life's epitome'; and in contemplating it with Yeats, we have moved from accident to meaning.

It is because of this leap that there occurs the 'had' of the last stanza.

> I *had* thought, seeing how bitter is that wind
> That shakes the shutter, to have brought to mind
> All those that manhood tried, or childhood loved
> Or boyish intellect approved,
> With some appropriate commentary on each;
> Until imagination brought
> A fitter welcome; but a thought
> Of that late death took all my heart for speech.

We have seen that Yeats sets out to provide a consecration of the life he and his wife are to lead in their new home, and that this consecration was to be achieved by a meditation on those friends whose lives provided an 'epitome' for living. The object of such a consecration is the creation in themselves of the sort of egotism that is a necessary condition for the creation in their own lives of the radical freedom that has been achieved by those that epitomise all life. But that egotism was already established before Yeats began to speak of Robert Gregory. Having achieved it, however, Yeats can examine the attempt to find it from a new angle. That is, once he is sure of his own status, once he is able to see his friends from the vantage point of his own greatness, the fact that he needed to use his friends to create his greatness becomes an embarrassment. He tells us what he 'had thought' to do, and the syntax suggests that he is giving up a plan of action. But he has already done just what he claims he is no longer intent on doing. The point is not that he is confused; but that the syntax is used to indicate a new delicacy of feeling that springs from the fact that 'imagination brought a fitter welcome'. Having made his soul he is now able to utter the formal sentiment that his own egotism – 'egotism' is here only the stronger form of 'magnanimity' – knows to be appropriate. He says, knowing that he has already spoken at considerable length, 'but a thought/of that late death took all my heart for speech'. This is not prevarication, not a desire to have it both ways, but simply the formal response to death that is necessary from his new perspective. He and his wife can now fall silent because they have recognised, and therefore achieved, for a period of time, the clarity and meaning that is life's 'epitome'. There is nothing left but to 'climb up the narrow winding stair to bed'.

'Hound Voice' and 'In Memory of Major Robert Gregory' are both poems that define human greatness. They are able to define that greatness (which is of necessity a tragic greatness, since all men die) because Yeats is able to imagine that greatness in particular men. Furthermore, in order to come to grips with that greatness he has had to assume the voice of the 'egotistical sublime'. From a standpoint less grand it would be impossible to freely acknowledge greatness; one would become either a naive flatterer or a sceptic. But we cannot assume that the egotism of the *persona* is only a literary device. For in reality, as well as in art, it is only when the individual has created in himself the mood of the egotistical sublime, that he can recognise the greatness of other men. Here we have the explanation of the word 'hysterical' at the beginning of 'Lapis Lazuli'. For Yeats has begun to write the poem in the 'egotistical sublime' just because he knows how dangerous, and how disastrously easy it is, to fail to create our own soul before dealing with 'social problems'. When he begins by caricaturing these women of conscience by calling them 'hysterical', he has already assumed the largeness of mind that is created in 'In Memory of Major Robert Gregory'.

That is, Yeats is prepared to value everything from the perspective of the soul's autonomy. Having made this decision death becomes a mere discourtesy. We are already our own images, we have already made the leap from accident to meaning. Having once chosen our own arrogance, death becomes just accident. It no longer interferes with the true business of the soul, the type of which is the gaiety of the artist.

> All men have aimed at, found and lost;
> Black out; Heaven blazing into the head:
> Tragedy wrought to its uttermost.
> Though Hamlet rambles and Lear rages,
> And all the drop-scenes drop at once
> Upon a hundred thousand stages,
> It cannot grow by an inch or an ounce.

The images are the same as those of 'The Municipal Gallery Revisited' and 'In Memory of Major Robert Gregory', and they are used to the same end. But it is too late – for we have already read the first stanza, and the irony and wit have annoyed us because we were not prepared then to view life and death from the perspective that we are given in Stanza II. I point out this fault in the poem because it is characteristic of the poem as a whole. Fine as it is, 'Lapis Lazuli' is not of the quality of Yeats's best poems. It assumes too much, it constantly rushes ahead of itself, and it does not provide enough context for the images in it (cf. especially Stanza II) to work completely independently of a context created by the reader's knowledge of Yeats's other poems.

However, in so far as technique and thought can be separated, its failure is a failure in technique rather than thought. Indeed, Yeats's clarity of thought is almost one of the difficulties. It is because he so clearly knows what the argument is that he takes so little pains with his fiction. What Yeats or any other poet usually wants to say is connected with the way he is going to say it, with the fact that he is writing poetry. In the case of 'Lapis Lazuli' Yeats is versifying an idea that on this occasion presents itself to him abstractly, and he fleshes out an argument with images, rather than thinking through a poem.

But, whatever the faults of the poem, it is still an impressive achievement. One of the more impressive aspects is the way that the third stanza indicates the social importance of the willingness to accept as a proper standpoint the egotistical sublime. The argument of the first two stanzas of the poem is that it is morally and personally correct to assume the attitude towards the individual that is documented in 'In Memory of Major Robert Gregory'. The hysteria of the women springs from their inability to see the victims of history as free to choose their own destiny, to leap into their freedom. In claiming that everyone chooses to play a role – to find a meaningful pattern in his life – Yeats insists that we recognise that human dignity springs from the quality of the individual. When he says that it cannot grow by an inch or an ounce he says what Hamlet says when he has discovered his own freedom (knowing that he is about to die):

Not a whit, we defy augury: there is a special providence in the fall of a sparrow. If it be now, 'tis not to come; if it be not to come, it will be now; if it be not now, yet it will come – the readiness is all. Since no man knows of aught he leaves, what is 't to leave betimes? Let be.

To pity a man is to reduce him to the status of victim; Yeats's point is that the only moral attitude, the only attitude that recognises humanity, is to acknowledge each individual's struggle against the accidents of life. The argument depends on a recognition that life can only be viewed qualitatively, and this recognition is possible only when we hold firmly to the knowledge that death is inevitable and universal.

The social value of taking the attitude that Yeats takes lies in the fact that death is inevitable. Nothing can be accomplished until we ignore the temporality of ourselves and our works 'All things fall and are built again,/And those that build them again are gay'. The meliorism of the women is not only a moral and personal red herring, but a socially destructive red herring. For it is only when we have achieved the kind of freedom involved in the 'black-out' of Stanza II that we can begin to create in the world. Those that create are 'gay'. On the level of social usefulness two things are put in opposition to the urgency and compassion of the women: the inevitability of death and the fact that it is only when we ignore our own destruction, only when we see that it does not matter, that we can begin to live creatively.

The fourth and fifth stanzas of the poem continue the line of argument that is begun in the third stanza. That is, they continue to explore the usefulness of the attitude of the autonomous soul in creating the possibilities of social life. The musician becomes the type of the artist of Stanza I, and provides paradoxically, something like the sort of relief from suffering that the hysterical women demanded. For the 'gaiety' that his artistry creates proves to be important in protecting us from the disasters that drive the women into this hysteria.

> Two Chinamen, behind them a third,
> Are carved in lapis lazuli,
> Over them flies a long-legged bird,
> A symbol of longevity;
> The third, doubtless a serving-man,
> Carries a musical instrument.
>
> Every discoloration of the stone,
> Every accidental crack or dent,
> Seems a water-course or an avalanche,
> Or lofty slope where it still snows
> Though doubtless plum or cherry-branch
> Sweetens the little half-way house
> Those Chinamen climb towards, and I
> Delight to imagine them seated there;
> There, on the mountain and the sky,
> On all the tragic scene they stare.
> One asks for mournful melodies;
> Accomplished fingers begin to play.
> Their eyes mid many wrinkles, their eyes,
> Their ancient, glittering eyes, are gay.

The culture of China is the oldest on the planet, and the artifact that Yeats meditates on contains a symbol for that longevity – the long-legged bird. But it is just the lack of 'hysteria' that produces the longevity of China and the longevity of the 'Chinamen' Yeats imagines. For they climb to a 'half-way house' that represents a mental space halfway between the 'black-out' of the tragic accept-ance of Hamlet, and the hysteria of the common perception of human limitation. Their wrinkled eyes 'stare' at the tragic scene with a wisdom born of their comprehension of the inevitability of tragedy. Given this knowledge as a datum, the 'tragic joy' of the arts becomes, not an aesthetic response, but the only healthy response, and the only pragmatic response. For the desire to do something 'drastic' springs from an inability to imagine fully the universality of death and destruction. Once we understand that 'all things fall' we are liberated from the pressure that is captured by the disruptive voices of the 'hysterical women', and are so free to create human society again – 'All things fall and are built again/ And those that built them again are gay'.

But the acceptance of destruction is not just the nihilism that frees the individual to create anew; it is also the necessary basis for the preservation of what we value. For the Chinese sages have grown old out of that tragic acceptance; their equanimity in the face of the 'tragic scene' is in itself a protection against time and destruction. It is the very gaiety with which they face their own and their society's ultimate destruction, that allows them to preserve it in the here and now.

It is because they know that all things fall that they call for 'mournful melodies'; art is an acknowledgement of reality and not an escape from it. And it is because they have come to grips with the inevitability of death and destruction that they can be gay: that is, can continue to live without hysteria. It is only in a society that understands that 'all things fall' that the artist can be 'a serving-man'. The women of the first stanza want art to serve by showing the way out of what is in fact a universal dilemma, although they feel it as something that can be averted.

The argument of the poem, then, can be summarised in the following manner: the first stanza describes as hysterical a meliorist attitude towards the specific evils of the age. The second stanza rejects that meliorism by insisting on the autonomy of the individual will as the source of all public, as well as private, value. The fourth and fifth stanzas return to the immediate problems posed by the first section in a different guise, and suggests that the attitude of mind that is captured by 'gay' in the poem is the most useful attitude to take to immediate problems, in that it releases us from the 'hysteria' of the first stanza, and so provides us with the intellectual and emotional balance that is necessary to preserve what we value. What is central to the whole argument is just the tension between a determinist view of man, and a view of man based on freedom of the will. Once we see that the 'hysteria' of the women is a function of the 'progressive' concern for man as victim, once we see that their hysteria is based upon the fact that for them men are nothing other than the creatures of their circumstance, we see what is dangerous in their position. What is paradoxical about their position is not just that it is self-contradictory (men are what their circumstances make them; therefore let us change their circumstances. Cast the net wide enough so that we are not exceptions and we will all just sit on our hands), nor that it provides no standard of value, but that it fails to follow through its own premise. For everyone and everything is destroyed: that is simply the most obvious fact about the phenomenal world. The point, once taken, allows us to begin thinking from the opposite side of the antinomy, where human values are given. Once the facts of destruction and death are accepted as phenomenal reality, and value is accepted as noumenal reality, we see that it is the duty of all men to be 'gay'; that is, to go on living for what is valuable in human existence despite the knowledge that 'all things fall'.

Of course, what makes the argument of the last two stanzas work is that Yeats's contemplation of the piece of lapis lazuli is itself the sort of act of mind that is exemplified on the stone. For he has achieved the kind of perspective that his Chinese sages have achieved, through his meditation upon the lapis lazuli. Furthermore, the insight is his; and not only something found in the stone. All the stone records is the aspiration of the Chinamen; their struggle towards the autonomy of soul that will provide perspective. But the achievement of that autonomy is Yeats's – 'I delight to *imagine* them seated there.' Once again we must notice the limited nature of the claim Yeats makes. He does not assume that men are free; he does not claim that we are able to decide our fate. What he maintains is that human activity only makes sense from within the conceptual framework of the soul's autonomy. The mountain, the sky, and the tragic scene are facts that remain facts. What has changed is the conceptual framework which provides the interpretation of the facts. Yeats wrote 'Lapis Lazuli' in 1939, the year of his death, and the year which began the Second World War. In imagining the Chinamen in their halfway house he has created for himself and his readers a point of balance which will allow both the painful acknowledgment of the many deaths to come (the poem is itself a 'mournful melody'), and a song celebrating human endeavour.

6

History as necessity

The poems discussed in Chapter 5 are best understood against the background of speculation about freedom and determinism. All of them have in common the belief that human action is best understood from within a conceptual structure that contains the notion of freedom of the will. In certain of these poems, for example 'The Municipal Gallery Revisited' and 'Lapis Lazuli', the relationship between Yeats's position *vis-à-vis* the problem of freedom and determinism and his notion of history becomes clear. For Yeats, history is the record of the realisation in the world of what is first intellect or thought.

> That civilisation may not sink,
> Its great battle lost,
> Quiet the dog, tether the pony
> To a distant post;
> Our master Caesar is in the tent
> Where the maps are spread,
> His eyes fixed upon nothing,
> A hand under his head.
> *Like a long-legged fly upon the stream*
> *His mind moves upon silence.*

One need only add that this notion of history is at odds with, say Marxism in that it regards intellect as free, as not part of a nexus of effects. Just as poems like 'Lapis Lazuli' are disturbing to many of Yeats's readers because man is thought of as free and not determined (i.e. not a victim to be pitied in his passive suffering), poems like 'Long-Legged Fly' seem silly to many readers because they cannot be assimilated to popular determinist notions of history – be they Marxist, positivist, metaphysical, or even the peculiar progressivism that is still popular although no one now will admit to holding it. It would be pointless to get involved in the whole question of historical explanations; but there are some marginal points that should be raised. It is generally accepted that historical explanations are causal explanations; that is, it is generally accepted by all but historians and philosophers of history. For those who know, the question is not just important, but open. I quote from W. H. Dray's book in the hope that the obvious respect and sympathy towards the idealist position exhibited there by one of the foremost contemporary philosophers of history will be counted as evidence that Yeats's position is neither peculiar nor simpleminded. Mr Dray's chapter on 'Causal Judgements in History' opens with the following remarks.

In the two preceding chapters we have discussed certain philosophical issues which arise out of the concepts of historical understanding and historical objectivity. It may be useful to conclude this brief introduction to philosophy of history on its critical side by going on to a problem which, in the view of some philosophers brings together in an even more troublesome and compelling way some of the issues already considered. This is the problem of the nature, meaning, status, and even legitimacy of the specifically causal judgments historians make in the conduct of their inquiries.

Few theoretical questions about their discipline seem to have bothered historians more than this one. There is, as Mandelbaum has observed, a widespread 'distrust' of causal judgment in history. On the part of some, this is due to what they regard as the extreme difficulty of making warrantable causal judgments. In the *Introduction* to his *Causes of the Civil War*, Kenneth Stamp declares: 'As one reflects upon the problem of causation, it becomes perfectly evident that historians will never know, objectively and with mathematical precision what caused the Civil War. Working with fragmentary evidence, possessing less than a perfect understanding of human behavior, and finding it impossible to isolate one historical factor to test its significance apart from all others, historians must necessarily be somewhat tentative and diffident in drawing their conclusions.' By others, however, the problem seems to be located less in the difficulty of the inquiry than in the concept of causation itself. Most historians, according to Crane Brinton, would reject the notion of 'cause' as an 'over-simplification'. Charles Beard objects that its application involves 'an arbitrary delimitation in time and space'. For G. J. Renier, causation is a 'postulate', which may easily encourage the 'superstitious belief' that historical events are predictable. And a group of American historians, a few years ago, agreed that 'cause' was 'an ambiguous term of varied and complex meaning' – 'a convenient figure of speech, describing motives, influences, forces, and other antecedent interrelations not fully understood'.[1]

[1] W. H. Dray, *Philosophy of History* (Englewood Cliffs, N.J.: Prentice-Hall, Inc., 1964), pp. 41–2.

One of the ways of dealing with the problem that Dray takes time to consider is Collingwood's:

He did not deny that historians properly make causal judgments. What he claimed was that they use the term 'cause' in a special sense. A specifically historical sense is needed, according to him, because what is caused in history are not natural events, but the actions of 'conscious and responsible' agents – or what is reducible to these. Causing a man to act, in this sense, 'means affording him a motive for doing it'. Depending on the motive involved, we may also speak in such cases of the agent being 'made', 'induced', 'persuaded', or 'compelled' to act. An example would be: 'Mr. Baldwin's speech caused the adjournment of the House.' 'In the same sense', Collingwood adds, 'we may say that a solicitor's letter causes a man to pay a debt or that bad weather causes him to return from an expedition.' It may seem a bit startling to find that it was an essential part of Collingwood's doctrine that what is caused in the present sense is always a free act. Since we are told, at the same time, that the causes in question can compel or make the agent act the way he does – indeed this turns out to be an essential feature – it is evident that the sense of freedom which Collingwood takes to be so closely bound up with the historian's sense of 'cause' cannot be freedom by contrast with coercion. It must be 'freedom of the will' in its traditional philosophical sense: a sense which denies that actions have 'sufficient conditions' in antecedent events.

There is obviously a connection between Collingwood's present doctrine and the account he gave of explanations in terms of the 'thought' of the historical agent. The explanation of actions is provided by reference to the agent's reason for acting. Collingwood now points out that such reasons can be causes in a special sense. Having been given by Baldwin's speech a reason for adjourning the House, the Speaker therefore adjourned it. If questioned later as to what caused him to do this, what he will try to make us see is the way the speech provided him with a very pressing reason for adjourning. The 'force' of causes in this sense might therefore be said to be a *rational* one. It is through the agent's recognition of the claim, in reason, which they make upon him to act, that they achieve what we call their effects. It follows that a 'cause' in the historical sense, might have failed to have an effect. For to be effective, the agent has to *accept* it as his cause, *make* it his cause. To put it another way: if an agent has cause to act, and acts accordingly, then what gave him cause to act may become a historical cause of his action. But we cannot, in advance, rule out the possibility that he will fail to act accordingly.

For Collingwood, then, a cause, if it is to be called a necessary condition of an action in history, is necessary not in the sense that without it the action *could not* have been performed: it is necessary only in the sense that without it there would not have been good reason to perform it. Similarly, if a cause is to be called a sufficient condition, it is to be called so, not in the sense that, given it, the action would necessarily be performed, but only in the sense that it renders the course of action in question 'rationally required'. To this it might be added that, since causes are conceived as 'forcing' people to act, only what offers sufficient reason doing what the agent otherwise does not want to do will count as causes in the rational, historical sense; for only these can properly be said to 'make', 'induce', or 'compel'. Because they are *causes*, they must inhibit the agent's freedom. But because they are causes of *actions*, they cannot, for Collingwood, be connected with their effects in the law-instantiating way; for this would cancel the 'free will' of the agent.[1]

Dray's analysis of Collingwood is used primarily as a foil to a positivist analysis of causation (e.g. Popper-Hempel). What is at stake is whether or not the notion of scientific explanation (Covering Laws plus Initial Conditions) developed in recent years is an adequate account of historical explanations. But the idealist theory itself is incompatible not only with a positivist account, but with any theory of history incompatible with 'freedom of the will' and incompatible with the traditional notions of human action that are compatible with freedom of the will. Yeats's historical poems, and his moral attitudes, are clearly based on a traditional notion of human action – yet he wrote *A Vision*. In the earlier chapters of this book I attempted to indicate how I thought *A Vision* should be taken. I suggested that *A Vision* was not a causal account of history, but a system of icons which presented in a systematic way the relationship between the way people thought and the sort of society they would produce, given that they thought what they did. *A Vision* includes both historical and psychological speculation of a peculiar kind in that the notions that are primary are not causal except in Collingwood's sense of cause. This point may be expanded with reference to all Yeats's 'psychological' speculations. In his poetry, in the theory of the mask, and in *A Vision* he uses concepts that are dependent upon the traditional notion of human action as opposed to notions that are deterministic (e.g. Marx, Freud, Skinner). Put too simply, he looks for reasons rather than causes. One example may help. We saw how 'The Municipal Gallery Revisited' and 'In Memory of Major Robert Gregory' were about the perception of freedom; how the poems documented Yeats's

---

[1] *Ibid.*, pp. 43–4.

renewal of belief in his own value through the contemplation of the lives of his friends. If we turn to the three subsidiary portraits in 'In Memory of Major Robert Gregory' (Stanzas III, IV, V, quoted on pp. 146–7) we can discover Yeats's theory of masks, and his theory of opposites, within the more general framework of traditional notions of human actions.

What Yeats is saying is that all these men deliberately set out to be more than they found themselves to be at a particular moment. That is, he explains their actions by reference to comprehensible, rational *motive* – the desire to be all that we can be – rather than by explaining it in terms of some sort of psychological mechanism (e.g. repression, Oedipal feelings, etc.). What he normally suggests about history is just that history will change as motives change.

V

Irish poets, learn your trade,
Sing whatever is well made,
Scorn the sort now growing up
All out of shape from toe to top,
Their unremembering hearts and heads
Base-born products of base beds.
Sing the peasantry, and then
Hard-riding country gentlemen,
The holiness of monks, and after
Porter-drinkers' randy laughter;
Sing the lords and ladies gay
That were beaten into the clay
Through seven heroic centuries;
Cast your mind on other days
That we in coming days may be
Still the indomitable Irishry.

from 'Under Ben Bulben'
(*Collected Poems*, p. 400)

The word 'normally' is important here. For Yeats knew the arguments for the other side as well as we do. Furthermore, he was willing to contemplate the unpleasant as well as the pleasant consequences of abandoning our normal concepts of human action; and the normal role that the concept of human action has in our thinking about history. Let me try to make plain what I mean by unpleasant consequences. Most of us, most of the time, use the language of freedom in some situations, and the language of determinism in others. This is not necessarily intellectual dishonesty: Strawson's argument is that it may be the case that our conceptual scheme, and our ontology, for good pragmatic reasons, should allow us both free will and causal explanations in a manner parallel to Quine's suggestions about the language of sense-data and the language of material objects. But unless we are willing to accept this at the very least questionable philosophical position, we are faced with a choice between one scheme or the other (that is not quite true, since there have been people who have argued a position called 'soft' determinism). But since most of us are prepared to accept determinist notions to some extent, we should have thought through what is entailed by our beliefs. Let me give an example, loaded I admit, that brings the point home on a personal level. Suppose we are willing to explain some one of our less savoury actions, to say to ourselves or our friends that we are conditioned to behave in certain ways and so should not be held responsible. Well, we all do it, don't we? But when we do something that we think praiseworthy we accept the praise. Our accepting the praise, feeling proud of what we did, etc., is only legitimate if what we did was done freely – for what one couldn't help doing should neither be blamed or praised. If we consistently apply the determinist argument we would have to give up much that is central to our notion of what it is to be a person, and, if we apply determinist notions beyond our own case, and to all men and women, we would be forced to give up other people's humanity, and the record of their humanity, i.e. history. 'Leda and the Swan' may be thought of as an attempt to think through the consequences of determinism.

LEDA AND THE SWAN

A sudden blow: the great wings beating still
Above the staggering girl, her thighs caressed
By the dark webs, her nape caught in his bill,
He holds her helpless breast upon his breast.

How can those terrified vague fingers push
The feathered glory from her loosening thighs?
And how can body, laid in that white rush,
But feel the strange heart beating where it lies?

A shudder in the loins engenders there
The broken wall, the burning roof and tower
And Agamemnon dead.

> Being so caught up,
> So mastered by the brute blood of the air,
> Did she put on his knowledge with his power
> Before the indifferent beak could let her drop?

>> (*Collected Poems*, p. 241)

A good way to begin thinking about this poem is to take notice of Ellmann's remarks about it.

> In Michelangelo what is expressed in the suave perfection of the union of human and divine. Under the pressure of Christian doctrine, there is no irony recognized in this union. Yeats has a different object, as he makes clear at once:

>> A sudden blow, the great wings beating still
>> Above the staggering girl ...

> For Yeats the significance of this mating is that it is not tender or easy; the bird, filled with divine power and knowledge, is still the brute blood of the air. The incongruities are glossed over by Michelangelo, in Yeats they are heightened. The sense of disproportion, of shock, of rape, is captured in those phrases which describe the blow, the flapping of huge wings, the strange dark webs, the catching of the helpless Leda. She is dazed and overcome, not cajoled, and the god, once the sexual crisis is past, lets her drop from his indifferent beak. I do not mean that Yeats is a naturalist as Michelangelo is an idealist; both of these positions are too easy. Rather what Yeats does is to let both views of the subject coalesce, to see them with double sight, and this is why his poem is modern as Michelangelo's painting is not. Mr. Melchiori shows intelligently how fond Yeats was of the personality of Michelangelo, but whether fond or not, Yeats belongs to a different persuasion from the Renaissance.[1]

Ellmann's remark gets us at once to the heart of the matter; the violence of the rape. However, it seems to me important to notice that Yeats takes considerable pains to dislodge from our memory any association between the swan and Zeus, any association with divinity, until the last two lines of the poem. Leda is being raped, not only by a god, but by history as a god. She is raped by history or god and as a result she is just a victim, not a person. The shudder in her loins 'engenders' the destruction of Troy. But all this happens to her; it catches her by surprise and is inflicted on her. It is the utter subjugation of the individual to history conceived as a

---

[1] Ellmann, *Identity of Yeats*, Preface, p. vi.

determined flow of events that is described in the octave. Leda does not make history, as do the artists of 'Lapis Lazuli'. Nor does she understand and co-operate with the makers of history as the boys and girls of 'The Statues'. Instead, history is made through her and on her, while she is confused and helpless. And history is conceived as merely bestial, as the brute blood of the air and nothing more. The swan is Zeus only in the context of the final question, and only so that the question can be asked. However, the question is ironic and ruthless; it is answered by what precedes it, by the terror and confusion described in the first stanza. The effect of the final question is to drive home the power and irrationality of history, of what is indifferent and beyond humanity, and to reinforce our sense of helplessness and confusion in the face of so much power.

The last question serves to underline Leda's absolute helplessness. She is 'mastered' and 'caught up'; that is, her life is simply part of a larger pattern that she cannot control. But if she could understand it her understanding would be a partial (and not very satisfactory) substitute for her freedom. That knowledge brings a sense of freedom is something we all know from experience. But the last question re-inforces the flapping, beating, jerky violence of the preceding lines. It forces us to remember than not the least important indignity is the sense of not understanding, not knowing, that often torments us in situations beyond our control. So the 'indifferent beak' becomes the final indignity, in that all this happened to her while she herself has been ignored. Raped, confused and ignored, Leda is 'let...drop'. She is not a person but a thing to be manipulated.

What Yeats finds terrifying is not the facts of mutability and change, but the possibility that the process of life may be utterly beyond human control, that history might be the result of something other than human consciousness. He can face the fact that all things fall if he can believe that what there is is in some sense human, in part a function of conscious human activity. The despair and anguish found in some of the poems about history and the historical process can be related to the degree to which history, the procession of events in the world, is seen as determined by something other than the nature of human consciousness.

The difference between the two views of history may be best illustrated if we look at the partial explanation Yeats gives of the Trojan War in 'Long-Legged Fly'.

That the topless towers be burnt
And men recall that face,
Move most gently if move you must
In this lonely place.
She thinks, part woman, three parts a child,
That nobody looks; her feet
Practise a tinker shuffle
Picked up on a street.
Like a long-legged fly upon the stream
Her mind moves upon silence.

We may notice that the passage depends upon the concept of human action that was central to the analysis of Collingwood quoted by Dray. Because Yeats is here able to see the destruction of Troy as the result of human action – Helen makes up her beauty, decides to be beautiful – we can regard the event with a bittersweet equanimity. History is tolerable because it is human.

One of the most impressive qualities of Yeats's poetry is his readiness to think things right through. In 'Leda and the Swan' he presents us with a vision of historical necessity that does not shrink from its conclusions. Yeats may have chosen to think differently most of the time, but in this poem he intends to examine the consequences of a position he knew to be arguable and serious. His ability to see what is involved in holding such a position is admirable; so, too, is the restraint which allows him to offer the poem without any disclaimer, without any palliative. The strength of the poem lies in that Yeats simply creates an image for historical determinism without offering an alternative theory. If we believe historical determinism is true, we must accept that our position is beneath the dark webs, that we are victims who will never be able to escape the next blow.

We saw earlier that from the standpoint of traditional concepts of human action anything that is not chosen can be derided as accident. 'The Second Coming' is like 'Leda and the Swan' in that it presents as horrible the consequences of determinism. But in the first stanza what is determined is seen as pure accident.

THE SECOND COMING

Turning and turning in the widening gyre
The falcon cannot hear the falconer;
Things fall apart; the centre cannot hold;
Mere anarchy is loosed upon the world,

> The blood-dimmed tide is loosed, and everywhere
> The ceremony of innocence is drowned;
> The best lack all conviction, while the worst
> Are full of passionate intensity.
>
> Surely some revelation is at hand;
> Surely the Second Coming is at hand.
> The Second Coming! Hardly are those words out
> When a vast image out of *Spiritus Mundi*
> Troubles my sight; somewhere in sands of the desert
> A shape with lion body and the head of a man,
> A gaze blank and pitiless as the sun,
> Is moving its slow thighs, while all about it
> Reel shadows of the indignant desert birds.
> The darkness drops again; but now I know
> That twenty centuries of stony sleep
> Were vexed to nightmare by a rocking cradle,
> And what rough beast, its hour come round at last,
> Slouches towards Bethlehem to be born?
>
> *(Collected Poems, pp. 210–11)*

To understand the poem we must be prepared to recognise that the poem is a fiction; that what is given as necessarily the course of history in the fiction is not grasped as determined by the *persona* of the poem who experiences the events given in the first stanza as 'mere' anarchy, and who is seen as hoping to discover a meaningful pattern in the events. But for the reader the pattern is already given in the first lines of the poem.

The difference in tone between the first and second stanzas represents a shift in the perspective of the *persona*. What is coming is, in the second stanza, not 'mere anarchy' but a determined destiny. But since 'The Second Coming' has received so much critical attention – some of it misguided – I will interrupt the argument for a line-by-line account of the poem. The first four lines present an image of the age from within the age. Because the perspective is limited the kinds of description offered are restricted. 'Things fall apart.' Are we entitled to ask what things – to ask this excitable man (the poem is a fiction – the speaker a character who must not be confused with Yeats) just what it is that disturbs him? But he cannot give us an answer – not yet. All he has to offer is 'mere anarchy'. For the proffered image is one of a giddy confusion rendered in a hallucinatory rhythm.

> Turning and turning in the widening gyre
> The falcon cannot hear the falconer.

There is no need to make heavy weather of 'gyre' – any dictionary will provide all we need to know. For the image is an image of anarchy, of the loss of control, and no more.[1] The first two lines state what is repeated in the next two images. Yeats is not after precision, nor exactitude. He is intent on creating a fiction which gives us a man in a state of bewilderment and anomie in which he can only claim to know that what is happening cannot be described as more than anarchy. The next four lines reiterate the horror of anarchy and formlessness in an even more forceful way. What is happening is formless, it is a tide. But it is a tide that sweeps through us, and which we respond to through our most basic and least controllable aspects. It is a 'blood-dimmed tide' in which consciousness and rationality are swept aside. In the normal course of events those who are rational have control, both in society and in their own lives, and those who are irrational are halt and confused, both in society (which for them is the mob) and in their own lives. But anarchy, the blood-dimmed tide, reverses this order.

> The blood-dimmed tide is loosed, and everywhere
> The ceremony of innocence is drowned;
> The best lack all conviction, while the worst
> Are full of passionate intensity.

What Yeats means by the ceremony of innocence can be observed in children at play. The sort of seriousness exhibited by a child is the 'ceremony of innocence', for in his innocence the child is able to invest whatever he does with a seriousness intrinsic to the activity, rather than something conferred from outside. The best are, for Yeats, those who can bring to their lives the seriousness of a child, and can bring with that seriousness and gravity a sense of importance that springs from their innocence, their lack of irony. It is exactly this quality that Yeats creates in himself in 'In Memory of Major Robert Gregory', and that he hopes his daughter will possess in 'A Prayer for my Daughter'. For Yeats perceives, rightly I think, that it is when men lose the sense of their greatness (that is, their innocence) and become sceptical about their stature and their motives, that civilisation is endangered.

[1] Once again, this is so from the perspective of the *persona*, and the reader's perspective is wider.

The first stanza, then, is simply a vision of anarchy. It is a vision of civilisation from within, when that civilisation cannot be seen to make sense. As such it is horrible: it is more than the speaker can bear.

> Surely some revelation is at hand;
> Surely the Second Coming is at hand.

Faced with anarchy, with the absence of meaning, the speaker clutches for a structure to give meaning. What he finds is probably still the most popular of all theories of history, Christianity. But because he has so fully absorbed the horror that he sees about him, he is not able to escape into the comfortable and familiar Christianity that he longs for. Instead, he has a vision of the future that is even worse than the present he longs to escape...

> Surely some revelation is at hand;
> Surely the Second Coming is at hand.
> The Second Coming! Hardly are those words out
> When a vast image out of *Spiritus Mundi*
> Troubles my sight: somewhere in sands of the desert
> A shape with lion body and the head of a man,
> A gaze blank and pitiless as the sun,
> Is moving its slow thighs, while all about it
> Reel shadows of the indignant desert birds.
> The darkness drops again; but now I know
> That twenty centuries of stony sleep
> Were vexed to nightmare by a rocking cradle,
> And what rough beast, its hour come round at last,
> Slouches towards Bethlehem to be born?

The progress of the beast is, we may notice, analogous to the activities of the Swan-Zeus in 'Leda and the Swan'. Its progress is inevitable, its gaze implacable – it is as inhuman and as natural as the behaviour of a planet. What is going to happen will happen as surely as the sun's rising and setting. And it is horrible; so horrible that the birds reel with indignation. It is even more offensive than anarchy. Then the 'darkness drops again'; the offensive thing is out of our sight. But not out of our minds, for it is a beast that comes from the *Spiritus Mundi*, from the world soul that is the collective mind of all of us. The gloss the speaker adds in the last four lines makes this clear.

now I know
That twenty centuries of stony sleep
Were vexed to nightmare by a rocking cradle,
And what rough beast, its hour come round at last,
Slouches towards Bethlehem to be born?

Yeats has created a simplified psychological determinism that can stand surrogate for any of the particular determinist psychologies one might care to mention. The role played by the *Spiritus Mundi* is the role that is played by the notion of id-ego-superego in Freud, or the collective unconscious of Jung, or the Elizabethan humours. That is, it simply stands for the principle of explanation. The particular explanation offered is simple, Let us, says the poem, suppose for a minute that the number of human desires or tendencies can be delimited – that there is a *Spiritus Mundi*. Furthermore, let us suppose that these tendencies are unchangeable and that the relationship that holds between them is not amenable to control. Then all we do when we act on one tendency is to repress the other. The beast has been sleeping in *Spiritus Mundi* – where it has been vexed by its opposite, by the symbol of love and affection that is the Christ-child, the rocking cradle. But since what we have is a determinist psychology, albeit a simple one, the repressed principle must eventually make itself felt. The beast is in us. It is not a force that can be located 'out there' as can the swan of 'Leda and the Swan'. Rather it is a part of our psyche that must find expression, which 'slouches' to Bethlehem to be born out of *Spiritus Mundi*, out of our consciousness, and into the world. Civilisation depends upon our being in control, it depends upon the fact that we can suit our actions to our reasons, and ignore or control our passions. What Yeats suggests in this poem is that the twenty centuries of Christianity, of the formal belief in Christian values, will simply be replaced by the rough beast because the nature of the psyche simply determines that ideals give way to their opposites, that human behaviour cannot in any significant way be controlled. There are at least two images in *Spiritus Mundi* – the beast and the cradle. They both demand an outlet, and since they are incompatible, in order that one be indulged the other must be suppressed. But enough psychic energy has been built up to change the direction of our actions – the beast's 'twenty centuries of stony sleep were vexed to nightmare by a rocking cradle'.

This particular poem has often been remarked as a prophecy of

Fascism. In a sense this is an adequate remark. But in seeing Fascism as a particular instantiation of what Yeats is talking of, we are in danger of missing the more general point. For Yeats is not saying just that there are people about who have too much conviction and not enough sense. He is talking about the beast that represents the opposite of our best selves, and he locates it in us. The poem jumps up and down with its perception that it is in us – in us – and not only in those general categories of people we can so easily make villains. And not only is it in us; it may be that it is in us in the sense that it is not something that we can control, but rather something that we shall be. Thus the irony that what was hoped for – the second coming of the Prince of Peace – has become its opposite. We are, collectively, an Anti-Christ. I said earlier that Yeats understood the issues that confront us when we think of the problem of freedom or determinism. The problem is not new, in that it exists as soon as we extend the notion of cause into human affairs. But with the growth of psychology it has taken on a new urgency. For psychology has suggested first that our actions are the product of psychological forces, and second that these psychological forces are not just amoral, but basically atavistic and bloodthirsty. We have grown accustomed to claims that, before Freud and Jung, would have terrified us. We can slip easily, for example, into the belief that we wish to kill our father and marry our mother, without ever recognising the horrors that we are if that is true. The virtue of 'The Second Coming' is that it presents to us, in a brilliant and brutal fashion, the nature of the claim.

If 'Leda and the Swan' and 'The Second Coming' are best thought of as poems which examine the consequences of determinism, it is, of course, true that most of the other poems that have been talked about deny the determinist position. This supposed contradiction will pose itself only if we think that poems are always expressions of the whole mind of the poet, or if we are busy using the poems as evidence in an attempt to characterise fixed positions in the poet's thought. I have not been trying to characterise Yeats's thought – though I do assume that isolating issues he habitually thought about will help in examining individual poems. Poems are individual acts of mind. Yeats normally writes from a position that starts from the notion of freedom of the will. But on occasion he was enough impressed, or horrified, by the consequences of determinism to write poems that embodied his fears. In saying

'what if. . . ?' he has done what poets necessarily do. For poems are
not arguments, although they share some characteristics of arguments. They provide an image that makes concrete a particular
conception about some part of our common experience. Yeats once
wrote that art is but a vision of reality. It is our job as readers to test
the vision against reality. That Yeats offers two ways of thinking,
two visions, of one of mankind's perennial problems, does not con-
vict him of inconsistency or of self-contradiction. He thought
differently at different times; he could sometimes regard himself
and his friends and humanity as free, and sometimes found himself
visited by our contemporary nightmare. So the fact that Yeats had
as he said once to Dorothy Wellesley, 'no answers', at least with
reference to these questions, does not matter, since he puts the
important questions with clarity, honesty, and vigour.

No poem examines these questions with quite the same in-
clusiveness as 'Nineteen Hundred and Nineteen'.

I

Many ingenious lovely things are gone
That seemed sheer miracle to the multitude,
Protected from the circle of the moon
That pitches common things about. There stood
Amid the ornamental bronze and stone
An ancient image made of olive wood –
And gone are Phidias' famous ivories
And all the golden grasshoppers and bees.

We too had many pretty toys when young:
A law indifferent to blame or praise,
To bribe or threat; habits that made old wrong
Melt down, as it were wax in the sun's rays;
Public opinion ripening for so long
We thought it would outlive all future days.
O what fine thought we had because we thought
That the worst rogues and rascals had died out.

All teeth were drawn, all ancient tricks unlearned,
And a great army but a showy thing;
What matter that no cannon had been turned
Into a ploughshare? Parliament and king
Thought that unless a little powder burned

The trumpeters might burst with trumpeting
And yet it lack all glory; and perchance
The guardsmen's drowsy chargers would not prance.

Now days are dragon-ridden, the nightmare
Rides upon sleep: a drunken soldiery
Can leave the mother, murdered at her door,
To crawl in her own blood, and go scot-free;
The night can sweat with terror as before
We pieced our thoughts into philosophy,
And planned to bring the world under a rule,
Who are but weasels fighting in a hole.

He who can read the signs nor sink unmanned
Into the half-deceit of some intoxicant
From shallow wits; who knows no work can stand,
Whether health, wealth or peace of mind were spent
On master-work of intellect or hand,
No honour leave its mighty monument,
Has but one comfort left: all triumph would
But break upon his ghostly solitude.

But is there any comfort to be found?
Man is in love and loves what vanishes,
What more is there to say? That country round
None dared admit, if such a thought were his,
Incendiary or bigot could be found
To burn that stump on the Acropolis,
Or break in bits the famous ivories
Or traffic in the grasshoppers or bees.

II

When Loie Fuller's Chinese dancers enwound
A shining web, a floating ribbon of cloth,
It seemed that a dragon of air
Had fallen among dancers, had whirled them round
Or hurried them off on its own furious path;
So the Platonic Year
Whirls out new right and wrong,
Whirls in the old instead;
All men are dancers and their tread
Goes to the barbarous clangour of a gong.

III

Some moralist or mythological poet
Compares the solitary soul to a swan;
I am satisfied with that,
Satisfied if a troubled mirror show it,
Before that brief gleam of its life be gone,
An image of its state;
The wings half spread for flight,
The breast thrust out in pride
Whether to play, or to ride
Those winds that clamour of approaching night.

A man in his own secret meditation
Is lost amid the labyrinth that he has made
In art or politics;
Some Platonist affirms that in the station
Where we should cast off body and trade
The ancient habit sticks,
And that if our works could
But vanish with our breath
That were a lucky death,
For triumph can but mar our solitude.

The swan has leaped into the desolate heaven:
That image can bring wildness, bring a rage
To end all things, to end
What my laborious life imagined, even
The half-imagined, the half-written page;
O but we dreamed to mend
Whatever mischief seemed
To afflict mankind, but now
That winds of winter blow
Learn that we were crack-pated when we dreamed.

IV

We, who seven years ago
Talked of honour and of truth,
Shriek with pleasure if we show
The weasel's twist, the weasel's tooth.

V

Come let us mock at the great
That had such burdens on the mind

And toiled so hard and late
To leave some monument behind,
Nor thought of the levelling wind.

Come let us mock at the wise;
With all those calendars whereon
They fixed old aching eyes,
They never saw how seasons run,
And now but gape at the sun.

Come let us mock at the good
That fancied goodness might be gay,
And sick of solitude
Might proclaim a holiday:
Wind shrieked – and where are they?

Mock mockers after that
That would not lift a hand maybe
To help good, wise or great
To bar that foul storm out, for we
Traffic in mockery.

VI

Violence upon the roads: violence of horses;
Some few have handsome riders, are garlanded
On delicate sensitive ear or tossing mane,
But wearied running round and round in their courses
All break and vanish, and evil gathers head:
Herodias' daughters have returned again,
A sudden blast of dusty wind and after
Thunder of feet, tumult of images,
Their purpose in the labyrinth of the wind;
And should some crazy hand dare touch a daughter
All turn with amorous cries, or angry cries,
According to the wind, for all are blind.
But now wind drops, dust settles; thereupon
There lurches past, his great eyes without thought
Under the shadow of stupid straw-pale locks,
That insolent fiend Robert Artisson
To whom the love-lorn Lady Kyteler brought
Bronzed peacock feathers, red combs of her cocks.

(*Collected Poems*, pp. 232–7)

It would be laborious and unrewarding to trace the now familiar issues through the poem. Sections one and two provide an analysis of the contemporary situation that is consistent with 'Leda and the Swan' and 'The Second Coming'. Both these poems present our inability to control our lives as a suddenly realised and horrible presentiment. In 'Nineteen Hundred and Nineteen' the realisation that we are 'weasels' is a surprise. Full of our own purposes we did not notice what we had become, and that becoming surprised us because we did not choose it – 'All men are dancers and their tread/ goes to the barbarous clangour of a gong'. The images of the gong, of the weasel, and of Robert Artisson, are similar in that they present us with man as simply the victim of a process of events, and consciousness as only a sort of epi-phenomenon. The horror of the concluding vision in the poem lies in the abasement of human intellect and will. The vision of evil is not specific, and is deliberately vague in that it can only be an intimation of what is to come, of a still unspecified evil. But the vision is primarily of men dominated and controlled by something that is beyond them. They are 'blind', their purpose 'in the labyrinth of the wind' (Section VI) and their condition is as victims only. They cannot choose, and are simply the victims of a mindless futility.

Sections V and VI of the poem function as proof for the conclusion of Section III, which is simply the claim that what Yeats says in 'The Statues' or 'Long-Legged Fly' or 'Under Ben Bulben' is not true. For in all these poems, what Yeats has affirmed is that man's consciousness, his desires, his conception of himself determine history. Shorn of the ability to control events, simply a pawn of a historical otherness, Yeats can find value only in the integrity of the individual consciousness. If man cannot control the process of his life, at least he may remain inviolable. If his works are simply a part of history, of that terrible otherness, then even his work, even his body, destroys his freedom.

III

Some moralist or mythological poet
Compares the solitary soul to a swan;
I am satisfied with that,
Satisfied if a troubled mirror show it,
Before that brief gleam of its life be gone,
An image of its state;

The wings half spread for flight,
The breast thrust out in pride
Whether to play, or to ride
Those winds that clamour of approaching night.

A man in his own secret meditation
Is lost amid the labyrinth that he has made
In art or politics;
Some Platonist affirms that in the station
Where we should cast off body and trade
The ancient habit sticks,
And that if our works could
But vanish with our breath
That were a lucky death,
For triumph can but mar our solitude.

The swan has leaped into the desolate heaven:
That image can bring wildness, bring a rage
To end all things, to end
What my laborious life imagined, even
The half-imagined, the half-written page;
O but we dreamed to mend
Whatever mischief seemed
To afflict mankind, but now
That winds of winter blow
Learn that we were crack-pated when we dreamed.

Instead of the creator man the poem can give us only the quixotic defiance of the man who leaps above historic necessity, above the nexus of history, of the world; and who in doing so loses all bonds with the world, all taint of the determined and inhuman world of events, bodies, works of intellect or hand. 'That', the flight of the man, were a lucky death because in taking nothing of the world with him, the swan escapes the web of necessity and finds some sort of freedom. The condition of freedom, however, is solitary. For everything in the world, being other than consciousness, re-introduces the same terrible limitation that consciousness seeks to avoid. To succeed in escaping the role of pawn it is necessary to leave the world behind; for to 'triumph' in preserving something would simply 'mar' the soul's freedom from necessity, its 'solitude'. Consciousness, the ability to choose, is for Yeats the supreme human value, and in a poem which sees the only possibility for maintaining that freedom in an escape from the world, in solitude, the poet suggests even the sacrifice of his poetry is not too great a price to pay for freedom; that the apocalypse itself is not too great a price.

7

'Among School Children'

In March of 1926 Yeats began to read Whitehead's *Science and the Modern World*. In the months of March, April, May and June he wrote a number of letters which communicate considerable excitement about Whitehead's book.

Read Whitehead's *Science and the Modern World*. I have now read the greater part of it and so far it seems to me my own point of view. He proves, as I think, that the mechanical theory of the world is untrue (though it works, like other untrue things) and substitutes a theory of organism. It is concentrated logic throughout and has the same intensity of thought – which is Beauty – that I find in Gentile. He is of course realist, but the difference between his point of view and that of Gentile does not seem to me of much moment until one gets to ultimates, and one does not do that in this book. Perhaps it is not great even then. It would not arise at all unless Whitehead were to insist that his world of 'eternal' objects, by which he means colours, sounds and so on, could remain were there no 'mind' present, and I judge from his whole doctrine of organism that he certainly does not mean this as he understands mind. Organism without mind – 'choice' – in some sense would be mechanism.[1]

In another letter he writes:

I have found a very difficult but profound person Whitehead, who seems to have reached my own conclusions about ultimate things. He has written down the game of chess and I, like some Italian prince, have made the pages and the court ladies have it out on the lawn. Not that he would recognise his abstract triumph in my gay rabble.[2]

The delight which Yeats expresses springs from the quality and scope of Whitehead's work. For in *Science and the Modern World* Whitehead tackles a problem that encompasses philosophy and history, especially the history of ideas, as well as the relationship between science, poetry and education. Whatever the final value of Whitehead's philosophical ideas, the book remains a monumental

[1] *Yeats–Moore Correspondence*, p. 89.
[2] *The Letters of W. B. Yeats*, ed. Allan Wade (London: Rupert Hart-Davis, 1954), p. 712.

effort of intellectual synthesis expressed in prose that often reaches
the level of art. What Yeats meant when he described the 'intensity of thought which is beauty' that he found in Whitehead
may be illustrated by this passage on the eighteenth century.

Sometimes it happens that the service rendered by philosophy is entirely
obscured by the astonishing success of a scheme of abstractions in expressing the dominant interests of an epoch. This is exactly what happened
during the eighteenth century. Les Philosophes were not philosophers.
They were men of genius, clear-headed and acute, who applied the seventeenth century group of scientific abstractions to the analysis of the un-
bounded universe. Their triumph, in respect to the circle of ideas mainly
interesting to their contemporaries, was overwhelming. Whatever did not
fit into their scheme was ignored, derided, disbelieved. Their hatred of
Gothic architecture symbolises their lack of sympathy with dim perspectives. It was the age of reason, healthy, manly, upstanding reason; but, of
one-eyed reason, deficient in its vision of depth. We cannot overrate the
debt of gratitude which we owe to these men. For a thousand years Europe
had been a prey to intolerant, intolerable visionaries. The common sense
of the eighteenth century, its grasp of the obvious facts of human suffering,
and of the obvious demands of human nature, acted on the world like a
bath of moral cleansing. Voltaire must have the credit, that he hated injustice, he hated cruelty, he hated senseless repression, and he hated hocus-
pocus. Furthermore, when he saw them, he knew them. In these supreme
virtues, he was typical of his century, on its better side. But if men cannot
live on bread alone, still less can they do so on disinfectants. The age had
its limitations; yet we cannot understand the passion with which some of
its main positions are still defended, especially in the schools of science,
unless we do full justice to its positive achievements. The seventeenth
century scheme of concepts was proving a perfect instrument for research.[1]

The subject-matter of Whitehead's book was of special interest
to Yeats; it was first of all a critique of the metaphysical and epistemological premises of seventeenth-century science, and Yeats
was delighted to write to T. Sturge Moore that

Whitehead describes the mechanical theory thus: 'The sense data or
sensations are projected by the mind so as to clothe appropriate bodies in
external nature...The poets are entirely mistaken...Nature is a dull
affair, soundless, scentless, colourless; merely the hurrying of material,
endlessly, meaninglessly (*Science and the Modern World*, p. 77).[2]

---

[1] Alfred North Whitehead, *Science and the Modern World* (New York: New American Library of World Literature, 1948), pp. 58–9.
[2] *Yeats–Moore Correspondence*, p. 87.

But the criticism of the empiricist epistemology which was the philosophical basis of scientific thought was offered in the context of a wide ranging examination of intellectual history. In Whitehead Yeats had found an ally against the empirical tradition of Locke, Hume and Russell who was able to talk with confidence and appreciation not only of philosophers, mathematicians and physicists, but of poets and artists as well. Furthermore, Whitehead's criticism of empiricism led him to a positive position that would lead to a 'system of thought basing nature upon the concept of organism, and not upon the concept of matter'. Ultimately, Whitehead's book is an exercise in speculative metaphysics combined with a systematic and sensitive approach to intellectual history. As such, it could not but appeal to Yeats, whose intellectual interests were exactly these, and who had previously found little reputable work in English in this area. It was exactly the absence of any first rate philosophical or meta-historical writing on the topics important to him which produced his interest in contemporary Italian idealism, in spiritualism, and in Spengler. If his philosophical position often seems unsophisticated, or if he seems often to be deliberately outrageous, he must be in part forgiven. For he was very much in the position of a prophet crying in the wilderness, and burdened by a sense of intellectual isolation. The relationship between Yeats's feeling of intellectual isolation, his tendency to make wild pronouncements, and his special delight in Whitehead can be traced through a letter of 23 June 1926. Without becoming involved in the point under discussion we can notice first Yeats's *cri de coeur* that 'proved' means 'accepted by the majority of teachers in English universities', his sudden announcement that we should weigh the old theory that the earth is flat and unmoving, and his relief at being back in the more congenial world of Whitehead and Gentile.

I certainly have not read your brother carefully. My special experience has shown me that the barrier which he assumes between images of sense and of the mind does not exist. I think therefore that he is not an author who has for me a special value. It is nothing to me that my special experience is not yet shared by the majority of teachers in universities (which is what is meant by 'proved'). What matters to me is that it is my experience. Your brother in that essay seems to give a validity to 'common sense' which it may not deserve, though of course we must discover why 'common sense' thinks these things, and in any case I am convinced that common sense, granted a special experience, puts the two cats, to 'a certain extent' as your brother would say, on an equality. Certainly neither common sense nor any other sense, granted the experience, justifies the belief that one cat and not the other has an external root. Your brother has not given the slightest reason for believing in this root in one case and not the other.

When the housemaid says her prayers after seeing a 'phantom' cat her common sense affirms its real existence just as much as mine, if I had said 'one picture was on the wall', would have affirmed the real existence of that picture, and neither affirmation may have objective philosophical value.

It may be of great importance to weigh the old conviction of the flatness and stillness of the earth, and Blake thought that still and flat earth true, the other a falsification of reason. Does not your brother contradict common sense, just as the astronomers did, when he suggests that both his 'images' have the like reality, which implies that matter is spatially fixed?

Your argument seems to be that I must not make this point because of your brother's first two propositions. I wish you would put them plainly for me. Gentile and Whitehead are difficult but if I read slowly I understand, but I admit that I do not feel that I understand your brother. When you explained that he considered Ruskin's cat unreal because only Ruskin saw it I understood, and was able to refute his position from my own memory.[1]

However, Yeats's interest in Whitehead was more specific than this general feeling of ease, of a common intellectual space. For although Yeats was aware, as he says in his letters to Sturge Moore, that he and Whitehead are not in complete agreement, he was able to find much to reinforce previous conclusions, and a new perspective for some old problems. I will try to indicate, in a brief and general way, Whitehead's position in *Science and the Modern World*, as far as possible in Whitehead's own words on the central points.

For Whitehead the most important single event in the history of Western culture is Pythagoras's discovery of the abstracting power of mathematics. In an interesting passage on ancient philosophy Whitehead talks of the three philosophers who find their way into stanza six of 'Among School Children'.

Pythagoras was the first man who had any grasp of the full sweep of this general principle. He lived in the sixth century before Christ. Our knowledge of him is fragmentary. But we know some points which established his greatness in the history of thought. He insisted on the importance of the utmost generality in reasoning, and he divined the importance of

---

[1] *Ibid.*, pp. 99–100.

number as an aid to the construction of any representation of the conditions involved in the order of nature. We also know that he studied geometry, and discovered the general proof of the remarkable theorem about
the right-angled triangle. The formation of the Pythagorean Brotherhood,
and the mysterious rumours as to its rites and its influence, afford some
evidence that Pythagoras divined, however dimly, the possible importance
of mathematics in the formation of science. On the side of philosophy he
started a discussion which has agitated thinkers ever since. He asked,
'What is the status of mathematical entities, such as numbers for example,
in the realm of things?' The number 'two', for example, is in some sense
exempt from the flux of time and the necessity of position in space. Yet
it is involved in the real world. The same considerations apply to geometrical notions – to circular shape, for example. Pythagoras is said to have
thought that the mathematical entities, such as numbers and shapes, were
the ultimate stuff out of which the real entities of our perceptual experience
are constructed. As thus baldly stated, the idea seems crude, and indeed
silly. But undoubtedly, he had hit upon a philosophical notion which has a
long history, and which had moved the minds of men, and has even entered
into Christian theology. About a thousand years separate the Athanasian
Creed from Pythagoras and about two thousand four hundred years
separate Pythagoras from Hegel. Yet for all these distances in time, the
importance of definite number in the constitution of the Divine Nature,
and the concept of the real world as exhibiting the evolution of an idea, can
both be traced back to the train of thought set going by Pathagoras.

The importance of an individual thinker owes something to chance. For
it depends upon the fate of his ideas in the minds of his successors. In this
respect Pythagoras was fortunate. His philosophical speculations reach us
through the mind of Plato. The Platonic world of ideas is the refined,
revised form of the Pythagorean doctrine that number lies at the base of
the real world. Owing to the Greek mode of representing numbers by
patterns of dots, the notions of number and of geometrical configuration
are less separated than with us. Also Pythagoras, without doubt, included
the shape-iness of shape, which is an impure mathematical entity. So today,
when Einstein and his followers proclaim that physical facts, such as
gravitation, are to be construed as exhibitions of local peculiarities of spatio-
temporal properties, they are following the pure Pythagorean tradition.
In a sense, Plato and Pythagoras stand nearer to modern physical science
than does Aristotle. The two former were mathematicians, whereas Aristotle was the son of a doctor, though of course he was not thereby ignorant
of mathematics. The practical counsel to be derived from Pythagoras, is to
measure, and thus to express quality in terms of numerically determined
quantity. But the biological sciences, then and till our own time, have been
overwhelmingly classificatory. Accordingly, Aristotle by his Logic throws
the emphasis on classification. The popularity of Aristotelian Logic re-

tarded the advance of physical science throughout the Middle Ages. If only the schoolmen had measured instead of classifying, how much they might have learnt.

Classification is a halfway house between the immediate concreteness of the individual thing and the complete abstraction of mathematical notions. The species take account of the specific character, and the genera of the generic character. But in the procedure of relating mathematical notions to the facts of nature, by counting, by measurement, and by geometrical relations, and by types of order, the rational contemplation is lifted from the incomplete abstractions involved in definite species and genera, to the complete abstractions of mathematics. Classification is necessary. But unless you can progress from classification to mathematics, your reasoning will not take you very far.[1]

Pythagoras is great just because it was he who discovered the intellectual tool which makes it possible to think about things in general, who made abstract thought possible. But, as Whitehead points out continually, abstract thought is about the world; it is not the world itself. This is a lesson that Yeats learned well, and which is reflected, not just in the poems already discussed, but in his prose; the idea occurs in the prose passage in *A Vision* on the figures that hold out to him the skeleton of a bird, as well as in 'Byzantium'. In Whitehead Yeats discovered both a love which he shared for abstract ideas, and a rigorous discussion of the sort of problems entailed by the use of abstractions. Central both to Whitehead's criticism of the metaphysics of science and to his own metaphysical scheme are a set of beliefs about the legitimate bounds of thought, and the status of the abstract entities used in thinking. The common error of taking an abstract entity too seriously, of refraining from strictly limiting the concepts we use to the areas in which they are operant, Whitehead calls the 'Fallacy of Misplaced Concreteness'. And in discussing what is misleading or wrong in the metaphysics of science Whitehead adduces a particular example of this fallacy which he calls the 'Fallacy of Simple Location'.

if we desired to obtain a more fundamental expression of the concrete character of natural fact, the element in this scheme which we should first criticise is the concept of *simple location*. In view therefore of the importance which this idea will assume in these lectures, I will repeat the meaning which I have attached to this phrase. To say that a bit of matter has *simple location* means that, in expressing its spatio-temporal relations, it is adequate

---

[1] Whitehead, *Science and the Modern World*, pp. 32–4.

to state that it is where it is, in a definite finite region of space, and throughout a definite finite duration of time, apart from any essential reference of the relations of that bit of matter to other regions of space and to other durations of time.

Again, this concept of simple location is independent of the controversy between the absolutists and the relativist views of space or of time. So long as any theory of space, or of time, can give a meaning, either absolute or relative, to the idea of a definite region of space, and of a definite duration of time, the idea of simple location had a perfectly definite meaning. This idea is the very foundation of the seventeenth century scheme of nature. Apart from it, the scheme is incapable of expression. I shall argue that among the primary elements of nature as apprehended in our immediate experience, there is no element whatever which possesses this character of simple location. It does not follow, however, that the science of the seventeenth century was simply wrong. I hold that by a process of constructive abstraction we can arrive at abstractions which are the simply-located bits of material, and at other abstractions which are the minds included in the scientific scheme. Accordingly, the real error is an example of what I have termed: The Fallacy of Misplaced Concreteness.

The advantage of confining attention to a definite group of abstractions, is that you confine your thoughts to clear-cut definite things, with clear-cut definite relations. Accordingly if you have a logical head, you can deduce a variety of conclusions respecting the relationships between these abstract entities. Furthermore, if the abstractions are well-founded, that is to say, if they do not abstract from everything that is important in experience, the scientific thought which confines itself to these abstractions will arrive at a variety of important truths relating to our experience of nature. We all know those clear-cut trenchant intellects, immovably encased in a hard shell of abstractions. They hold you to their abstractions by the sheer grip of personality.

The disadvantage of exclusive attention to a group of abstractions, however well-founded, is that, by the nature of the case, you have abstracted from the remainder of things. In so far as the excluded things are important in your experience, your modes of thought are not fitted to deal with them. You cannot think without abstractions; accordingly, it is of the utmost importance to be vigilant in critically revising your modes of abstractions. It is here that philosophy finds its niche as essential to the healthy progress of society. It is the critic of abstractions. A civilization which cannot burst through its current abstractions is doomed to sterility after a very limited period of progress. An active school of philosophy is quite as important for the locomotion of ideas, as is an active school of railway engineers for the locomotion of fuel.[1]

---

[1] Whitehead, *Science and the Modern World*, pp. 57–8.

Whitehead argues that if we think of bits of matter located in space-time without reference to other bits of matter in other bits of space-time, then Hume's problems with induction and causality necessarily follow. But we do not have to follow Whitehead in the specificity of his argument, to note that according to *Science and the Modern World* the empiricist position is merely a specific example of the fallacy of misplaced concreteness. When Whitehead expounds his own metaphysical doctrines he finds it necessary to talk about 'eternal objects'. These 'eternal objects' are what are normally referred to as universals and in his chapter on 'abstraction' Whitehead is careful to demonstrate what sorts of ontological claims can be safely made about 'eternal objects'.

Whitehead's positive theory conceives of nature as an organic system of interpenetrating events or occasions. In order to make sense of the world we need a notion of entities being bound together and interacting. Any events abstracted from the continuum of entities in space–time are connected to the whole continuum, and the continuum is reality – but a reality of process. So we can say that each entity 'takes account of' the rest of reality, or prehends it. Cognition and perception are, for Whitehead, particular examples of the business of taking account, when the taking account occurs between two entities, one of which is a mind. In his book Whitehead claims that this conception of 'taking account' was possible before the general acceptance of the metaphysics of science'.

My discussion of the epoch will be best introduced by a quotation from Francis Bacon, which forms the opening of Section (or 'Century') IX of his *Natural History*, I mean his *Silva Silvarum*. We are told in the contemporary memoir by his chaplain, Dr. Rawley, that this work was composed in the last five years of his life, so it must be dated between 1620 and 1626. The quotation runs thus:

'It is certain that all bodies whatsoever, though they have no sense, yet they have perception; for when one body is applied to another, there is a kind of election to embrace that which is agreeable, and to exclude or expel that which is ingrate; and whether the body be alternant, evermore a perception precedeth operation; for else all bodies would be like one to another. And sometimes this perception, in some kind of bodies, is far more subtile than sense; so that sense is but a dull thing in comparison of it: we see a weather glass will find the least difference of the weather in heat or cold, when we find it not. And this perception is sometimes at a distance, as well as upon the touch; as when the loadstone draweth iron;

or flame naptha of Babylon, a great distance off. It is therefore a subject of a very noble enquiry, to enquire of the more subtile perceptions; for it is another key to open nature, as well as the sense; and sometimes better. And besides, it is a principal means of natural divination; for that which in these perceptions appeareth early, in the great effects cometh long after.'

There are a great many points of interest about this quotation, some of which will emerge into importance in succeeding lectures. In the first place, note the careful way in which Bacon discriminates between perception, or taking account of, on the one hand, and sense, or cognitive experience, on the other hand. In this respect Bacon is outside the physical line of thought which finally dominated the century. Later on, people thought of passive matter which was operated on externally by forces. I believe Bacon's line of thought to have expressed a more fundamental truth than do the materialistic concepts which were then being shaped as adequate for physics.[1]

For Whitehead cognition is merely a special kind of prehension, and Whitehead claims both to have made clear what is valuable in Berkeley, and to have produced a philosophy of organism which 'inverts' Kant, which discovers the subjective only after a process which proceeds from the objective world.

Thus we know ourselves as a function of unification of a plurality of things which are other than ourselves. Cognition discloses an event as being as activity, organising a real togetherness of alien things. But this psychological field does not depend on its cognition; so that this field is still a unit event as abstracted from its self-cognition. Accordingly, consciousness will be the function of knowing. But what is known is already a prehension of aspects of the one real universe. These aspects are aspects of other events as mutually modifying, each the others. In the pattern of aspects they stand in their pattern of mutual relatedness.

The aboriginal data in terms of which the pattern weaves itself are the aspects of shapes, of sense-objects, and of other eternal objects whose self-identity is not dependent on the flux of things. Wherever such objects have ingression into the general flux, they interpret events, each to the other. They are here in the perceiver; but, as perceived by him, they convey for him something of the total flux which is beyond himself. The subject-object relation takes its origin in the double role of these eternal objects. They are modifications of the subject, but only in their character of conveying aspects of other subjects in the community of the universe. Thus no individual subject can have independent reality, since it is a prehension of limited aspects of subjects other than itself.

The technical phrase 'subject-object' is a bad term for the fundamental

---

[1] Whitehead, *Science and the Modern World*, pp. 43–4.

situation disclosed in experience. It is really reminiscent of the Aristotelian 'subject-predicate'. It already presupposes the metaphysical doctrine of diverse subjects qualified by their private predicates. This is the doctrine of subjects with private worlds of experience. If this be granted, there is no escape from solipsism. The point is that the phrase 'subject-object' indicates a fundamental entity underlying the objects. Thus the 'objects' as thus conceived, are merely the ghosts of Aristotelian predicates. The primary situation disclosed in cognitive experience is 'ego-objects amid objects'. By this I mean that the primary fact is an impartial world transcending the 'here-now' which marks the ego-object, and transcending the 'now' which is the spatial world of simultaneous realization. It is a world also including the actuality of the past, and the limited potentiality of the future, together with the complete world of abstract potentiality, the realm of eternal objects which transcends, and finds exemplification in and comparison with, the actual course of realization. The ego-object, as consciousness here-now, is conscious of its experient essence as constituted by its internal relatedness to the world of realities, and to the world of ideas. But the ego-object, in being thus constituted, is within the world of realities, and exhibits itself as an organism requiring the ingression of ideas for the purpose of this status among realities. The question of consciousness must be reserved for treatment on other occasion.

The point to be made for the purpose of the present discussion is that a philosophy of nature as organic must start at the opposite end to that requisite for a materialistic philosophy. The materialistic starting point is from independently existing substances, matter and mind. The matter suffers modifications of its external relations of locomotion, and the mind suffers modifications of its contemplated objects. There are, in this materialistic theory, two sorts of independent substances, each qualified by their appropriate passions. The organic starting point is from the analysis of process as the realization of events disposed in an interlocked community. The event is the unit of things real. The emergent enduring pattern is the stabilization of the emergent achievement so as to become a fact which retains its identity throughout the process. *It will be noted that endurance is not primarily the property of enduring beyond itself, but of enduring within itself. I mean that endurance is the property of finding its pattern reproduced in the temporal parts of the total event* [my italics]. It is in this sense that a total event carries an enduring pattern. There is an intrinsic value identical for the whole and for its succession of parts. Cognition is the emergence, into some measure of individualised reality, of the general substratum of activity, poising before itself possibility, actuality, and purpose.[1]

We shall see that this concept of 'endurance' is central to 'Among School Children', for it is in enduring, that is reproducing a pattern

[1] *Ibid.*, pp. 136–7.

within themselves, that the chestnut tree and the dance become apt symbols for a proper attitude to the process of human life. In his last chapter Whitehead discusses how 'eternal ideas and values' form a part of the cognitive process of recognising the endurance of a pattern. The ideas in this passage are also important to an understanding of 'Among School Children'.

A complete occasion includes that which in cognitive experience takes the form of memory, anticipation, imagination, and thought. These elements in an experient occasion are also modes of inclusion of complex eternal objects in the synthetic prehension, as elements in the emergent value. They differ from the concreteness of full inclusion. In a sense this difference is inexplicable; for each mode of inclusion is of its own kind, not to be explained in terms of anything else. But there is a common difference which discriminates these modes of inclusion from the full concrete ingression which has been discussed. This *differentia* is *abruptness*. By 'abruptness' I mean that what is remembered, or anticipated, or imagined, or thought, is exhausted by a finite complex concept. In each case there is one finite eternal object prehended within the occasion as the vertex of a finite hierarchy. This breaking off from an actual illimitability is what in any occasion marks off that which is termed mental from that which belongs to the physical event to which the mental functioning is referred.

In general there seems to be some loss of vividness in the apprehension of the eternal objects concerned; for example, Hume speaks of 'faint copies'. But this faintness seems to be a very unsafe ground for differentiation. Often things realized in thought are more vivid than the same things in inattentive physical experience. But the things apprehended as mental are always subject to the condition that we come to a stop when we attempt to explore ever higher grades of complexity in their realized relationships. We always find that we have thought of just this – whatever it may be – and of no more. There is a limitation which breaks off the finite concept from the high grades of illimitable complexity.

Thus an actual occasion is a prehension of one infinite hierarchy (its associated hierarchy) together with various finite hierarchies. The synthesis into the occasion of the infinite hierarchy is according to its specific mode of realization, and that of the finite hierarchies is according to various other specific modes of realization. There is one metaphysical principle which is essential for the rational coherence of this account of the general character of an experient occasion. I call this principle, 'The Translucency of Realization.' By this I mean that any eternal object is just itself in whatever mode of realization it is involved.[1]

---

[1] *Ibid.*, pp. 154–5.

I shall contend that 'Among School Children' should be read in the light of Whitehead's position. But before I turn to the poem there is one other issue which should be considered. It is clear that Whitehead's position, although it makes much of abstract thought and the universals which are the subjects of abstract thought, is profoundly anti-Platonic. For in Whitehead's scheme what is real is the prehended experience, and abstraction serves only as a means of thinking about the prehended experience.

It is generally recognised that the parable of the second stanza of 'Among School Children' is a reference to Aristophanes's speech in Plato's *Symposium*; what is not recognised is that the poem alludes in a systematic way to the conversation of Socrates and Diotima in the dialogue. Diotima first convinces Socrates that love must be love of what is unchanging or immortal. She goes on to say that it is the desire for immortality which prods men to desire children,

'For love, Socrates, is not, as you imagine, the love of the beautiful only' 'What then?' 'The love of generation and the birth of beauty.' 'Yes,' I said. 'Yes, indeed,' she replied. 'But why of generation?' 'Because to the mortal creature, generation is a sort of eternity and immortality,' she replied; 'and if, as has been already admitted, love is of the everlasting possession of the good, all men will necessarily desire immortality together with good: Wherefore love is of immortality.'

All this she taught me at various times when she spoke of love. And I remember her once saying to me, 'What is the cause, Socrates, of love, and the attendant desire? See you not how all animals, birds, as well as beasts, in their desire of procreation, are in agony when they take the infection of love, which begins with the desire of union; whereto is added the care of offspring, on whose behalf the weakest are ready to battle against the strongest even to the uttermost, and to die for them, and will let themselves be tormented with hunger or suffer anything in order to maintain their young? Man may be supposed to act thus from reason; but why should animals have these passionate feelings? Can you tell me why?' Again I replied that I did not know. She said to me: 'And do you expect ever to become a master in the art of love, if you do not know this?' 'But I have told you already, Diotima, that my ignorance is the reason why I come to you; for I am conscious that I want a teacher; tell me then the cause of this and of the other mysteries of love.' 'Marvel not,' she said, 'if you believe that love is of the immortal, as we have several times acknowledged; for here again, and on the same principle too, the mortal nature is seeking as far as is possible to be everlasting and immortal: and this is only to be attained by generation, because generation always leaves behind a new existence in the pace of the old. Nay, even in the life of the same individual there is succession and not absolute unity: a man is called the same, and yet in the short interval which elapses between youth and age, and in which every animal is said to have life and identity, he is undergoing a perpetual process of loss and reparation – hair, flesh, bones, blood, and the whole body are always changing. Which is true not only of the body, but also of the soul, whose habits, tempers, opinions, desires, pleasures, pains, fears, never remain the same in any one of us, but are always coming and going; and equally true of knowledge, and what is still more surprising to us mortals, not only do the sciences in general spring up and decay, so that in respect of them we are never the same; but each of them individually experiences a like change. For what is implied in the word "recollection", but the departure of knowledge, which is ever being forgotten, and is renewed and preserved by recollection, and appears to be the same although in reality new, according to that law of succession by which all mortal things are preserved, not absolutely the same, but by substitution, the old worn-out mortality leaving another new and similar existence behind – unlike the divine, which is always the same and not another? And in this way, Socrates, the mortal body, or mortal anything, partakes of immortality; but the immortal in another way. Marvel not then at the love which all men have of their offspring; for that universal love and interest is for the sake of immortality.'[1]

Yeats, in Stanza V of 'Among School Children', asks what mother would think an old man worth the trouble of his birth and youth. Later in the Dialogue Diotima points out that the immortality of the body cannot be achieved. Yeats agrees with Plato that the desire for what is immortal and unchanging cannot be satisfied in this world. But he does not come to the same conclusions about how we should respond to this. Diotima continues by saying that those who are 'pregnant in body only' betake themselves to women to beget children, but those who are 'souls which are pregnant' seek immortality in other ways. Diotima ends by saying that the love of beauty, the desire of immortality leads us to the world of immutable unchanging forms.

'These are the lesser mysteries of love, into which even you, Socrates, may enter; to the greater and more hidden ones which are the crown of these, and to which, if you pursue them in a right spirit, they will lead, I know not whether you will be able to attain. But I will do my utmost to inform you, and do you follow if you can. For he who would proceed aright in this

---

[1] *Dialogues of Plato*, ed. J. D. Kaplans (New York: Affiliated Publishers, Inc., 1955), pp. 212–14.

matter should begin in youth to visit beautiful forms; and first, if he be guided by his instructor aright, to love one such form only – out of that he should create fair thoughts; and soon he will of himself perceive that the beauty of one form is akin to the beauty of another; and then if beauty of form in general is his pursuit, how foolish would he be not to recognize that the beauty in every form is one and the same! And when he perceives this he will abate his violent love of the one, which he will despise and deem a small thing, and will become a lover of all beautiful forms: in the next stage he will consider that the beauty of the mind is more honourable than the beauty of the outward form. So that if a virtuous soul have but a little comeliness, he will be content to love and tend him, and will search out and bring to the birth thoughts which may improve the young, until he is compelled to contemplate and see the beauty of institutions and laws, and to understand that the beauty of them all is of one family, and that personal beauty is a trifle; and after laws and institutions he will go on to the sciences, that he may see their beauty, being not like a servant in love with the beauty of one youth or man or institution, himself a slave mean and narrow-minded, but drawing towards and contemplating the vast sea of beauty, he will create many fair and noble thoughts and notions in boundless love of wisdom; until on that shore he grows and waxes strong, and at last the vision is revealed to him of a single science, which is the science of beauty everywhere. To this I will proceed; please give me your very best attention:

'He who has been instructed thus far in the things of love, and who has learned to see the beautiful in due order and succession, when he comes towards the end will suddenly perceive a nature of wondrous beauty (and this, Socrates, is the final cause of all our former toils) – a nature which in the first place is everlasting, not growing and decaying, or waxing and waning: secondly, not fair in one point of view and foul in another, or at one time or in one relation or at one place fair, at another time or in another relation or at another place foul, as if fair to some and foul to others, or in the likeness of a face or hands or any other part of the bodily frame, or in any form of speech or knowledge, or existing in any other being, as, for example, in an animal, or in heaven, or in earth, or in any other place but beauty absolute, separate, simple, and everlasting, which without diminution and without increase, or any change, is imparted to the ever-growing and perishing beauties of all other things. He who from these ascending under the influence of true love, begins to perceive that beauty, is not far from the end. And the true order of going, or being led by another, to the things of love, is to begin from the beauties of earth and mount upwards for the sake of that other beauty, using these as steps only, and from one going on to two, and from two to all fair forms, and from fair forms to fair practices, and from fair practices to fair notions, until from fair notions he arrives at the notion of absolute beauty, and at last knows what the essence of beauty is. This, my dear Socrates,' said the stranger of Mantineia, 'is that life above all others which man should live, in the contemplation of beauty absolute; a beauty which if you once beheld, you would see not to be after the measure of gold, and garments, and fair boys and youths, whose presence now entrances you; and you and many an one would be content to live seeing them only and conversing with them without meat or drink, if that were possible – you only want to look at them and to be with them. But what if man had eyes to see the true beauty – the divine beauty, I mean, pure and clear and unalloyed, not clogged with the pollutions of mortality and all the colours and vanities of human life – thither looking, and holding converse with the true beauty simple and divine? Remember how in that communion only, beholding beauty with the eye of the mind, he will be enabled to bring forth, not images of beauty, but realities (for he has hold not of an image but of a reality) and bringing forth and nourishing true virtue to become the friend of God and be immortal, if mortal man may. Would that be an ignoble life?'[1]

Essentially, this is the pattern of Stanzas II to VII of 'Among School Children'. For we proceed from the love of beautiful forms, the Ledaean body, and immediately discover that these forms are insufficient just in that they are subject to change. In Stanza V we discover that the attempt to perpetuate what we love through procreation is not sufficient. And in Stanzas VI and VII we discover the love of nuns and philosophers. But Yeats's allusions to the Platonic dialogue should not be taken as evidence that he accepts the Platonic view of love, or of reality. For the poem is essentially a Whiteheadian rebuttal of the Platonic doctrine. The poem is a reverie in which certain 'eternal ideas' suggest themselves. As we have seen, for Whitehead, complex eternal ideas manifest themselves in the form of 'memory, anticipation, imagination and thought'. In the context of a visit to a school Yeats remembers Maud Gonne, thinks about his present bodily condition, and thinks about the relationship of these eternal ideas, in the poem called 'presences' and 'images', and their relationship to human life, 'labour'. And the conclusion that he reaches is that if we take the 'eternal ideas', the presences, that symbolise all heavenly glory, to be anything other than abstractions, if we hold, with Plato, that we have found reality instead of an image, then they can only serve to break hearts. For we live in a complex world of process, and the process can only seem senseless and hostile unless we see the connexity or prehensive unity, which holds both event and eternal

[1] *Dialogues of Plato*, ed. Kaplans, pp. 216–18.

object in a continuing relationship with what has gone before and after. So that the poem may be regarded as an attempt to illustrate how the 'fallacy of misplaced concreteness', the reification of abstractions, serves continually to alienate the individual from his experience of himself, and from the kind of joyous intellectual perception of pattern that is possible once we understand that reality is a prehensive unity of experience rather than a series of discrete moments unconnected by an inherent structure.

AMONG SCHOOL CHILDREN

I

I walk through the long schoolroom questioning;
A kind old nun in a white hood replies;
The children learn to cipher and to sing,
To study reading-books and histories,
To cut and sew, be neat in everything
In the best modern way – the children's eyes
In momentary wonder stare upon
A sixty-year-old smiling public man.

II

I dream of a Ledaean body, bent
Above a sinking fire, a tale that she
Told of a harsh reproof, or trivial event
That changed some childish day to tragedy –
Told, and it seemed that our two natures blent
Into a sphere from youthful sympathy,
Or else, to alter Plato's parable,
Into the yolk and white of the one shell.

III

And thinking of that fit of grief or rage
I look upon one child or t'other there
And wonder if she stood so at that age –
For even daughters of the swan can share
Something of every paddler's heritage –
And had that colour upon cheek or hair,
And thereupon my heart is driven wild:
She stands before me as a living child.

IV

Her present image floats into the mind –
Did Quattrocento finger fashion it
Hollow of cheek as though it drank the wind

And took a mess of shadows for its meat?
And I though never of Ledaean kind
Had pretty plumage once – enough of that,
Better to smile on all that smile, and show
There is a comfortable kind of old scarecrow.

V

What youthful mother, a shape upon her lap
Honey of generation had betrayed,
And that must sleep, shriek, struggle to escape
As recollection or the drug decide,
Would think her son, did she but see that shape
With sixty or more winters on its head,
A compensation for the pang of his birth,
Or the uncertainty of his setting forth?

VI

Plato thought nature but a spume that plays
Upon a ghostly paradigm of things;
Solider Aristotle played the taws
Upon the bottom of a king of kings;
World-famous golden-thighed Pythagoras
Fingered upon a fiddle-stick or strings
What a star sang and careless Muses heard:
Old clothes upon old sticks to scare a bird.

VII

Both nuns and mothers worship images,
But those the candles light are not as those
That animate a mother's reveries,
But keep a marble or a bronze repose.
And yet they too break hearts – O Presences
That passion, piety, or affection knows,
And that all heavenly glory symbolise –
O self-born mockers of man's enterprise;

VIII

Labour is blossoming or dancing where
The body is not bruised to pleasure soul,
Nor beauty born out of its own despair,
Nor blear-eyed wisdom out of midnight oil.
O chestnut-tree, great-rooted blossomer,
Are you the leaf, the blossom or the bole?
O body swayed to music, O brightening glance,
How can we know the dancer from the dance?

(*Collected Poems*, pp. 242–5)

The first stanza gives us a formal setting, an official occasion which is really a performance in which everyone pretends to some sort of attention and interest in an immediate occasion, but is really performing in a meaningless and pointless ritual. The school inspector walks through the schoolroom 'questioning' – that is, he does what school inspectors are supposed to do, he inspects, he seems to take an interest in what is happening in the room. But of course this is only the official visit of a 'sixty-year-old smiling public man', and the real activity of the man lies hidden behind the mask. The nun too is involved in the public performance of this ritual, and in response to the formal situation of question and answer, she 'replies'. But her reply, though it is first of all the correct formal response within the public ritual, also functions as an explanation of the genesis of this sort of ritual. For the children are learning those abstract ways of thinking that eventually result in our inability to connect the individual bits of our experience to each other.

> The children learn to cipher and to sing,
> To study reading-books and histories,
> To cut and sew, be neat in everything
> In the best modern way –

The difficulty we have in making sense of our experience, of seeing how any individual object or event is connected to the ambience of our experience and the world, is already manifest in these children. For the old man they see is something alien to them, something that makes no sense. So they can only 'stare', blank and uncomprehending, in 'momentary wonder', not upon a man, or a shape like their shape in sixty years, but upon a 'sixty-year-old smiling public man'.

But the inspector of schools is no more able to make sense of his experience of them than they are of him. He begins by feeling at best as alien as they feel him to be, for he too lives in a world in which each moment is separate from each other moment, he too has learned to 'cut and sew, be neat in everything'.

> And I though never of Ledaean kind
> Had pretty plumage once – enough of that,
> Better to smile on all that smile, and show
> There is a comfortable kind of old scarecrow.

Because he accepts as real not the whole process of life, not a prehensive unity, but this particular moment, because he is in effect reasoning in the way that Whitehead characterised as the fallacy of misplaced concreteness, he can only regret his past. Because he is committed to the abstract notion of this very minute, because he believes he can capture his essential being in an abstract simple location in space-time, he thinks he is nothing but a scarecrow. And because he believes, correctly, that his audience is committed to the same way of seeing, he can only regret the passing of what he was, and make what he is as 'comfortable', as undisturbing, as possible.

So we have on the one hand an abstract figure, a public scarecrow, and on the other hand a man who escapes the boundary of this minute, this performance, who is connected to past and future even as he performs as the 'comfortable scarecrow'. And the whole man behind the mask is seen as withdrawing from this particular moment to an earlier moment that has occupied his attention and influenced his development. What he remembers is the moment when he decided to love, when he created the figure, the eternal object, which would remain with him for the rest of his life.

> I dream of a Ledaean body, bent
> Above a sinking fire, a tale that she
> Told of a harsh reproof, or trivial event
> That changed some childish day to tragedy –
> Told, and it seemed that our two natures blent
> Into a sphere from youthful sympathy,
> Or else, to alter Plato's parable,
> Into the yolk and white of the one shell.

It is important to realise that what is remembered is a picture, a kind of snapshot, of a single moment. He remembers Maud Gonne – who the woman is should not really occupy our attention – as a body bent above a sinking fire. She is still, because this is a remembered scene, and a single emotion. So he does not remember just what she said, just what caused them to feel the unity of first love. Instead he remembers the eternal moment, when this choice was made. Throughout the section of the poem which deals with the poet's reverie we see eternal ideas as snapshots. We are presented with 'a Ledaean body bent above a sinking fire' or a girl who 'stands before me as a living child' or 'her present image' still as a Quattrocento painting. Whitehead says that what distinguishes these eternal ideas is not that they are Hume's 'faint copies', but that they are abrupt. They are truly just what they are and not a part of the flux of things. So the poet's images of Maud Gonne are isolated from each other, and because they are isolated and unchanging, they are like the images of nuns and philosophers and mothers; they break hearts.

In the first two stanzas we are given the public figure and the passionate life of the man behind the public figure. And since the two do not stand in a relationship to each other, have not been seen as part of a pattern, the disparity between them can only be painful. The Platonic lover, the man in search of a fit eternal object for his love, looks at the children and tries to find some way of unifying the memory of the Ledaean body, the memory of his own youth, now made mythical and eternal, made immortal in the figure of the Ledaean body, the body visited by the Gods, by Zeus himself, and his present experience.

> And thinking of that fit of grief or rage
> I look upon one child or t'other there
> And wonder if she stood so at that age –
> For even daughters of the swan can share
> Something of every paddler's heritage –
> And had that colour upon cheek or hair,
> And thereupon my heart is driven wild:
> She stands before me as a living child.

Since he is thinking in terms of stasis, and not in terms of process, his attempt leads him not to an understanding of how and why he is here, leads him not to an understanding of himself and the woman but to another snapshot, another eternal idea. And the desperate and hopeless desire for possession, the mixture of desire with the recognition that desire is pointless, produce not just the image, but the passionate hopeless desire for the image. So that the last two lines of the stanza break in upon the meditative mood of the preceding lines with a rush of emotion that is necessarily and immediately associated with the image. In fact, the emotion in the verse reaches us even before the image:

> And thereupon my heart is driven wild:
> She stands before me as a living child.

The stanza begins with the poet looking for something like the mental image of the previous stanza. He begins by thinking of that moment, and while thinking, looks upon the children in the school-room for something answerable to the presence he has created. Which of these children, he wonders, is most like her, which of these children is most easily changed into the eternal and perfect mythic woman of his memory? For there must be some connection between the real and the imagined perfect, there must be something that the image shares with everyday reality. For even daughters of the swan, even the mythic creature, must first have been real, must first have been the paddler, the ugly duckling of the fairy tale. But in looking for his perfect creature in the real world, the poet finds not real children but another image. *She*, already the fabled creature, not the real world of the classroom, stands before him.

And since this image is another snapshot, an eternal idea, it cannot lead him back into the world of process, of smooth and equable time, but leads him to another image.

> Her present image floats into the mind –
> Did Quattrocento finger fashion it
> Hollow of cheek as though it drank the wind
> And took a mess of shadows for its meat?
> And I though never of Ledaean kind
> Had pretty plumage once – enough of that,
> Better to smile on all that smile, and show
> There is a comfortable kind of old scarecrow.

It is important to notice that the present image is given in more detail than the image of the child or the Ledaean body. But before we begin to notice the details, we must realise that even though the image is given to us in some detail it is still given to us as another eternal idea. What we are presented with is not the thought of a woman, *but an image as an object of thought*. It floats before the poet, and is thought about as the object of aesthetic appreciation as if it had been painted by a Quattrocento finger. In dealing with the details of the image we must first take account of what is meant by 'Ledaean kind'. To be Ledaean, first of all, is to be beautiful. But this in itself will not get us very far in the passage. In the preced-ing poem, 'Leda and the Swan', Yeats talks about the rape of Leda by Zeus in terms of an annunciation. Leda is suddenly forced out of her normal human role as participant in history, and is sud-denly placed in the role of determinant. She 'put(s) on' the power of Zeus, if not his knowledge. For she becomes, living, as fixed and permanent and eternal as the images worshipped by the nuns. The whole of the sestet of the poem deals with the moment when centuries of history are made. And Leda has been taken up, fixed into the moment – 'caught up/Mastered'. In Stanza IV of 'Among School Children' the woman is Ledaean in that she has, still alive, fixed her attention on an image, and so has become, like Leda, a monument to the power of what is other than human, of what is not immediate in normal experience. So her present image is

> Hollow of cheek as though it drank the wind
> And took a mess of shadows for its meat?

This is life lived through abstraction, life feeding on something as unsubstantial as wind. The normal ordinary kinds of sustenance given to all, the normal daily life which may be no more glorious than the mess of pottage for which Esau traded his birthright, is at worst merely sustenance. But what feeds this Ledaean woman who cannot live in the world because she wants to make it into the image she drinks, into the mess of shadows which she feeds on? There is a temptation to involve what is known about Maud Gonne, and Yeats's relationship to her, in discussing this poem. While it is probably the case that Yeats's model for the 'Ledaean body' in 'Among School Children' was Maud Gonne, and that these lines are occasioned by his uneasiness and unhappiness about the sort of political activity she was involved in ('A Helen of social welfare dream/Climb on a wagonette to scream') the lines stand by themselves, and can be read without any biographical speculation.

In comparison to what has befallen his lover, the *persona* of the poem has escaped some of the more unhappy consequences. For he was never of Ledaean kind, never so beautiful – though he had pretty plumage once – and never possessed in quite the same way by the object or thought that possessed her. For although, as he has told us in the second stanza, they seem united by some 'harsh reproof or trivial event', he is not so possessed by the abstract desire for something out of life that possesses her. So he regrets what he can still imagine, but no longer have – that is, both the moment remembered in Stanza II and physical vigour, and is able to concentrate on the more normal problems of all men and women when they grow old. He will not surrender to the longing for the eternal ideal, the Ledaean body that he loved and the pretty plumage he loved with, but will strive to show that there is a 'comfortable kind of old scarecrow'. But having determined to do this, having stated his intention to continue playing out the ritual of public behaviour, 'to smile on all that smile', the reverie continues.

But we notice a difference in that the anguish of personal memory has been replaced with a meditative consideration of the problem as one for all mankind. The context has broadened, and the mood of personal anguish is replaced by the measured, meditative rhetoric of Stanzas v and vi. But before proceeding to these stanzas it is important to notice the continual use of bird imagery throughout the section of personal reminiscence. For the world of nature, and or process, is given to us in terms of bird imagery. When the poet searches for the 'Ledaean body' among the children, hoping to find one who looks like her as a young girl, he talks of discovering among these 'paddlers' one who will turn out to be daughter of the swan, alluding to the story of the ugly duckling. And in Stanza IV the poet sees the transformation wrought by ageing in terms of a transformation from a bird with 'pretty plumage' to a scarecrow. The development of this image prepares the ground for the poet's realisation in Stanza VI that it is abstraction which is the scarecrow, that men live in nature and process, and that he is a bird, a natural creature after all.

The more general questions are dealt with in Stanzas v and vi.

> What youthful mother, a shape upon her lap
> Honey of generation had betrayed,
> And that must sleep, shriek, struggle to escape
> As recollection or the drug decide,
> Would think her son, did she but see that shape
> With sixty or more winters on its head,
> A compensation for the pang of his birth,
> Or the uncertainty of this setting forth?

Old age faces every human being. But, by and large, we are able to put it out of mind until we are old. In Stanza v Yeats directs our attention to both old age and to our desire not to think about growing old. He asks what mother could bear to think of her son with 'sixty or more winters' on his head, knowing that the answer will be – none. And so Yeats forces the reader to anticipate the conclusion in Stanza VII – that women like nuns and philosophers worship images, and that the image a mother worships is not that of an old man, but of a man at the peak of his powers. Before Diatima tells Socrates the right way of going about the business of loving, she tells him that love is not love of the beautiful only:

'For love, Socrates, is not, as you imagine, the love of the beautiful only.' 'What then?' 'The love of generation and the birth of beauty.' 'Yes,' I said. 'Yes, indeed,' she replied. 'But why of generation?' 'Because to the mortal creature, generation is a sort of eternity and immortality', she replied; 'and if, as has been already admitted, love is of the everlasting possession of the good, all men will necessarily desire immortality together with good: Wherefore love is of immortality.'[1]

In Stanza v Yeats's rhetorical question assumes a truth that we all know and try to avoid, that to have children is not to achieve an immortality of bodily perfection. So far as the mother bears her child with a perfect immortal 'image' in mind, she will be disappointed. For men are creatures of mortality, organisms which wax and wane in the natural world. They are not self-born images, but a part of the changing world of mutability.

> What youthful mother, a shape upon her lap...
> Would think her son, did she but see that shape
> With sixty or more winters on its head,
> A compensation for the pang of his birth,
> Or the uncertainty of his setting forth?

The question posed in this stanza assumes the same mode of thought present throughout the section of personal reminiscence. What mother, faced with the image of an old man, would think that image worth the pangs and uncertainty of childbirth and parenthood? But the image is a selection from the whole process of life, as such it is another example of the fallacy of misplaced concreteness. For in thinking of that image, we leave out all that has passed between birth and old age, which is most of life. But once the question is posed, the conclusion that the pain and suffering were unjustified is inevitable. Of course, the constant assumption that life is not process, but progress towards a goal, a 'setting forth', is one of the primary sources of human anguish. For mothers, and Yeats does not need to say fathers, though we are quite safe in extending the meaning to include fathers, often worship such images. There are fewer jokes more often rehearsed in North

[1] *Dialogues of Plato*, ed. Kaplans, p. 212.

America than the one of the proud parent introducing a young child as either a lawyer or a football star. And there are few adolescents who do not await anxiously the day when they will be 'adult', and, they think, 'finished'. Many lives are lived as attempts to reach and hold some image of oneself, to become this or become that. So Yeats points out that if we think in terms of 'becoming' something, we must face the fact that what will become, our final metamorphosis, is an old man.

But within the passage the language that Yeats has chosen suggests that the image of the old man and the image that the mother worships are both abstractions. For the baby is described as a 'shape'. This is accurate, in that young babies do exhibit the absence of individuality that makes it possible to think about them in a way that will lead to the creation of an eternal idea. This formlessness is an invitation to us to create a form for them. So the baby in Stanza V is just a 'shape', a bunch of human stuff that will grow and change. Yet the old man that the baby will become, is, in line 5 described as 'that shape'. The point of the repeated use of 'shape' is that something other than the two moments is given to us in the poem.

Despite the gap created by the juxtaposition of young child and old man, Yeats forces us to take account of the continuum between. Lines 2–4 of this stanza are about this gap, in a way that merges with the Platonic superstructure of the poem. For we have seen how, in Diotima's discourse on love, the notion of recollection has already been introduced. Yeats brought to his reading of the *Symposium* a thorough understanding of the Platonic tradition and the role that reminiscence or recollection played in it. According to Plato and his commentators, true knowledge was a property of the soul, and the soul of each man had existed in heaven before his present life on earth. When we learn things on earth we are not really learning them but rather dreaming back to out previous knowledge of all things when we were heavenly souls. But in coming to this life we had been blinded to our heavenly knowledge. The fall into the world of matter and generation was seen as a fall away from true knowledge, because of a love for the temporary and material and this love was often symbolised as a drunkeness (cf. the earlier discussion of 'A Dialogue of Self and Soul'). The complex of ideas and symbols alluded to in this passage appears throughout the Platonic and neo-Platonic tradition, but in a note Yeats adduces a specific source – Porphyry's essay 'On the Cave of the Nymphs'.

I have taken the 'honey of generation' from Porphyry's essay on 'The Cave of the Nymphs', but find no warrant in Porphyry for considering it the 'drug' that destroys the 'recollection' of pre-natal freedom. He blamed a cup of oblivion given in the zodiacal sign of Cancer.

(Collected Poems, p. 535)

In almost all Platonic and neo-Platonic writing the 'drug' or wine which binds the soul to generation destroys the soul's knowledge of heaven and the forms. The point of all this in neo-Platonism was to make clear the choice of the individual soul in the world. The choice was between the material and the spiritual world, since we had all tasted of the drug that bound us to the world of matter, and since we all might recollect, if we gave our attention to the task, our knowledge of heaven. So in Stanza V Yeats talks of the child who

> Honey of generation had betrayed,
> And that must sleep, shriek, struggle to escape
> As recollection or the drug decide...

The honey of generation is the neo-Platonic drink which binds us to the world of generation. The sexual overtones of the image are present, not just in Yeats's poem, but in his source as well. Furthermore, the child is faced with the neo-Platonic choice between continuing existence in this world, and love for this world, or the desire to 'escape' from the world because of his recollection of pre-natal freedom. The passage presents this dichotomy as a determined course of events. The child will 'sleep, shriek, struggle to escape/As recollection or the drug decide.'

Once we recover from the initial strangeness of Yeats's imagery we can see why he has chosen so recondite an image. For the child is faced with a choice that is really no choice. For he can, blinded by the honey of generation, strive for a kind of immortality in the world, and will then find his physical decrepitude as painful as that of the old man in the first four stanzas, and as disappointing as the mother in Stanza V, or he will desire the sort of heavenly image prompted by recollection, that broke the hearts of nuns, or turned philosophers into scarecrows. But in either case he will find in life no blossoming or dancing; but will merely 'sleep, shriek, or struggle to escape'.

The heavenly abstractions that destroy the possibility of healthy, human activity, intellectual or otherwise, are the subject of Stanza VI.

> Plato thought nature but a spume that plays
> Upon a ghostly paradigm of things;
> Solider Aristotle played the taws
> Upon the bottom of a king of kings;
> World-famous golden-thighed Pythagoras
> Fingered upon a fiddle-stick or strings
> What a star sang and careless Muses heard:
> Old clothes upon old sticks to scare a bird.

Here, Yeats, in an ironic and witty manner, reviews the accomplishments of the philosophical tradition, and finds it wanting. But in doing so, he discovers that possibility of healthy human activity which he has not found in his own experience. The stanza begins by examining the platonic theory of forms. According to Plato, what was real were the eternal unsubstantial forms, and the world of nature was an inferior copy of them. Yeats reformulates the doctrine by comparing the relationship between nature and the forms to the relationship between the unsubstantial spume thrown up when a wave breaks over a rock, and the solid rock itself. But he reminds us that this rock is a 'ghostly paradigm' – an abstract, perfect example. So the comparison promised by the first line is made ludicrous by what follows:

> Plato thought nature but a spume that plays
> Upon a ghostly paradigm of things:

By providing us with the comparison, and then refusing to follow the imaginative chain of thought he has begun, Yeats captures the emotional appeal of Platonism (cf. Wordsworth's 'Fallings from us – vanishings') in the haunting quality of the verse, and provides the pithiest possible comment on the absurdity of Platonic thought.

Aristotle is, by comparison, solider. For though he preserves much of his teacher's ontological and metaphysical doctrine, he was primarily interested in classifying and thinking about the things of this world. So his primary interests were quasi-scientific (biological), logical and political. And in his metaphysics this practical interest produced a bastard Platonism in which the Platonic sea of perfect and immutable forms were discovered to inhere in the particulars of this world, and the form of the good became a sort of lazy god, an unmoved mover, who did nothing, yet was a final cause. It is this mixture of metaphysical longing and common sense that leads Russell to say of Aristotle that Plato and common sense do not mix. So we have the Aristotle of Yeats's poem, 'solider' than Plato, concerned with a more worldly abstraction, the state, the political life of man. Yeats symbolises a certain sort of abstract passion by reminding us that Aristotle taught Alexander. Politics, like religion, is abstract.

As Diotima tells Socrates:

'Souls which are pregnant – for there certainly are men who are more creative in their souls than in their bodies – conceive that which is proper for the soul – to conceive or contain. And what are these conceptions? – wisdom and virtue in general. And such creators are poets and all artists who are deserving of the name inventor. But the greatest and fairest sort of wisdom by far is that which is concerned with the ordering of states and families, and which is called temperance and justice. And he who in youth has the seed of these implanted in him and is himself inspired, when he comes to maturity desires to beget and generate. He wanders about seeking beauty that he may beget offspring – for in deformity he will beget nothing – and naturally embraces the beautiful rather than the deformed body; above all, when he finds a fair and noble and well-nurtured soul, he embraces the two in one person, and to such as one he is full of speech about virtue and the nature and pursuits of a good man; and he tries to educate him; and at the touch of the beautiful which is ever present to his memory, even when absent, he brings forth that which he had conceived long before, and in company with him tends that which he brings forth; and they are married by a far nearer tie and have a closer friendship than those who beget mortal children, for the children who are their common offspring are fairer and more immortal.'[1]

But this striving after immortality, though seemingly solider than Plato's, is treated just as ironically.

> Solider Aristotle played the taws
> Upon the bottom of a king of kings...

The attempt to capture virtue and make it immortal is nothing more than whipping a schoolboy. The process of building empires, the magic of conquest and the glory of the state, are reduced to a schoolboy's 'bottom'. The 'king of kings' is envisaged, not as a glorious monarch, but as a child's bum. The effect of the description of Aristotle's philosophical position is roughly the same as that of

---

[1] *Dialogues of Plato*, ed. Kaplans, p. 215.

Plato's. In both cases something normally thought of as important is made to seem absurd. We may notice, in both cases, that a device used with particular effectiveness is the deliberate use of the word 'play'. In both the description of nature, and that of Aristotle's pedagogical activities, 'play' is used in a manner that accurately describes the activities by pointing out that they are rule-governed. But the activities are unlike those usually evoked by the word 'play', in that they are solemn. The considerations that arise from the way 'play' is used, and not used, in the description of the activities of Plato and Aristotle, are centrally connected with the argument of the poem. For the activity of Pythagoras is also a sort of 'play', since what he is doing is playing upon a musical instrument. But it too is not joyous, but solemn. It is not until the last stanza that we find activity that preserves anything of the joy normally associated with play; but in that stanza the joyous activity is called 'labour'.

Pythagoras's play receives more attention and sympathy, than that of Plato or Aristotle. Whitehead finds Pythagoras admirable because he was the first to understand the power of abstraction. But Whitehead points out what Yeats probably knew from other sources, including Plato, that Pythagoras not only discovered the abstracting power of numbers, but went on to create a metaphysical system in which number and relation became ontologically supreme. So Pythagoras is, as Whitehead and others suggest, a pre-Platonic Plato. But there is this difference; that at least in the conventional view of Plato, what he is supposed to have reified was the idea of things and abstractions (the form of the horse, and the form of the good), while Pythagoras makes number, proportions and relation his ontological prime. So we have the Pythagoras of the poem, who listens to and abstracts the pattern from the flux of things, but who is immobile; who is interested not in the whole of experience, the dance, but simply in the pattern of the dance.

> World-famous golden-thighed Pythagoras
> Fingered upon a fiddle-stick or strings
> What a star sang and careless Muses heard:
> Old clothes upon old sticks to scare a bird.

'Golden-thighed' is a classical epithet often applied to Pythagoras, expressing the perfection of soul he had supposedly achieved. But here it marks off the difference between an abstract interest in pattern, and the ability to live by the pattern that may be found in the real world. For 'golden-thighed' Pythagoras can only 'finger' on a 'fiddle-stick' what in the world is sung. The image is of fixity and absence of motion; of an activity disturbing because of its loss of motion. And opposed to this intellectual pattern, to a pattern merely noticed, we have the music of the spheres which is the pattern and the flux together. So Pythagoras can only finger what a star 'sang'. But in fingering the pattern, in looking at relationships instead of isolated objects, Pythagoras is preferable to Plato. For it is not necessary to follow Pythagoras in making only the pattern important. For a proper attention to the right kind of abstraction will allow us to think both generally and concretely at the same time – to preserve both the pattern and the flux of things, and the intellectual imaginative unity that allows us to grasp into a prehensive unity any particular event; to preserve both the event and the before and after. This is what the star sang (not just pattern but a patterning of the flux of things) and what the Muses heard. Poetry is the type of finding pattern in the flux of things and reproducing that pattern in a concrete way. But the condition for this joyous perception of patterning, as opposed to the perception of pattern or form, what Whitehead calls the 'eternal idea', is a willingness to avoid the attempt to make immortal the objects within the pattern. The 'muses' are careless because they are too busy finding pattern and meaning in what happens to try to make immortal and unchanging what they are celebrating. So this man full of care, this man musing on the ravages of time, and meditating on the 'eternal ideas' of passion, piety and affection, suddenly realises that it is in the letting go, the refusal to countenance those abstractions, that poetry is born. And he becomes careless himself, becomes the bird that sings and in singing embodies the pattern, becomes a whole man again. For although he no longer has 'pretty plumage' he is a creature of this world, and the 'eternal idea' he has of himself as a young man, or of the 'Ledaean body', are like the 'eternal ideas' of the philosophers: simply abstractions, scarecrows, which prevent him entering into the world of unified experience. So he dismisses the philosophers as 'Old clothes upon old sticks to scare a bird.'

The last line of this stanza marks a turning point in the verse. With the sudden insight that the poet has gained he is not only able to dismiss the scarecrow philosophers, but the other images of

perfection and immortality as well. So Stanza VII begins by conso-
lidating this new knowledge, and ends with the poet's rhetorical
denunciation of the image. For now he is able to tell how life must
be led, to tell them what the condition of dancing or blossoming
involves.

> Both nuns and mothers worship images,
> But those the candles light are not as those
> That animate a mother's reveries,
> But keep a marble or a bronze repose.
> And yet they too break hearts – O Presences
> That passion, piety, or affection knows,
> And that all heavenly glory symbolise –
> O self-born mockers of man's enterprise. . .

The image that the mother worships is the image of her son as
a man in the full flower of his life. The image that she worships is
an 'eternal idea' – it does not change. But what is like it in the
world does change; her son eventually will have 'sixty or more
winters' on his head. So what might be enjoyed, the process of
living in the world, is exchanged for an image that, because it is
timeless, represents not the process of life, but a kind of false hiatus,
a kiss like that of the lover in Keats's 'Ode on a Grecian Urn',[1]
who loves forever only because he never possesses what he loves.

The mother's image breaks her heart because it is an image of
heavenly perfection in life; because it insists that the world of
change be unchanging. To imagine perfection and immortality
of the body is to demand too much. So what might otherwise be
enjoyed, the process of living, is ignored, and the mother's image
breaks her heart.

If the image that the mother cherishes preserves all the vibrancy
of life, the religious images that the nuns worship hold out something more austere, less involved with normal human activity, and
since they are less desirable, the gap between what one can conceive of having, and what one has is smaller and less painful. Yet
'they too break hearts' for they draw us away from the world of
process and change. To come to them, to come to light the candle

[1]   Fair youth, beneath the trees, thou canst not leave
        Thy song, nor ever can those trees be bare;
        Bold Lover, never, never canst thou kiss,
        Though winning near the goal – yet, do not grieve;
        She cannot fade, though thou hast not thy bliss,
        For ever wilt thou love, and she be fair

and illumine their repose, is to try to withdraw from the world of change and action. And because we live in a world of actions and change we can never enter their stillness, their unchanging, immortal perfection. The mother worships perfection and immortality in life, and the nun worships perfection and immortality out of life, but both live in a world of process and change.

In discovering that he is a 'bird' after all, the poet has come to terms with the personal anguish of his own ageing, and with the role of the sort of abstract thought – philosophy – that interests him. In the early part of this stanza he has come to terms with the impersonal situation given to us in Stanza I. For in thinking of nuns and mothers, and the images they worship, he has come to understand the situation of the children in the schoolroom. For their 'education' consists of learning to do homage to the images of the nuns who teach them, and the mothers that bore them. When he thinks of the images worshipped by mother and nun he is, after all, thinking of the very children in front of him. In the earlier stanzas of the poem he has not really seen the children; they were simply an unintegrated aspect of his experience that gave rise to the reverie primarily because it was not understood. But now the whole experience has been comprehended and he is able to repudiate the way of thinking that has produced both the painful experience of being regarded as an abstract image himself (the smiling public man), and the painful reverie that has arisen because he thinks in terms of 'eternal ideas' too. So the crippling 'eternal ideas' are taken up into the vision of harmonious pattern, into a vision of what is possible in time. The vision is possible because the images are understood to be just that. They are 'presences', ephemeral and haunting, because they are outside the world of time and change, although they arise and can be thought only because of what is actual in the world of his poem.

> O Presences
> That passion, piety, or affection knows,
> And that all heavenly glory symbolise –
> O self-born mockers of man's enterprise...

The image of the Ledaean body has grown out of passion, and can be 'known' only by passion. So too, the images of piety and affection are known, respectively, by nun and mother. But despite the fact that they grow out of, and are known by, normal experience, they are out of normal experience, they are abstractions from experience. They are therefore removed from the flux of time. They need nothing else in order to be themselves. They qualify, therefore, as fit objects for the sort of love that Diotima describes to Socrates in *The Symposium*; they symbolise all heavenly glory. But it is exactly this quality of immutability that makes them repugnant to the poet. For they can only 'mock' the enterprise, the activity, of living in the world. They are self-born, outside the flux of actuality. They are still, and perfect, and they symbolise 'heavenly glory'. But here, in this life, they only serve to distract us from the only enterprise we have.

So the poet rejects them in favour of the harmonious vision of life led in its complex actuality.

> Labour is blossoming or dancing where
> The body is not bruised to pleasure soul,
> Nor beauty born out of its own despair,
> Nor blear-eyed wisdom out of midnight oil.
> O chestnut-tree, great-rooted blossomer.
> Are you the leaf, the blossom or the bole?
> O body swayed to music, O brightening glance,
> How can we know the dancer from the dance?

The poet speaks his new wisdom to the presences of the preceding stanza; he rejects them by choosing to live within the prehended unity of vision which unites all the aspects of the individual life, and the eternal objects that guide the perception of life, into a harmonious event that moves through and in the flux of time. To move, in a patterned way, through time, is what is meant by blossoming or dancing. But this blossoming or dancing is nothing but the normal process of events, the life of mother, child, and poet, that seemed so terrible in the preceding stanzas. For this labour blossoms or dances when we abjure the passion for 'heavenly glory'. Then, in the moment of renunciation of timelessness or immortality, the normal life of man partakes of secular blessedness, the vision of the self as opposed to the soul. So in 'Among School Children', as in 'A Dialogue of Self and Soul'; the poet tells us that when we cast out remorse, the desire for heavenly perfection that makes our life in time seem terrible, then (from 'A Dialogue of Self and Soul'):

> So great a sweetness flows into the breast
> We must laugh and we must sing,

> We are blest by everything,
> Everything we look upon is blest.

So the labour of this stanza catches both the process of birth in
time, the child's labour as he learns in school, and the school inspector's labour as he thinks his way back to the condition of the
bird that sings of life in time. But though this is labour, it is joyous. It is this play that could only be imitated when approached
from the abstract point of view of the philosophers. For what they
did was play primarily in the sense of being not the real thing,
being merely a shadowy reflection of the proper activity. And in
the final stanza we are given, not an abstraction, not a pattern
imitated, but the joyous participation in life of the whole man.

> Labour is blossoming or dancing where
> The body is not bruised to pleasure soul,
> Nor beauty born out of its own despair,
> Nor blear-eyed wisdom out of midnight oil.

In these lines the poem singles out some of the abstractions that
have marred the enterprise or labour of the race. The religious
abnegation of the nuns, because it requires us to abjure the desires
of the flesh, 'bruises' the body to pleasure soul, as do the quasi-
philosophical, quasi-theological doctrines of Plato and Pythagoras.
The wisdom of the schoolchildren, or the philosophers, is 'blear-
eyed', can only be gained by ignoring all that exists apart from the
particular abstractions under scrutiny. The image of 'blear-eyed'
wisdom born out of painful study at midnight, in the 'mad
abstract dark', suggests that this wisdom is false because it leaves
out, or blurs, so much of normal experience. Nor is the blossoming
or dancing of 'labour' like the beauty 'born out of its own despair'.
For this beauty is discovered in the search for an eternal object, and
is born out of the despair that comes from the search for the timeless in a world of time.

Against the pain caused by the fragmentation of reality and process in the search for something immortal, the poet places before
us the symbol of the chestnut tree which endures through time,
and which embodies pattern. The tree is a 'blossomer'. It produces not something eternal, but something fragile and transient.
But in doing so it is 'rooted' in what has passed and it gives pro-
mise for the future; it is an example of fruitfulness in time, a 'great-
rooted blossomer'. And it is introduced to us in the third hortatory

gesture of the poem. For the poet has begun with an intense mood of personal reminiscence which conjures up the fragmented eternal ideas of his past. And the effect produced is like that of looking at still pictures. We are not given the fragments of the past as a history, but as scenes caught forever in an unchanging medium. The movement of the lines echoes the sense in that the verse too has a stillness about it.

> I dream of a Ledaean body, bent
> Above a sinking fire...
> Her present image floats into the mind –

After the stillness and individuality of the private reminiscences we move to the quiet measured rhetoric of the next few stanzas. But once the poet has recognised himself as poet, the quality of the poetry changes drastically. For in Stanza VII the new truth produces a new vigour in the verse. The voice fills with confidence and anger as he rails against the abstractions that have caused so much despair.

> O Presences
> That passion, piety, or affection knows,
> And that all heavenly glory symbolise –
> O self-born mockers of man's enterprise...

And when the poet addresses the presences to speak to them of the life in process, in time, the verse begins to move more freely; with a quickening movement.

> Labour is blossoming or dancing where
> The body is not bruised to pleasure soul,
> Nor beauty born out if its own despair,
> Nor blear-eyed wisdom out of midnight oil.
> O chestnut-tree, great-rooted blossomer,
> Are you the leaf, the blossom or the bole?
> O body swayed to music, O brightening glance,
> How can we know the dancer from the dance?

But the rhetorical force of 'O chestnut-tree' and 'O body swayed to music' is that of ecstasy, not, as in the preceding stanzas, that of rejection. For the 'great-rooted blossomer' is in time, is the unity of leaf, blossom and bole in time, the *enduring* pattern, and enduring stuff, of reality.

So too the body swayed to music moves through time, an enduring object that moves in the world. And its motion serves to mark it off from the bodies of the preceding stanzas. For in the stanza on the woman he loved the poet has been able to conceive of her only as a monumental object, or in arrested motion, as in a snapshot – she stands, or floats, or bends, but she is seen as static, caught in a single moment in the abstraction of simple location.

But of all the images of stasis in the poem, none is more remarkable than that of Pythagoras. He sits, immobile, almost a statue, for he has thighs of gold, fingering, reducing to stasis, the music of the spheres. And in opposition to the figure of Pythagoras we have the body swayed to music of the last stanza. For it is in the conjoining of flux and pattern that we discover reality. However important we think Pythagoras's discovery of pattern, and however preferable Pythagoras's vision of it is to Plato's vision of the forms, it remains an abstraction. What is important is not the pattern, but the prehended unity in which we discover it. The dance is more than the choreographer's marks, more than a path traced in space. And the description of pattern inhering in the flux of stuff is the grasping into a prehended unity which is the 'brightening glance'. The glance discovers that we cannot discover the dancer without the enduring pattern of real events.

'The organic starting point is from the analysis of process as the realisation of events disposed in an interlocked community. The event is the unit of things real. The emergent enduring pattern is the stabilisation of the emergent achievement so as to become a fact which retains its identity throughout the process. It will be noted that endurance is not primarily the property of enduring beyond itself, but of enduring within itself. I mean that endurance is the property of finding its pattern reproduced in the temporal parts of the total event. It is in this sense that a total event carries an enduring pattern. There is an intrinsic value identical for the whole and for its succession of parts. Cognition is the emergence, into some measure of individualised reality, of the general substratum of activity, poising before itself possibility, actuality, and purpose.'[1]

For, as Whitehead said earlier in this passage, what is known must be 'a prehension of aspects of the one real universe'. The brightening glance (Whitehead's cognition) is possible only when we recognise the connexity of things. The children have looked up from their cutting and sewing to 'stare', without understanding, at

[1] Whitehead, *Science and the Modern World*, p. 138.

the figure of an aged man. And the aged man, lost in his personal reverie, has not been able to see them. For both he and they were lost in a knowledge that was 'blear-eyed', that could only see one thing at the expense of the others. But the 'brightening glance' is the recognition of connexity; the word glance itself suggests motion, as opposed to the fixity of a 'stare' or the blankness of 'blear-eyed'.

What is comprehended by the glance is the entire ambient, not dance only, not dancer only, but dancer and dance. For we cannot locate the dancer, outside the process. If we try to 'tell' the person apart from the enduring pattern we will find a 'Ledaean body' or a 'present image', that is only an abstraction, an 'eternal object', and not a dancer. And the image of the dance insists on the pattern as inhering in the actual event, and inseparable from it. For we may find an object that is the fiddle that we play, but there is no object that can be identified as a 'dance'. The body that sways to music 'dances', but when the body is removed there is no dance remaining. For the pattern must inhere in something. A pattern is a series of relationships and a series of relative positions, and in order to speak of pattern we must give up the notion of simple location. The brightening glance finds pattern in the flux of things, but finds it only because the attempt to find an immortal eternal object has been put aside. So the poem ends with two questions that have been answered even before they are asked. The blossomer is a 'great-rooted blossomer', and the glance is a brightening glance; one is a prehension of aspects of the one real universe, the other the cognition of a prehension of aspects of the one real universe. The tree, already described as a 'great-rooted blossomer' makes the question addressed to it tautologous, answers the question just by being the 'great-rooted blossomer'. In the same way, the glance, just be being bright, by encompassing the whole activity, places the question that is addressed to it in perspective. It asks of the glance that makes the universe into a unity, if the universe is a unity, which is not really to ask a question at all.

II

The two poems that immediately follow 'Among School Children' are both written out of the central perceptions embodied in it. I consider first the second of the two, 'Wisdom'.

The true faith discovered was
When painted panel, statuary,
Glass-mosaic, window-glass,
Amended what was told awry
By some peasant gospeller;
Swept the sawdust from the floor
Of that working-carpenter.
Miracle had its playtime where
In damask clothed and on a seat
Chryselephantine, cedar-boarded,
His majestic Mother sat
Stitching at a purple hoarded
That He might be nobly breeched
In starry towers of Babylon
Noah's freshet never reached.
King Abundance got Him on
Innocence; and Wisdom He.
That cognomen sounded best
Considering what wild infancy
Drove horror from His Mother's breast.

(*Collected Poems*, pp. 246–7)

If we keep in our minds what Christianity meant in the history of Western Europe, the poem is sardonic enough. Christianity was first of all a 'fabulous, formless darkness', the recredescence of the elementary human passions that had been, if not controlled, at least held partially in check by Roman civilisation. Again and again Yeats stresses the violence, the essential mystery, involved in the story of Christ. In 'A Stick of Incense' Yeats insists that the only way to understand the events of the Christ story are to place it in a context of human passion and lust, to see Christianity as an eruption from the passionate world that underlies whatever patterns men are able to impose on their experience, and not as an instance of divine intervention.

A STICK OF INCENSE

Whence did all that fury come?
From empty tomb or Virgin womb?
Saint Joseph thought the world would melt
But liked the way his finger smelt.

(*Collected Poems*, p. 383)

We have seen how, in the poems in which Yeats expresses pessimism and fear because of what seems to be the direction and progress of history, the force which seems to threaten man is not some malevolent god, but rather the turbulence and hatred of man himself. 'Wisdom' insists on this conception of Christ and Christianity. Christ has been bred out of innocence, the murderous innocence of the absence of pattern, not the innocence of custom and ceremony, and abundance, the energy and passion of man. We know this by virtue of the wildness of his infancy. This wildness is so frightening that it does not horrify his mother, but stupefies her (drives horror from her breast), and so it must be disguised. So we get the irony of 'cognomen'. Faced with this horror, this fall into barbarism, we call the child 'wisdom'. And the 'true faith' is discovered in the act of denying the horror. Instead of the pain, frustration and waste that accompany the major historical and intellectual upheaveals in society – the sawdust of the working carpenter – we have the image that keeps a marble or a bronze repose. Instead of the terrible infant we have the 'eternal idea', 'nobly breeched/In starry towers of Babylon'. The absurdity of all this is made clear with we are told that the starry towers are towers that 'Noah's freshet never reached.' The irony of the poem concentrates our attention on the process by which the 'eternal idea' is created out of the mess, the flux of things, and how, once it is created, it is enthroned in a splendour and seriousness and stillness above the flux of events (the sawdust created by the working carpenter, or Noah's freshet). But once enthroned in this splendour it becomes a pretty and irrelevant joke. It isn't true, but it is the lie that we want. So it is the 'true faith' enshrined 'on a seat/Chryselephantine, cedar-boarded,' and misnamed wisdom, which disguises the central facts of experience which provided the original impetus to faith.

'Wisdom' is simply an ironic recapitulation of the human capacity to abjure the living reality for a mental construct. But in 'Colonus' Praise' Yeats explores the point of view discussed in the last stanza of 'Among School Children'.

COLONUS' PRAISE

Chorus. Come praise Colonus' horses, and come praise
The wine-dark of the wood's intricacies
The nightingale that deafens daylight there,

If daylight ever visit where,
Unvisited by tempest or by sun,
Immortal ladies tread the ground
Dizzy with harmonious sound,
Semele's lad a gay companion.

And yonder in the gymnasts' garden thrives
The self-sown, self-begotten shape that gives
Athenian intellect its mastery,
Even the grey-leaved olive-tree
Miracle-bred out of the living stone;
Nor accident of peace nor war
Shall whither that old marvel, for
The great grey-eyed Athene stares thereon.

Who comes into this country, and has come
Where golden crocus and narcissus bloom,
Where the Great Mother, mourning for her daughter
And beauty-drunken by the water
Glittering among grey-leaved olive-trees,
Has plucked a flower and sung her loss;
Who finds abounding Cephisus
Has found the loveliest spectacle there is.

Because this country has a pious mind
And so remembers that when all mankind
But trod the road, or splashed about the shore,
Poseidon gave it bit and oar,
Every Colonus lad or lass discourses
Of that oar and of that bit;
Summer and winter, day and night,
Of horses and horses of the sea, white horses.

I ignore certain theoretical questions in contemplating this poem.
Since 'Colonus' Praise' was published as part of Yeats's translation
of Sophocles's play, one might be tempted to treat the poem as
essentially part of the play, and essentially Sophocles's. But Yeats
published this poem independently, and I shall treat it as an independent production; I assume that we may safely ask what Yeats
meant, and ignore Sophocles.

Let us begin with the olive-tree of the second stanza. It is instructive to note that the olive-tree in this poem embodies the value of
abstraction; it becomes a symbol for Platonic Forms or Abstract
Ideas, for the whole world of intellectual self-sufficiency that is

embodied in the 'presences' of 'Among School Children'. Just as these presences are 'self-born', the olive-tree is 'self-sown' and 'self-begotten'. The olive-tree becomes a symbol for the ontological difference that marks off ideas from anything considered from within the manifold of time and space. But the olive-tree, like the presences of 'Among School Children', is not found in an independently subsisting world that can be captured by an analogy between that special world and the world of sense. Ideas or concepts or forms are independent of space and time just because they don't exist in the world in the way objects, persons etc., exist. They are part of our conceptual apparatus and it is just because they are a part of our conceptual apparatus that they resist change.

> Nor accident of peace nor war
> Shall wither that old marvel, for
> The great grey-eyed Athene stares thereon.

It is the stare that fructifies and guarantees the abstract; it is the human mind that, by attending to the abstract and formal, creates the pattern of existence, and so makes possible the prehended unity of human experience. So we see that this appreciation of the role of abstractions in human life springs from the perception that Yeats struggles[1] towards in 'Among School Children'. For in that poem he is interested in presenting a reasoned argument for abandoning one sort of notion about the role of abstract thought for another which he thinks more valuable. But 'Colonus' Praise' assumes as given the conceptual scheme that is discovered in 'Among School Children'. For the equivalent to the dance that concludes 'Among School Children', is given to us in the first stanza of 'Colonus' Praise'.

> Unvisited by tempest or by sun,
> Immortal ladies tread the ground
> Dizzy with harmonious sound,
> Semele's lad a gay companion.

Perhaps the most effective way to place this poem is to examine the intellectual superstructure through which Yeats probably viewed Sophocles. Yeats's familiarity with the tradition of neo-Platonism has been discussed; and one source in particular, Porphyry's essay 'On the Cave of the Nymphs' (cf. Appendix B, p. 240)

---

[1] We are, of course, talking about poetic strategy and not about how Yeats's ideas really developed.

has been given special prominence. The emphasis on this essay is arbitrary, in that the ideas and images in the essay were known to Yeats from a great many sources. But the emphasis is Yeats's in that he himself cites the essay whenever he talks of his sources. The 'honey of generation' that he talks of in 'Among School Children', was a common image that Yeats knew from a number of separate sources, but in his note he specifies Porphyry's essay as his source. In his essay on Shelley's neo-Platonism he again concentrates his attention on this particular essay, rather than talking more widely of the tradition. One important reason Yeats may have had for making the essay his touch-stone for the neo-Platonic tradition was that it is unusual in that instead of being just the adumbration of doctrine, it is a formal piece of literary criticism, in which Porphyry sets out to explicate a passage of fourteen lines from Homer. Both as a source of Platonic images and as one of the oldest examples of literary criticism the essay is interesting. If one were to put aside the question of Porphyry's obvious belief in neo-Platonism, one might take the essay as the first example of 'new criticism', or at least the first serious attempt at *explication de texte*, in that Porphyry carefully examines every image in the passage as part of a deliberate fiction that has to be interpreted. For instance:

One particular, however, remains to be explained, and that is the symbol of the olive planted at the top of the cavern; since Homer appears to indicate something very admirable by giving it such a position. For he does not merely say that an olive grows in this place, but that it flourishes on the summit of the cavern.

> 'High at the head a branching olive grows,
> Beneath, a gloomy grotto's cool recess.'

But the growth of the olive in such a situation, is not fortuitous, as some one may suspect, but contains the enigma of the cavern. For since the world was not produced rashly and casually, but is the work of divine wisdom and an intellectual nature, hence an olive, the symbol of this wisdom, flourishes near the present cavern, which is an image of the world. For the olive is the plant of Minerva; and Minerva is wisdom. But this Goddess being produced from the head of Jupiter, the theologist has discovered an appropriate place for the olive, by consecrating it at the summit of the port; signifying by this, that the universe is not the effect of a casual event, and the work of irrational fortune, but that it is the offspring of an intellectual nature and divine wisdom, which is separated, indeed, from it [by a difference of essence], but yet is near to it, through being established on the summit of the whole port...

Yeats's interest in neo-Platonism sprang from the fact that the tradition was rich in images that could be manipulated within a poetry that was not necessarily Platonic in spirit. Yeats found, in Porphyry's essay, a kind of attention to poetry, and a lexicon of images, that he could find nowhere else. That is, in this essay the relevance of neo-Platonic habits (of manipulating images and interpreting them within a philosophical framework) to poetry is made explicit. The realisation of the value of these habits did not mean, of course, that Yeats was convinced by Porphyry that Homer was a Platonist. Nor does Yeats's use of his neo-Platonist reading to provide a structure of meaning for Sophocles's choral song mean that he thought Sophocles's poetry should be given a neo-Platonic reading. He simply uses what comes to hand in order to write his own poem. The images of 'Colonus' Praise' are all interpreted in Porphyry's essay, and indeed in the tradition as a whole. What Yeats wants in the first stanza of the poem is to create an image of fecundity and sensuality. Given Sophocles's text, and Taylor's footnote in Yeats's edition of Porphyry's essay –

'Nymphs', says Hermias, in his Scholia on the Phaedrus of Plato, 'are Goddesses who preside over regeneration, and are ministrant to Bacchus, the offspring of Semele. Hence they dwell near water, that is, they are conversant with generation. But this Bacchus supplies the regeneration of the whole sensible world.'

– Yeats can create the luxurious verse of the first stanza, with its intricacy of pattern, its luxuriant song, and its womb-like darkness.

> *Chorus.* Come praise Colonus' horses, and come praise
> The wine-dark of the wood's intricacies,
> The nightingale that deafens daylight there,
> If daylight ever visit where,
> Unvisited by tempest or by sun,
> Immortal ladies tread the ground
> Dizzy with harmonious sound,
> Semele's lad a gay companion.

The relationship between the fecundity of the first stanza, and the abstract clarity of the second is inherent in the relationship between the tree and the stone, on the one hand, and the tree and Athene's stare on the other.

And the world being spontaneously produced (i.e. being produced by no external, but from an internal cause), and being also self-adherent, is allied to matter; which, according to a secret signification, is denominated a *stone* and a rock on account of its sluggish and repercussive nature with respect to form: the ancients, at the same time, asserting that matter is infinite through its privation of form.

The 'living stone' of the second stanza represents the harshness of the world without the addition of form. The stone is simply what is given, the world as an intransient and ongoing entity, that is harsh and formless.

Through matter, therefore, the world is obscure and dark; but through the connecting power, and orderly distribution of form, from which also it is called *world*, it is beautiful and delightful...

The perception of form is, in Yeats's poem, bred out of the stone. For the Platonist form is prior to, and more important than, the world. It is imposed from above, as it were. But in Yeats's poem form springs from matter; Athene's tree is 'miracle-bred out of the living stone'. Form is apprehended as 'inherent' in all experience, and inseparable from the possibility of experience. But form remains epistemologically of a different order than the objects of experience – the tree cannot 'wither' – just because form is a necessary condition of experience, just because the 'stare' of Athene is itself the symbol for the epistemic necessity of form. In the prehended unity of perception that Whitehead talks of, form is given in perception as a part of what we perceive; it is 'miracle-bred out of the living stone'. This is because form is the basis of perception. But, from the point of view of the kind of existence possessed by ideas as opposed to things, forms are 'self-sown, self-begotten'. All the philosophical complexities of 'Among School Children' are caught up and abbreviated in the second stanza of 'Colonus' Praise'.

The third stanza of the poem is, if possible, even more wrought than the first two. Those stanzas exhibited Yeats's talent for creating rhythmic verse about the most complex of issues. In the third stanza the verse has an added power that springs from the dramatic effect created by the way the poem avoids naming Oedipus ('who comes into this country, and has come...'). The regular rhythm in the stanza, and the repetitive use of 'who', create a rhetorical strength that does not disturb the delicacy of the lyric. In terms of sound, this stanza, indeed the whole poem, is Yeats's finest. But the poem is far more than sound. To see how the stanza works we might consider a passage from 'A Packet for Ezra Pound':

I send you the introduction of a book which will, when finished, proclaim a new divinity. Oedipus lay upon the earth at the middle point between four sacred objects, was there washed as the dead are washed, and thereupon passed with Theseus to the wood's heart until amidst the sound of thunder earth opened, 'riven by love', and he sank down soul and body into the earth. I would have him balance Christ who, crucified standing up, went into the abstract sky soul and body, and I see him altogether separated from Plato's Athens, from all that talk of the Good and the One, from all that cabinet of perfection, an image from Homer's age.[1]

The passion of Oedipus represents for Yeats the application of the whole mind to this life, and the passion of Christ represents for him the process of abstraction from life that he finds in both Platonism and Christianity. Once we are prepared to acknowledge the continuing force of Christianity and Platonism in our intellectual traditions, and in our daily life, we see why Yeats writes so often and so passionately of these issues. Before we can fully understand this stanza, however, we must ask what we are to make of the other 'characters' in the poem. What, for instance, does the story of Demeter and Persephone have to do with the issues under discussion?

The traditional Greek myths play a major role in the neo-Platonic system of imagery. A number of these stories were used to explicate a particular difficulty that appears as a consequence of their sort of idealism. Given that forms are, for the Platonist, really existent entities that are not in space and time, there is a hiatus between the world of sense and the world of ideas that cannot be closed. Without becoming embroiled in the philosophical issues raised for the Platonists one may note that they multiply myths to indicate the nature of the relationship between ideas and reality. Since ideas are not in space or time, figures like Apollo and Athene can be spoken of as intellectual Gods. But they are, for that reason, unable to act in the world. The job of 'energizing providentially', that is of creating the (for the Platonist) similitude between the two worlds of formed matter and ideas, falls in the province of lower Gods (e.g. the naiads of Porphyry's essay), and into the province of those Gods who die, or are otherwise not so clearly heavenly as Apollo or Athene. Thus Porphyry says

Thus, also, Proserpine, who is the inspective guardian of every thing produced from seed, is represented by Orpheus as weaving a web; and the

---

[1] Yeats, *A Vision*, p. 27.

heavens are called by the ancients a veil, in consequence of being, as it were, the vestment of the celestial Gods.

And the footnote that Taylor adds goes on to explain.

The theological meaning of this Orphic fiction is beautifully unfolded by Proclus, as follows: 'Orpheus says that the vivific cause of partible natures [i.e. Prosperpine], while she remained on high, weaving the order of celestials, was a nymph, as being undefiled; and in consequence of this connected with Jupiter, and abiding in her appropriate manners; but that, proceeding from her proper habitation, she left her webs unfinished, was ravished; having been ravished, was married; and being married she generated, in order that she might animate things which have an adventitious life. For the unfinished state of her webs indicates, I think, that the universe is imperfect or unfinished, as far as to perpetual animals [i.e. The universe would be imperfect if nothing inferior to the celestial Gods was produced]. Hence Plato says, that the one Demiurgus calls on the many Demiurgi to weave together the mortal and immortal natures; after a manner reminding us, that the addition of the mortal genera is the perfection of the textorial life of the universe, and also exciting our recollection of the divine Orphic fable, and affording us interpretative causes of the unfinished webs of Prosperpine'. See vol. ii. p. 356, of my translation of Proclus on the Timaeus.

This interpretation of the Rape of Persephone is one of the more important neo-Platonic images, and it forms part of a group that contains amongst other stories, the story of Bacchus, and Narcissus's fall into generation when he fell in love with his own image in water (i.e. matter). Of course, the Narcissus story is obliquely relevant to the verse in that the narcissus flowers 'bloom' in the region where Yeats locates the Great Mother and Oedipus. What Yeats is after may be described as a kind of instantiation in which form is seen as firmly wedded to matter. The reason that Yeats speaks of the Great Mother as 'beauty-drunken by the water' can be garnered from these passages.

As soon, therefore, as the soul gravitates towards body in this first production of herself, she begins to experience a material tumult, that is, matter flowing into her essence. And this is what Plato remarks in the Phaedo, that the soul is drawn into body staggering with recent intoxication; signifying by this, the new drink of matter's impetuous flood, through which the soul, becoming defiled and heavy, is drawn into a terrene situation.

Thus, too, Ceres educated Prosperpine, with her Nymphs, in a cave;

and many other particulars of this kind may be found in the writings of
theologists. But that the ancients dedicated caverns to Nymphs, and
especially to the Naiades, who dwell near fountains, and who are called
Naiades from the streams over which they preside, is manifest from the
hymn to Apollo, in which it is said: 'The Nymphs residing in caves shall
deduce fountains of intellectual waters to thee, (according to the divine
voice of the Muses,) which are the progeny of a terrene spirit. Hence waters,
bursting through every river, shall exhibit to mankind perpetual effusions
of sweet streams.'

'Abounding Cephisus' then becomes a symbol for the inter-play
between matter and form. More exactly, we should say that it is a
symbol for the inextricability of one from the other in the world.
For Yeats is not interested in the abstract pattern of Christian
thought, nor in Plato's cabinet of perfection. His poem is a celebration of the intricate pattern of life itself.

The richness and complexity of the pattern of the actual as it
displays itself through time presents itself as a kind of salvation
because what we need to be saved from is the mistaken attempt to
locate ideas and form outside the pattern of the actual, in order to
find 'heavenly glory'. The 'labour' of 'Among School Children'
is only possible in the world of Oedipus, the world of the marriage
of form and matter that is 'the loveliest spectacle there is'.

The neo-Platonists took the sea to be a symbol for the material
world. In the last stanza we are told of the intellectual discipline
that will make possible the discovery of the 'loveliest spectacle',
the discovery of the union of matter and form.

> Because this country has a pious mind
> And so remembers that when all mankind
> But trod the road, or splashed about the shore,
> Poseidon gave it bit and oar,
> Every Colonus lad or lass discourses
> Of that oar and of that bit;
> Summer and winter, day and night,
> Of horses and horses of the sea, white horses.

According to Porphyry Poseidon is the guardian of middle
natures; his realm lies between that of his heavenly brother and his
hellish brother. In Section 17 of Porphyry's essay Yeats would have
learned, if he had not already known it, that for the neo-Platonist
'the deep, the sea, and a tempest are images of a material nature'.
In this section Porphyry uses the traditional neo-Platonist gloss of

the Ulysses story to illustrate the way that man can free himself from this world.

On this account, too, a seat under the olive is proper to Ulysses, as to one who implores divinity, and would appease his natal daemon with a suppliant branch. For it will not be simply, and in a concise way, possible for any one to be liberated from this sensible life, who blinds this daemon, and renders his energies inefficacious; but he who dares to do this, will be pursued by the anger of the marine and material Gods, whom it is first requisite to appease by sacrifices, labours, and patient endurance; at one time, indeed, contending with the passions, and at another employing enchantments and deceptions, and by these, transforming himself in an all-various manner; in order that, being at length divested of the torn garments [by which his true person was concealed], he may recover the ruined empire of his soul. Nor will he even then be liberated from labours; but this will be effected when he has entirely passed over the raging sea, and, though still living, becomes so ignorant of marine and material works [through deep attention to intelligible concerns], as to mistake an oar for a corn-van.

For the neo-Platonist this life is a trap, and the god that presides over it is to be placated, so that eventually we may escape him. But Yeats's piety is not of this sort. The gifts of Poseidon are to be welcomed because they allow men to live in this world. The bit and oar are symbols for man's love of this world, and for his strenuous commitment to the world. The sinuous and muscular rhythm of the section is in itself a symbol for our commitment to the rhythm of physical existence embodied in the natural rhythms of summer and winter, day and night. Rather than achieving that abstract apotheosis of the heavens, we choose the passionate incarnation of Oedipus. We have a love of form in matter that exults in the play of time and change, a love of that fluid and elastic interplay of form in matter that has always found its symbol in the movements of a horse or the regularity and strength of the sea. We have come to love our life, to love 'horses, and horses of the sea, white horses'.

8

Conclusions

My original object in writing this book was to show how what Yeats had written in the twentieth century placed him squarely in the tradition of English romanticism. I took 'romanticism' to be a term best handled by reference to certain ideas which I characterised as Kantian. During the period in which the book was written there have been developments both in literary criticism and in other fields which have made my task easier. It is to these peripheral matters that I briefly turn my attention.

That English philosophy has been dominated by the empirical turn of mind best represented by Locke and Hume has long been a truism. The fact that those who were philosophers were less sure of the truism than those who were not in no way mitigated the scorn generally felt in the English-speaking world for ideas that lay outside the English empiricist tradition. It is my guess that the negative reaction to Yeats's 'ideas' was based, at least in part, on the belief widely held by those interested in literature, that Yeats's philosophical speculations, just because they lay outside the empirical tradition, were not only wrong, but not worth considering seriously. When Auden wrote of Yeats 'you were silly like us' he was expressing a sentiment often expressed – that Yeats wrote good poetry although what he believed, and therefore said, was nonsense. His gift, or his poetry, according to Auden and others, 'survived' the unfortunate fact that what he said was non-sense.

In Chapter 3 I discussed the role of historical British empiricism and of its most popular modern manifestation, logical positivism, in creating a climate in which it was possible to suppose that poetry should be excluded from the realm of meaningful discourse. The fact that it has been widely held that poetry is 'pseudo-statement' provided a psychological excuse for a weak-minded approach to the relationship between Yeats's ideas and his thought, and to the question of meaning and poetry in general. Strictly speaking, if you accept Richards's notion of pseudo-statement, or any other notion that separates poetry from meaningful discourse, there is no problem. If all poetry is meaningless, then all poetry is meaningless; and the particular ideas of a particular poet are of no matter to the literary critic as distinct from the biographer or historian, since they cannot be found in his poems. However, what has happened is that a general climate has been created in which it is possible to believe that poetry and ideas have some tenuous connections, but that the value of the poetry is independent of the value of the ideas. Now, as I argued in Chapter 3, it seems to me that this position has, as a matter of historic fact, been a response to the pressures that have arisen from the empiricist notion of meaning, and the widely held belief that that notion of meaning showed that poetry was meaningless. But as a reply to a logical positivist who claims that poetry is meaningless (and for that particular reason only, worthless) the argument, if it is an argument, doesn't get off the ground. However, it is normally coupled with a claim about the value of 'art', and that argument at least could do what the anti-positivists hope to do – which is show that poetry has a value. But although one might make a case for the value of poetry without claiming that it is meaningful, you can't simply backtrack and re-introduce meaning just because you have claimed poetry is valuable. To do so is simply to return to the original position without offering any real defence. We could ignore this particular bit of sloppy thinking if it were not the case that because people have held a position like this they could claim both that Yeats was a great poet, and that what his poems said was nonsense.[1] For anyone who holds, as I do, that poetry is a form of meaningful discourse, there is a *prima facie* case that anything that counts against what a poem 'says' counts against the value of the poem. That is, if poetry is a form of meaningful discourse, the value of what is said must be one of the important criteria for judging the value of a poem. Yvor Winters agrees with Auden that what Yeats says in his poems is silly; but Winters has the grace to conclude that silly poetry is bad poetry. Conversely, for anyone who believes that poetry is meaningful discourse, an essential element in establishing the worth of a body of poetry is to understand it, and show how it makes sense. That is a more general objective than to demonstrate that Yeats's poetry belongs in the tradition of Western romanticism, but one

---

[1] If you take Richards's position, Yeats's poetry does not mean anything at all, and to ask what it means is 'an incorrect response'.

which is equally adequate as a description of what I have attempted in this book.

The question which follows almost immediately from what I have said is one about the relationship between 'making sense' and truth and falsity. I am not here referring to the question whether or not there are true and false propositions in poems – that question was discussed in Chapter 3. I am interested in considering the natural doubt that occurs to anyone who believes that poetry is meaningful; does that mean that some are simply false? The question can be reformulated in terms of what was said in Chapter 3: it is not the poem or the statement in the poem which would then be false, but the statements in an adequate interpretation which would be true or false. But that would not answer the doubt which prompted the question because the doubt was prompted by the feeling that some poems are good even though we thoroughly disagree with them. This difficulty arises because we have a simplified model of intellectual activity in non-literary fields. If we remember that we take e.g. Marx, Freud, and Hume seriously, even though we are not Marxists, Freudians and so on, we see that the simple model of the white-coated scientist ticking off true and false conclusions is a trap. We do not totally reject Marx because we think that he is wrong *simpliciter*: what he said is too complex, interesting and powerful to be so dismissed. So may we react to a poem or novel that seems to us to be 'wrong'. What we normally do is use a more adequate and complicated model of intellectual activity than the one we are prepared to state. In fact, when we examine the way we make intellectual judgments we realise it is only rarely that we are prepared to abandon criteria like coherence, breadth, originality and complexity.[1]

In effect, what I have been doing in this book fits this general description. I have not been arguing that Yeats is 'right' *simpliciter*; but only that he speaks from within a tradition that has a legitimate claim on our attention, and that his poetry shares the characteristics that give the tradition a right to our serious attention. In claiming that Yeats's position as an 'idealist' in philosophy was respectable I made in effect, two claims. One was that, from within the frame-

---

[1] Only propositions can be true or false. Theories are adequate or inadequate, powerful or weak, etc...Poems should be regarded as theory-like, and our characterisation of them as cognitive constructs should be in the terms we use to describe theories and not propositions.

work of idealism what Yeats said was coherent and intelligent, and the second was that idealism itself is, not simply true or false, but a coherent and respectable approach to genuine philosophical problems. In attempting the task I have run a risk inherent in literary criticism. Literary studies has as its object the interpretation of works of fiction. In this it differs from mathematics or physics and most traditional disciplines, which have as the object of study either natural phenomena or a certain sort of human behaviour or the manipulation of a closed system. The critic must follow where the poet or novelist leads, and the poet or novelist leads where he will. Yeats talks of large philosophical issues, and I, who have no philosophical credentials, have had to follow. What professional competence I or any other critic can muster is useful in determining the interpretation of an individual poem. But with respect to deciding about the worth of the ideas expressed in a poem or novel neither I nor any other critic can claim a special competence or training. And it is for this reason that I have avoided as far as possible any claims about the philosophical questions that have been raised in the book. I will not now throw that prudence to the wind – but I will address myself to a related question – that of the role and place of idealist beliefs in the English-speaking world.

In the last decade the easy belief in the English-speaking world that empiricism made obvious sense and idealism obvious nonsense has been challenged. The challenge has come from a number of quarters; from academic philosophy, from anthropology, from linguistics, and from literary criticism. One might begin by considering 'the new linguistics', which seems to be in the process of discovering Descartes's universal grammar, or Lévi-Strauss's structuralism, or the philosophers' re-discovery of Kant and what Strawson calls 'descriptive metaphysics', or Quine's marvellous pragmaticism,[1] a pragmaticism that seems to claim that there is in the world exactly what we need to think the thoughts we want to think and no more and no less. What unites these disparate areas

---

[1] Quine is clearly in the empiricist tradition. But Quine's empiricism is not the sort that Yeats found objectionable because it provides the sort of scope for what Quine calls the 'creative imagination' that Yeats's idealism was intended to provide. When I speak of a rationalist revival I am thinking primarily of developments outside philosophy. Within the discipline of philosophy as practised in English-speaking universities it would be more proper to speak of an empiricism that has turned itself inside out, so that it is able to accommodate ideas that previously seemed tenable only within the idealist tradition.

of thought is the re-introduction of ideas that are profoundly un-empirical, that belong properly to the rationalist and idealist tradition of Western thought. Whether, 300 years from now, people will speak of the second half of the twentieth century as a rationalist or idealist revival I do not know. But if the thinkers prominent in their minds when they speak of our age are men like Chomsky, Lévi-Strauss, Quine, and the numerous literary critics working on, e.g. neo-Platonism and the Romantics, they will. Yeats's poetry is properly viewed as an early example of the shift that is now taking place from an empiricist to an idealist or rationalist model. Many of the issues now being canvassed in these areas are canvassed in his poetry. If what has happened is that we have begun to escape an empiricist strait-jacket that had become more of a disadvantage than an advantage, then it will be possible for Yeats's future audience to read his poetry without our contemporary sense of reading something strange and outlandish.

It is only when we are familiar with Yeats's philosophical ideas that we can begin to appreciate his foremost virtue – his largeness of mind. Yeats's speculations about philosophical questions are, I believe, especially useful in thinking about his poetry because they occupy a level of generality not achieved in, say, his love poetry. But this level of generality is useful only because Yeats's thought is all of a piece; because he did not think of philosophical issues on Monday, and love on Wednesday, but thought of both with his whole mind. We have seen how the thrust of Yeats's philosophical poems is to discover the nature of mental activity, and to develop a critique of abstraction that does justice to the importance of ideas, but which at the same time delivers us from what Whitehead called the 'fallacy of misplaced concreteness'. When we examine poems like 'For Anne Gregory' or 'Michael Robartes and the Dancer', or 'Solomon and the Witch' we find the same issues raised. In 'For Anne Gregory', for example, Yeats is able to see clearly the relationship between certain traditional problems in Western philosophy and the agony of growing up in our contemporary world.

FOR ANNE GREGORY

'Never shall a young man,
Thrown into despair
By those great honey-coloured

Ramparts at your ear,
Love you for yourself alone
And not your yellow hair.'

'But I can get a hair-dye
And set such colour there,
Brown, or black, or carrot,
That young men in despair
May love me for myself alone
And not my yellow hair.'

'I heard an old religious man
But yesternight declare
That he had found a text to prove
That only God, my dear,
Could love you for yourself alone
And not your yellow hair.'

(*Collected Poems*, p. 277)

What is in current psychological jargon called an identity crisis, is for Yeats the product of that traditional Western essentialism that begins with Plato and Pythagoras. In using the almost redundant phrase 'yourself alone' he can create the illusion of youthful earnestness striving towards the central mystery that we all recognise as one of the central experiences of adolescence. The sense of striving toward a central mystery is furthered by the use of the word 'ramparts'. The girl's beauty (her hair) is a sort of perversely natural and unwanted barricade to her essential self. In suggesting that 'only God' can love the girl in the way she wishes to be loved – 'only God, my dear/Could love you for yourself alone' – Yeats compresses the whole argument of 'Among School Children'. For he is reminding us that life as all of us must live it is composed of the full panoply of the physical world; that it is only God who can deal in essences. We are aware that we are the sum total of our life, the product of all we have experienced, and that our essential self is only an abstraction...But we must notice the tact of the poem. For the man speaking to the girl does not make a personal claim to this wisdom. He says he heard this from an 'an old religious man'. In the fictional speaker we have a tolerant man who recognises that the adolescent desire of the young girl has something in common with the religious impulse behind Christianity. So he invokes an authority that the girl will trust. Of course, for the reader, the effect is more complicated. For we have been enlisted in the struggle to

235

educate the earnest and beautiful young lady, and to co-operate in inventing, with the speaker, the old religious man. We are wiser than both the religious man and the girl, for we share the wisdom of the speaker, who is so far from being taken in by religion and other forms of essentialism that he can choose this tactful way to caution the girl, rather than a more direct approach. And, if we fall in fully with the mood of the poem, there is one more gentle irony. We are manipulated into the realisation that if this girl must not be loved for her essential self, then we must maintain a certain distance from a God that could love her for herself alone. We are placed firmly in the world of yellow hair. An examination of Yeats's love poems would show that often they are about issues related to philosophical issues in a fashion similar to 'For Anne Gregory'. But that does not mean that they are philosophical poems in disguise. It is simply that Yeats has seen a connection between personal life and the tradition of Western thought that illuminates both. The same remark can be made about his political poetry, for political ideals such as that of a free Ireland may be a 'presence' that breaks hearts, or an idea that shapes the future, or both

> We know their dream; enough
> To know they dreamed and are dead;
> And what if excess of love
> Bewildered them till they died?
> I write it out in a verse –
> MacDonagh and MacBride
> And Connolly and Pearse
> Now and in time to be,
> Wherever green is worn,
> Are changed, changed utterly:
> A terrible beauty is born.
>
> from 'Easter 1916' (*Collected Poems*, p. 205)

In a sense it is true to say that Yeats wrote the same poem time after time – for at a certain high level of generality we can reduce the poems to a doctrine. But because he had so firm a grasp of the complexities of life he was able to root his philosophical specula-tions in the full range of human experience. For example, it is possible to say of 'Solomon and the Witch' that it simply means that ideals are useful as ideals and not as estimates of what is really possible; that recognising that they are *only* ideals is a precondition of their usefulness. Said so, the poem is no more interesting than

Browning's homily about reaches, heavens, and grasps. But Browning can only deal with the question in a heavy-handed way. Yeats's poem is about a man and a woman deciding to make love once more, and in being about something at once as trivial as copulation, and as important as love ('O! Solomon! let us try again'), Yeats is able to show us a way to a freedom from the tyranny of ideals without denigrating their importance. His greatness is partly his ability to think through his position, and to see connections that most of us have not been prepared to see, and so to deliver us into a world that is a complex whole.

> Labour is blossoming or dancing where
> The body is not bruised to pleasure soul,
> Nor beauty born out of its own despair,
> Nor blear-eyed wisdom out of midnight oil.
> O chestnut-tree, great-rooted blossomer,
> Are you the leaf, the blossom or the bole?
> O body swayed to music, O brightening glance,
> How can we know the dancer from the dance?

'The Genealogical Tree of Revolution'

I

NICHOLAS OF CUSA
KANT RESTATES THE ANTINOMIES
HEGEL BELIEVES THAT HE HAS SOLVED THEM WITH HIS
DIALECTIC THESIS: ANTITHESIS: SYNTHESIS
ALL THINGS TRANSPARENT TO REASON

II

DIALECTICAL MATERIALISM
(KARL MARX AND SCHOOL)
a. Nature creates Spirit.
Brain creates Mind.
Only the reasonable should
exist.
Evolution.
b. Dialectic as conflict of classes.
Each class denied by its
successor.
History, a struggle for food;
science, art, religions, but
cries of the hunting pack.

c. The past is criminal.
Hatred justified.
The Party is above the State.

d. Final aim: Communism.
Individual, class, nations
lost in the whole.
e. The Proletariat justified, because,
having nothing, it
can reject all.

III

ITALIAN PHILOSOPHY
(INFLUENCED BY VICO)
a. Spirit creates Nature.
Mind creates Brain.
All that exists is
reasonable.
Platonic reminiscence.
b. Dialectic rejected.
Conflicts are between
positives ('distincts').
Civilisation, the rise of
classes and their return
to the mass bringing
their gifts.
c. The past is honoured.
Hatred is condemned.
The State is above the
Party.
d. Final aim: Fascism.
Individual, class, nation
a process of the whole.
e. History, now transparent
to reason, justified.

IV

A RACE PHILOSOPHY

The antinomies cannot be solved.
Man cannot understand Nature because he has not made it. (Vico.)
Communism, Fascism, are inadequate because society is the struggle of two
forces not transparent to reason – the family and the individual.
From the struggle of the individual to make and preserve himself comes intel-
lectual initiative.

From the struggle to found and preserve the family come good taste and good habits.

Equality of opportunity, equality of rights, have been created to assist the individual in his struggle.

Inherited wealth, privilege (*sic*), precedence, have been created to preserve the family in its struggle.

The business of Government is not to abate either struggle but to see that individual and family triumph by adding to Spiritual and material wealth.

Materially and Spiritually uncreative families or individuals must not be allowed to triumph over the creative.

Individual and family have a right to their gains but Government has a right to put a limit to those gains.

If a limit is set it must be such as permits a complete culture to individual and family; it must leave to the successful family, for instance, the power to prolong for as many years as that family thinks necessary the education of its children.

It must not be forgotten that Race, which has for its flower the family and the individual, is wiser than Government, and that it is the source of all initiative.[1]

[1] Yeats, Unpublished paper quoted by Ellmann in *The Identity of Yeats*, p. 351.

Thomas Taylor's edition of Porphyry's essay 'On the Cave of the Nymphs, in the thirteenth book of the Odyssey'

1. What does Homer obscurely signify by the cave in Ithaca, which he describes in the following verses?

> High at the head a branching olive grows,
> And crowns the pointed cliffs with shady boughs.
> A cavern pleasant, though involv'd in night,
> Beneath it lies, the Naiades' delight:
> Where bowls and urns of workmanship divine
> And massy beams in native marble shine;
> On which the Nymphs amazing webs display,
> Of purple hue, and exquisite array.
> The busy bees within the urns secure
> Honey delicious, and like nectar pure.
> Perpetual waters through the grotto glide,
> A lofty gate unfolds on either side;
> That to the north is pervious to mankind;
> The sacred south t' immortals is consign'd.

That the poet, indeed, does not narrate these particulars from historical information, is evident from this, that those who have given us a description of the island, have, as Cronius[a] says, made no mention of such a cave being found in it. This likewise, says he, is manifest, that it would be absurd for Homer to expect, that in describing a cave fabricated merely by poetical license, and thus artificially opening a path to Gods and men in the region of Ithaca, he should gain the belief of mankind. And it is equally absurd to suppose, that nature herself should point out, in this place, one path for the descent of all mankind, and again another path for all the Gods. For, indeed, the whole world is full of Gods and men: but it is impossible to be persuaded, that in the Ithacensian cave men descend, and Gods ascend. Cronius, therefore, having premised thus much, says, that it is evident, not only to the wise but also to

---

[a] This Cronius, the Pythagorean, is also mentioned by Porphyry, in his Life of Plotinus.

the vulgar, that the poet, under the veil of allegory, conceals some mysterious signification; thus compelling others to explore what the gate of men is, and also what is the gate of the Gods: what he means by asserting that this cave of the Nymphs has two gates; and why it is both pleasant and obscure, since darkness is by no means delightful, but is rather productive of aversion and horror. Likewise, what is the reason why it is not simply said to be the cave of the Nymphs, but it is accurately added, of the Nymphs which are called Naiades? Why, also, is the cave represented as containing bowls and amphoræ, when no mention is made of their receiving any liquor, but bees are said to deposit their honey in these vessels as in hives? Then, again, why are oblong beams adapted to weaving placed here for the Nymphs; and these not formed from wood, or any other pliable matter, but from stone, as well as the amphoræ and bowls? Which last circumstance is, indeed, less obscure; but that, on these stony beams, the Nymphs should weave purple garments, is not only wonderful to the sight, but also to the auditory sense. For who would believe that Goddesses weave garments in a cave involved in darkness, and on stony beams; especially while he hears the poet asserting, that the purple webs of the Goddesses were visible. In addition to these things likewise, this is admirable, that the cave should have a twofold entrance; one made for the descent of men, but the other for the ascent of Gods. And again, that the gate, which is pervious by men, should be said to be turned towards the north wind, but the portal of the Gods to the south; and why the poet did not rather make use of the west and the east for this purpose; since nearly all temples have their statues and entrances turned towards the east; but those who enter them look towards the west, when standing with their faces turned towards the statues, they honour and worship the Gods. Hence, since this narration is full of such obscurities, it can neither be a fiction casually devised for the purpose of procuring delight, nor an exposition of a topical history; but something allegorical must be indicated in it by the poet, who likewise mystically places an olive near the cave. All which particulars the ancients thought very laborious to investigate and unfold; and we, with their assistance, shall now endeavour to develope the secret meaning of the allegory. Those persons, therefore, appear to have written very negligently about the situation of the place, who think that the cave, and what is narrated concerning it, are nothing more than a fiction of the poet.

But the best and most accurate writers of geography, and among these Artemidorus the Ephesian, in the fifth book of his work, which consists of eleven books, thus writes: 'The island of Ithaca, containing an extent of eighty-five stadia,[b] is distant from Panormus, a port of Cephalenia, about twelve stadia. It has a port named Phorcys, in which there is a shore, and on that shore a cave, in which the Phæacians are reported to have placed Ulysses.' This cave, therefore, will not be entirely an Homeric fiction. But whether the poet describes it as it really is, or whether he has added something to it of his own invention, nevertheless the same inquiries remain; whether the intention of the poet is investigated, or of those who founded the cave. For, neither did the ancients establish temples without fabulous symbols, nor does Homer rashly narrate the particulars pertaining to things of this kind. But how much the more any one endeavours to show that this description of the cave is not an Homeric fiction, but prior to Homer was consecrated to the Gods, by so much the more will this consecrated cave be found to be full of ancient wisdom. And on this account it deserves to be investigated, and it is requisite that its symbolical consecration should be amply unfolded into light.

2. The ancients, indeed, very properly consecrated a cave to the world, whether assumed collectively, according to the whole of itself, or separately, according to its parts. Hence they considered earth as a symbol of that matter of which the world consists; on which account some thought that matter and earth are the same; through the cave indicating the world, which was generated from matter. For caves, are for the most part, spontaneous productions, and connascent with the earth, being comprehended by one uniform mass of stone; the interior parts of which are concave, but the exterior parts are extended over an indefinite portion of land. And the world being spontaneously produced, [*i.e.* being produced by no external, but from an internal cause,] and being also self-adherent is allied to matter; which, according to a secret signification, is denominated a stone and a rock, on account of its sluggish and repercussive nature with respect to form: the ancients, at the same time, asserting that matter is infinite through its privation of form. Since, however, it is continually flowing, and is of itself destitute of the supervening investments of form, through which it partici-

[b] *i.e.* Rather more than ten Italian miles and a half, eight stadia making an Italian mile.

pates of *morphe*,[c] and becomes visible, the flowing waters, darkness, or, as the poet says, obscurity of the cavern, were considered by the ancients as apt symbols of what the world contains, on account of the matter with which it is connected. Through matter, therefore, the world is obscure and dark; but through the connecting power, and orderly distribution of form, from which also it is called *world*, it is beautiful and delightful. Hence it may very properly be denominated a cave; as being lovely, indeed, to him who first enters into it, through its participation of forms, but obscure to him who surveys its foundation, and examines it with an intellectual eye. So that its exterior and superficial parts, indeed, are pleasant, but its interior and profound parts are obscure, [and its very bottom is darkness itself]. Thus also the Persians, mystically signifying the descent of the soul into the sublunary regions, and its regression from it, initiate the mystic [or him who is admitted to the arcane sacred rites] in a place which they denominate a cavern. For, as Eubulus says, Zoroaster was the first who consecrated, in the neighbouring mountains of Persia, a spontaneously produced cave, florid, and having fountains, in honour of Mithra, the maker and father of all things; a cave, according to Zoroaster, bearing a resemblance of the world, which was fabricated by Mithra. But the things contained in the cavern being arranged according to commensurate intervals, were symbols of the mundane elements and climates.

3. After this Zoroaster likewise, it was usual with others to perform the rites pertaining to the mysteries in caverns and dens, whether spontaneously produced, or made by the hands. For, as they established temples, groves, and altars, to the celestial Gods, but to the terrestrial Gods, and to heroes, altars alone, and to the subterranean divinities pits and cells; so to the world they dedicated caves and dens; as likewise to Nymphs,[d] on account of the water which trickles, or is diffused in caverns, over which the Naiades, as we shall shortly observe, preside. Not only, however, did the ancients make a cavern, as we have said, to be a symbol of the world, or of a generated and sensible nature; but they also

[c] In the original, δι ον μο̄ζφουται. But *morphe*, as we are informed by Simplicius, pertains to the colour, figure, and magnitude of superficies.

[d] 'Nymphs', says Hermias, in his Scholia on the Phædrus of Plato, 'are Goddesses who preside over regeneration, and are ministrant to Bacchus, the offspring of Semele. Hence they dwell near water, that is, they are conversant with generation. But this Bacchus supplies the regeneration of the whole sensible world.'

assumed it as a symbol of all invisible powers; because, as caverns are obscure and dark, so the essence of these powers is occult. Hence Saturn fabricated a cavern in the ocean itself, and concealed in it his children. Thus, too, Ceres educated Proserpine, with her Nymphs, in a cave; and many other particulars of this kind may be found in the writings of theologists. But that the ancients dedicated caverns to Nymphs, and especially to the Naiades, who dwell near fountains, and who are called Naiades from the streams over which they preside, is manifest from the hymn to Apollo, in which it is said: 'The Nymphs residing in caves shall deduce fountains of intellectual waters to thee, (according to the divine voice of the Muses,) which are the progeny of a terrene spirit. Hence waters, bursting through every river, shall exhibit to mankind perpetual effusions of sweet streams.'[e] From hence, as it appears to me, the Pythagoreans, and after them Plato, showed that the world is a cavern and a den. For the powers which are the leaders of souls, thus speak in a verse of Empedocles:

Now at this secret cavern we're arrived.

And by Plato, in the 7th book of his Republic, it is said, 'Behold men as if dwelling in a subterraneous cavern, and in a den-like habitation, whose entrance is widely expanded to the admission of the light through the whole cave.' But when the other person in the Dialogue says, 'You adduce an unusual and wonderful similitude,' he replies, 'The whole of this image, friend Glauco, must be adapted to what has been before said, assimilating this receptacle, which is visible through the sight, to the habitation of a prison; but the light of the fire which is in it to the power of the sun.'

4. That theologists therefore considered caverns as symbols of the world, and of mundane powers, is, through this, manifest. And it has been already observed by us, that they also considered a cave as a symbol of the intelligible essence; being impelled to do so by different and not the same conceptions. For they were of opinion, that a cave is a symbol of the sensible world, because caverns are dark, stony, and humid; and they asserted, that the world is a thing of this kind, through the matter of which it consists, and through its repercussive and flowing nature. But they thought it to be a symbol of the intelligible world, because that world is invisible

---

[e] These lines are not to be found in any of the hymns now extant, ascribed to Homer.

to sensible perception, and possesses a firm and stable essence. Thus, also, partial powers are unapparent, and especially those which are inherent in matter. For they formed these symbols, from surveying the spontaneous production of caves, and their nocturnal, dark, and stony nature; and not entirely, as some suspect, from directing their attention to the figure of a cavern. For every cave is not spherical, as is evident from this Homeric cave with a two-fold entrance. But since a cavern has a twofold similitude, the present cave must not be assumed as an image of the intelligible, but of the sensible essence. For in consequence of containing perpetu-ally-flowing streams of water, it will not be a symbol of an in-telligible hypostasis, but of a material essence. On this account also, it is sacred to Nymphs, not the mountain, *or rural[f] Nymphs*, or others of the like kind, but to the Naiades, who are thus denomin-ated from streams of water. For we peculiarly call the Naiades, and the powers that preside over waters, Nymphs; and this term, also, is commonly applied to all souls descending into generation. For the ancients thought that these souls are incumbent on water which is inspired by divinity, as Numenius, says, who adds, that on this account, a prophet asserts, that the Spirit of God moved on the waters. The Egyptians likewise, on this account, represent all dæmons, and also the sun, and, in short, all the planets,[g] not standing on any thing solid, but on a sailing vessel; for souls descending into generation fly to moisture. Hence, also, Heraclitus says, 'that moisture appears delightful and not deadly to souls;' but the lapse into generation is delightful to them. And in another place [speaking of unembodied souls], he says, 'We live their death, and we die their life.' Hence the poet calls those that are in generation *humid*, because they have souls which are *profoundly* steeped in moisture. On this account, such souls delight in blood and humid seed; but water is the nutriment of the souls of plants. Some like-

---

[f] In the original, ουδα αχζαςων; but for αχζαιων, I read, αγζαιων.

[g] In the original, τους τε Αιγυπτιους δια τουτο τους δαιμονας απαντας ουχ εττανια επι στεςεου, αλλα παντας επι πλοιου, και τον ηλιον, και απλως παντας, ους τινας ειδεναι χςη τας ψυχας επιποτωμενας τω υγςω, τας εις γενεσιν κατιουτας. But after the words και απλως παντας, it appears to me to be requisite to insert τως πλανητας. For Martianus Capella, in lib. ii. De Nuptiis Philologiæ, speaking of the sun, says: 'Ibi quandam navim, totius naturæ cursibus diversa cupiditate moderantem, cunctaque flammarum congestione plenissimam, beatis circumac-tam mercibus conspicatur. Cui *nautæ septem* germani, tamen suique consimiles præsidebant,' &c. For in this passage the seven sailors are evidently the seven planets.

wise are of opinion, that the bodies in the air, and in the heavens, are nourished by vapours from fountains and rivers, and other exhalations. But the Stoics assert, that the sun is nourished by the exhalation from the sea; the moon from the vapours of fountains and rivers; and the stars from the exhalation of the earth. Hence, according to them, the sun is an intellectual composition formed from the sea; the moon from river waters; and the stars from terrene exhalations.

5. It is necessary, therefore, that souls, whether they are corporeal or incorporeal, while they attract to themselves body, and especially such as are about to be bound to blood and moist bodies, should verge to humidity, and be corporalized, in consequence of being drenched in moisture. Hence the souls of the dead are evocated by the effusion of bile and blood; and souls that are lovers of body, by attracting a moist spirit, condense this humid vehicle like a cloud. For moisture condensed in the air constitutes a cloud. But the pneumatic vehicle being condensed in these souls, becomes visible through an excess of moisture. And among the number of these we must reckon those apparitions of images, which, from a spirit coloured by the influence of imagination, present themselves to mankind. But pure souls are averse from generation; so that, as Heraclitus says, '*a dry soul is the wisest*'. Hence, here also, the spirit becomes moist and more aqueous through the desire of coition, the soul thus attracting a humid vapour from verging to generation. Souls, therefore, proceeding into generation, are the Nymphs called Naiades. Hence it is usual to call those that are married Nymphs, as being conjoined to generation, and to pour water into baths from fountains, or rivers, or perpetual rills.

6. This world, then, is sacred and pleasant to souls who have now proceeded into nature, and to natal dæmons, though it is essentially dark and *obscure*: [ηεζοειδῆς]; from which some have suspected that souls also are of an *obscure* nature, [αεζωδως,] and essentially consist of air. Hence a cavern, which is both pleasant and dark, will be appropriately consecrated to souls on the earth, conformably to its similitude to the world; in which, as in the greatest of all temples, souls reside. To the Nymphs likewise, who preside over waters, a cavern, in which there are perpetually flowing streams, is adapted. Let, therefore, this present cavern be consecrated to souls, and, among the more partial powers, to nymphs, that preside over streams and fountains, and who, on this account,

are called *fontal* and *Naiades*. What, therefore, are the different
symbols, some of which are adapted to souls, but others to the
aquatic powers, in order that we may apprehend that this cavern is
consecrated in common to both? Let the stony bowls, then, and the
amphorae, be symbols of the aquatic Nymphs. For these are, indeed, the symbols of Bacchus, but their composition is fictile, *i. e.*
consists of baked earth; and these are friendly to the vine, the gift
of the God; since the fruit of the vine is brought to a proper maturity by the celestial fire of the sun. But the stony bowls and amphorae, are in the most eminent degree adapted to the Nymphs who
preside over the water that flows from rocks. And to souls that
descend into generation, and are occupied in corporeal energies,
what symbol can be more appropriate than those instruments pertaining to weaving? Hence, also, the poet ventures to say, 'that on
these the Nymphs weave purple webs, admirable to the view.' For
the formation of the flesh is on and about the bones, which in the
bodies of animals resemble stones. Hence these instruments of weaving consist of stone, and not of any other matter. But the purple
webs will evidently be the flesh which is woven from the blood.
For purple woollen garments are tinged from blood; and wool is
dyed from animal juice. The generation of flesh, also, is through and
from blood. Add, too, that the body is a garment with which the
soul is invested, a thing wonderful to the sight, whether this refers
to the composition of the soul, or contributes to the colligation of
the soul [to the whole of a visible essence]. Thus, also, Proserpine,
who is the inspective guardian of every thing produced from seed,
is represented by Orpheus as weaving a web;[h] and the heavens are

---

[h] The theological meaning of this Orphic fiction is beautifully unfolded by
Proclus, as follows: 'Orpheus says that the vivific cause of partible natures
(*i.e.* Proserpine), while she remained on high, weaving the order of celestials, was
a nymph, as being undefiled; and in consequence of this connected with Jupiter,
and abiding in her appropriate manners; but that, proceeding from her proper
habitation, she left her webs unfinished, was ravished; having been ravished, was
married; and that being married she generated, in order that she might animate
things which have an adventitious life. For the unfinished state of her webs
indicates, I think, that the universe is imperfect or unfinished, as far as to perpetual animals (*i.e.* The universe would be imperfect if nothing inferior to the
celestial Gods was produced). Hence Plato says, that the one Demiurgus calls on
the many Demiurgi to weave together the mortal and immortal natures; after a
manner reminding us, that the addition of the mortal genera is the perfection of
the textorial life of the universe, and also exciting our recollection of the divine
Orphic fable, and affording us interpretative causes of the unfinished webs of
Proserpine.' – See vol. ii. p. 356, of my translation of Proclus on the Timæus.

called by the ancients·a veil, in consequence of being, as it were, the vestment of the celestial Gods.

7. Why, therefore, are the amphoræ said not to be filled with water, but with honey-combs? For in these Homer says the bees deposit their honey. But this is evident from the word τιθαιξωσσειν, which signifies τιθεναι την βοσιν; i.e. to deposit aliment. And honey is the nutriment of bees. Theologists, also, have made honey subservient to many and different symbols, because it consists of many powers; since it is both cathartic and preservative. Hence, through honey, bodies are preserved from putrefaction, and inveterate ulcers are purified. Farther still, it is also sweet to the taste, and is collected by bees, who are ox-begotten, from flowers. When, therefore, those who are initiated in the Leontic sacred rites, pour honey instead of water on their hands; they are ordered [by the initiator] to have their hands pure from every thing productive of molestation, and from every thing noxious and detestable. Other initiators [into the same mysteries] employ fire, which is of a cathartic nature, as an appropriate purification. And they likewise purify the tongue from all the defilement of evil with honey. But the Persians, when they offer honey to the guardian of fruits, consider it as the symbol of a preserving and defending power. Hence some persons have thought that the nectar and ambrosia,[1] which

---

The *unfinished webs* of Proserpine are also alluded to by Claudian, in his poem De Raptu Proserpinæ, In the following verse:

Sensit adesse Deas, *imperfectumque laborem Deserit.*

I only add, that, by ancient theologists, the shuttle was considered as a signature of *separating*, a cup of *vivific*, a sceptre of *ruling*, and a key of *guardian* power.

[1] The theological meaning of nectar and ambrosia, is beautifully unfolded by Hermias, in his Scholia on the Phædrus of Plato, published by Ast, Lips. 1810, p. 145, where he informs us, ' that *ambrosia* is analogous to dry nutriment, and that, on this account, it signifies an establishment in causes; but that *nectar* is analogous to moist food, and that it signifies the providential attention of the Gods to secondary natures; the former being denominated, according to *a privation of the mortal and corruptible [κατα στεσητιν του βσοτου και φθαστον]*; but the latter, according to *a privation of the funeral and sepulchral [κατα στεσησιν του κτεσιος εισημενον και του ταφου]*.' And when the Gods are represented as energizing providentially, they are said to drink nectar. Thus Homer, in the beginning of the 4th book of the Iliad:

Οι δε θεοι πας Ζηνι καθημενοι ηγοσοωνθο
Χσυτεῳ εν δαπεδῳ, μετα δε σφισι ποτνια Ηβη
Νεκτας εῳνοχοει τοι δε χσυσεοις δεπαεσσι
Δειδεχατ' αλληλους, Τσῳων πολιν εισοσοωντες.

the poet pours into the nostrils of the dead, for the purpose of preventing putrefaction, is honey; since honey is the food of the Gods. On this account, also, the same poet somewhere calls nectar $\epsilon\zeta\upsilon\theta\zeta o\nu$; for such is the colour of honey, [viz. it is a deep yellow]. But whether or not honey is to be taken for nectar, we shall elsewhere more accurately examine. In Orpheus, likewise, Saturn is ensnared by Jupiter through honey. For Saturn, being filled with honey, is intoxicated, his senses are darkened, as if from the effects of wine, and he sleeps; just as Porus, in the Banquet of Plato, is filled with nectar; for wine was not (says he) yet known. The Goddess Night, too, in Orpheus, advises Jupiter to make use of honey as an artifice. For she says to him—

> When stretch'd beneath the lofty oaks you view
> Saturn, with honey by the bees produc'd,
> Sunk in ebriety,[k] fast bind the God.

This, therefore, takes place, and Saturn being bound, is castrated in the same manner as Heaven; the theologist obscurely signifying by this, that divine natures become through pleasure bound, and drawn down into the realms of generation; and also that, when dissolved in pleasure, they emit certain seminal powers. Hence Saturn castrates Heaven, when descending to earth, through a desire of coition.[1] But the sweetness of honey signifies, with theologists, the

> Now with each other, on the golden floor
> Seated near Jove, the Gods converse; to whom
> The venerable Hebe nectar bears,
> In golden goblets; and as these flow round,
> Th' immortals turn their careful eyes on Troy.

For then they providentially attend to the Trojans. The possession, therefore, of immutable providence by the Gods is signified by their drinking nectar; the exertion of this providence, by their beholding Troy; and their communicating with each other in providential energies, by receiving the goblets from each other.

[k] Ebriety, when ascribed to divine natures by ancient theologists, signifies a deific superessential energy, or an energy superior to intellect. Hence, when Saturn is said by Orpheus to have been intoxicated with honey or nectar, the meaning is, that he then energized providentially, in a deific and super-intellectual manner.

[1] Porphyry, though he excelled in philosophical, was deficient in theological knowledge; of which what he now says of the castrations of Saturn and Heaven, is a remarkable instance. For ancient theologists, by things preternatural, adumbrated the transcendent nature of the Gods; by such as are irrational, a power more divine than all reason; and by things apparently base, incorporeal beauty. Hence, in the fabulous narrations to which Porphyry now alludes, the genital parts must be considered as symbols of prolific power; and the castration of these parts as signifying the progression of this power into a subject order. So that the

same thing as the pleasure arising from copulation, by which Saturn, being ensnared, was castrated. For Saturn, and his sphere, are the first of the orbs that move contrary to the course of Cœlum, or the heavens. Certain powers, however, descend both from Heaven [or the inerratic sphere] and the planets. But Saturn receives the powers of Heaven, and Jupiter the powers of Saturn. Since, therefore, honey is assumed in purgations, and as an antidote to putrefaction, and is indicative of the pleasure which draws souls downward to generation; it is a symbol well adapted to aquatic Nymphs, on account of the unputrescent nature of the waters over which they preside, their purifying power, and their co-operation with generation. For water co-operates in the work of generation. On this account the bees are said, by the poet, to deposit their honey in bowls and amphoræ; the bowls being a symbol of fountains, and therefore a bowl is placed near to Mithra, instead of a fountain; but the amphoræ are symbols of the vessels with which we draw water from fountains. And fountains and streams are adapted to aquatic Nymphs, and still more so to the Nymphs that are souls which the ancients peculiarly called bees, as the efficient causes of sweetness. Hence Sophocles does not speak unappropriately when he says of souls—

> In swarms while wandering, from the dead,
> A humming sound is heard.

8. The priestesses of Ceres, also, as being initiated into the mysteries of the terrene Goddess, were called by the ancients bees; and Proserpine herself was denominated by them *honied*. The moon, likewise, who presides over generation, was called by them a bee, and also a bull. And Taurus is the exaltation of the moon. But bees are ox-begotten. And this appellation is also given to souls proceeding into generation. The God, likewise, who is occultly connected with generation, is a stealer of oxen. To which may be added, that honey is considered as a symbol of death, and on this account, it is usual to offer libations of honey to the terrestrial Gods; but gall is considered as a symbol of life; whether it is obscurely signified by this, that the life of the soul dies through pleasure, but through bitterness the soul resumes its life, whence,

fable means that the prolific powers of Saturn are called forth into progression by Jupiter, and those of Heaven by Saturn; Jupiter being inferior to Saturn, and Saturn to Heaven. – See the Apology for the Fables of Homer, in vol. i. of my translation of Plato.

also, bile is sacrificed to the Gods; or whether it is, because death liberates from molestation, but the present life is laborious and bitter. All souls, however, proceeding into generation, are not simply called bees, but those who will live in it justly, and who, after having performed such things as are acceptable to the Gods, will again return [to their kindred stars]. For this insect loves to return to the place from whence it first came, and is eminently just and sober. Whence, also, the libations which are made with honey are called sober. Bees, likewise, do not sit on beans, which were considered by the ancients as a symbol of generation proceeding in a right line, and without flexure; because this leguminous vegetable is almost the only seed-bearing plant, whose stalk is perforated throughout without any intervening knots.ᵐ We must therefore admit, that honey-combs and bees are appropriate and common symbols of the aquatic Nymphs, and of souls that are married [as it were] to [the humid and fluctuating nature of] generation.

9. Caves, therefore, in the most remote periods of antiquity, were consecrated to the Gods, before temples were erected to them. Hence, the Curetes in Crete dedicated a cavern to Jupiter; in Arcadia, a cave was sacred to the Moon, and to Lycean Pan; and in Naxus, to Bacchus. But wherever Mithra was known, they propitiated the God in a cavern. With respect, however, to this Ithacensian cave, Homer was not satisfied with saying that it had two gates, but adds, that one of the gates was turned towards the north, but the other, which was more divine, to the south. He also says, that the northern gate was pervious to descent, but does not indicate whether this was also the case with the southern gate. For of this, he only says, 'It is inaccessible to men, but it is the path of the immortals.'

10. It remains, therefore, to investigate what is indicated by this narration, whether the poet describes a cavern which was in reality consecrated by others, or whether it is an enigma of his own invention. Since, however, a cavern is an image and symbol of the world, as Numenius and his familiar Cronius assert, there are two extremities in the heavens, viz. the winter tropic, than which nothing is more southern, and the summer tropic, than which nothing is more northern. But the summer tropic is in Cancer, and

---

ᵐ Hence, when Pythagoras exhorted his disciples to abstain from beans, he intended to signify, that they should beware of a continued and perpetual descent into the realms of generation.

the winter tropic in Capricorn. And since Cancer is nearest to us, it is very properly attributed to the Moon, which is the nearest of all the heavenly bodies to the earth. But as the southern pole, by its great distance, is invisible to us, hence Capricorn is attributed to Saturn, the highest and most remote of all the planets. Again, the signs from Cancer to Capricorn, are situated in the following order: and the first of these is Leo, which is the house of the Sun; afterwards Virgo, which is the house of Mercury; Libra, the house of Venus; Scorpius, of Mars; Sagittarius, of Jupiter; and Capricornus, of Saturn. But from Capricorn in an inverse order, Aquarius is attributed to Saturn; Pisces, to Jupiter; Aries, to Mars; Taurus, to Venus; Gemini, to Mercury; and, in the last place, Cancer to the Moon.

11. Theologists therefore assert, that these two gates are Cancer and Capricorn; but Plato calls them entrances. And of these, theologists say, that Cancer is the gate through which souls descend; but Capricorn that through which they ascend. Cancer is indeed northern, and adapted to descent; but Capricorn is southern, and adapted to ascent.[n] The northern parts, likewise, pertain to souls

[n] Macrobius, in the 12th chapter of his Commentary on Scipio's Dream, has derived some of the ancient arcana which it contains from what is here said by Porphyry. A part of what he has farther added, I shall translate, on account of its excellence and connexion with the above passage. 'Pythagoras thought that the empire of Pluto began downwards from the milky way, because souls falling from thence appear to have already receded from the Gods. Hence he asserts, that the nutriment of milk is first offered to infants, because their first motion commences from the galaxy, when they begin to fall into terrene bodies. On this account, since those who are about to descend are yet in *Cancer*, and have not left the milky way, they rank in the order of the Gods. But when, by falling, they arrive at the *Lion*, in this constellation they enter on the exordium of their future condition. And because, in the *Lion*, the rudiments of birth, and certain primary exercises of human nature, commence; but *Aquarius* is opposite to the *Lion*, and presently sets after the *Lion* rises; hence, when the sun is in *Aquarius*, funeral rites are performed to departed souls, because he is then carried in a sign which is contrary or adverse to human life. From the confine, therefore, in which the zodiac and galaxy touch each other, the soul, descending from a round figure, which is the only divine form, is produced into a cone by its defluxion. And as a line is generated from a point, and proceeds into length from an indivisible, so the soul, from its own point, which is a monad, passes into the duad, which is the first extension. And this is the essence which Plato, in the Timæus, calls impartible, and at the same time partible, when he speaks of the nature of the mundane soul. For as the soul of the world, so likewise that of man, will be found to be in one respect without division, if the simplicity of a divine nature is considered; and in another respect partible, if we regard the diffusion of the former through the world, and of the latter through the members of the body.

' As soon, therefore, as the soul gravitates towards body in this first production

descending into generation. And the gates of the cavern which are turned to the north, are rightly said to be pervious to the descent of men; but the southern gates are not the avenues of the Gods, but of souls ascending to the Gods. On this account, the poet does not

of herself, she begins to experience a material tumult, that is, matter flowing into her essence. And this is what Plato remarks in the Phædo, that the soul is drawn into body staggering with recent intoxication; signifying by this, the new drink of matter's impetuous flood, through which the soul, becoming defiled and heavy, is drawn into a terrene situation. But the starry *cup* placed between Cancer and the Lion, is a symbol of this mystic truth, signifying that descending souls first experience intoxication in that part of the heavens through the influx of matter. Hence oblivion, the companion of intoxication, there begins silently to creep into the recesses of the soul. For if souls retained in their descent to bodies the memory of divine concerns, of which they were conscious in the heavens, there would be no dissension among men about divinity. But all, indeed, in descending, drink of oblivion; though some more, and others less. On this account, though truth is not apparent to all men on the earth, yet all exercise their opinions about it; because *a defect of memory is the origin of opinion.* But those discover most who have drank least of oblivion, because they easily remember what they had known before in the heavens.

'The soul, therefore, falling with this first weight from the zodiac and milky way into each of the subject spheres, is not only clothed with the accession of a luminous body, but produces the particular motions which it is to exercise in the respective orbs. Thus in Saturn, it energizes according to a ratiocinative and intellective power; in the sphere of Jove, according to a practic power; in the orb of the Sun, according to a sensitive and imaginative nature; but according to the motion of desire in the planet Venus; of pronouncing and interpreting what it perceives in the orb of Mercury; and according to a plantal or vegetable nature, and a power of acting on body, when it enters into the lunar globe. And this sphere, as it is the last among the divine orders, so it is the first in our terrene situation. For this body, as it is the dregs of divine natures, so it is the first animal substance. And this is the difference between terrene and supernal bodies (under the latter of which I comprehend the heavens, the stars, and the more elevated elements,) that the latter are called upwards to be the seat of the soul, and merit immortality from the very nature of the region, and an imitation of sublimity; but the soul is drawn down to these terrene bodies, and is on this account said to die when it is enclosed in this fallen region, and the seat of mortality. Nor ought it to cause any disturbance that we have so often mentioned the death of the soul, which we have pronounced to be immortal. For the soul is not extinguished by its own proper death, but is only overwhelmed for a time. Nor does it lose the benefit of perpetuity by its temporal demersion. Since, when it deserves to be purified from the contagion of vice, through its entire refinement from body, it will be restored to the light of perennial life, and will return to its pristine integrity and perfection.'

'The powers, however, of the planets, which are the causes of the energies of the soul in the several planetary spheres, are more accurately described by Proclus, in p. 260 of his admirable Commentary on the Timæus, as follows: ει δε βουλει και οτι των αγαθων πλανητων Σεληνη μεν αιτια τοις θνητοις της φυσεως, το αυτοπΙον αγαλμα ουσα της πηγαιας φυτεως· Ηλιος δε δημιουργος των αισθησεων πασων, διοτι και του οζαν και του οζατθαι αιτιος. Ζζμης δι των της φαντασιας κινητεων· τυτης γας της φαντασΙικης ουσιας, ως μιας ουσης αισθησεως και φαντασιας, Ηλιος

say that they are the avenues of the Gods, but of immortals; this appellation being also common to our souls, which are *per se*, or essentially, immortal. It is said, that Parmenides mentions these two gates in his treatise On the Nature of Things; as likewise, that they are not unknown to the Romans and Egyptians. For the Romans celebrate their Saturnalia when the Sun is in Capricorn; and during this festivity, slaves wear the shoes of those that are free, and all things are distributed among them in common; the legislator obscurely signifying by this ceremony, that through this gate of the heavens, those who are now born slaves will be liberated through the Saturnian festival, and the house attributed to Saturn, *i.e.* Capricorn, when they live again, and return to the fountain of life. Since, however, the path from Capricorn is adapted to ascent,[o] hence the Romans denominate that month in which the Sun, turning from Capricorn to the east, directs his course to the north, Januarius, or January, *from janua*, a gate. But with the Egyptians, the beginning of the year is not Aquarius, as with the Romans, but Cancer. For the star Sothis, which the Greeks call the Dog, is near to Cancer. And the rising of Sothis is the new moon with them, this being the principle of generation to the world. On this account, the gates of the Homeric cavern are not dedicated to the east and west, nor to the equinoctial signs, Aries and Libra, but to the north and south, and to those celestial signs which, towards the south, are most southerly, and, towards the north, are most northerly; because this cave was sacred to souls and aquatic Nymphs. But these places are adapted to souls descending into generation, and afterwards separating themselves from it. Hence, a

υποστατης· Αφροδιτη δε των επιθυμητικων ορεξεων· Αξης δε των θυμοειδων κινησεων ταν κατα φυσιν εκασΙοις· κοινη δε των μεν ζωτικων πασων δυναμεων Ζευς, των δε γνωσΙικων Κξονος, διηζηται γας ωαντα τα ειδη τα αλογα εις ταυτας, *i.e.* 'If you are willing, also, you may say, that of the beneficent planets, the Moon is the cause to mortals of nature, being herself the visible statue of fontal nature. But the Sun is the Demiurgus of every thing sensible, in consesequence of being the cause of sight and visibility. Mercury is the cause of the motions of the phantasy; for of the imaginative essence itself, so far as sense and phantasy are one, the Sun is the producing cause. But Venus is the cause of epithymetic appetites [or of the appetites pertaining to desire]; and Mars, of the irascible motions which are conformable to nature. Of all vital powers, however, Jupiter is the common cause; but of all gnostic powers, Saturn. For all the irrational forms are divided into these.'

[o] For καταβατικη, in this place, it appears to me to be obviously necessary to read αναβατικη. For Porphyry has above informed us, that Capricorn is the gate through which souls ascend.

place near to the equinoctial circle was assigned to Mithra as an appropriate seat. And on this account he bears the sword of Aries, which is a martial sign. He is likewise carried in the Bull, which is the sign of Venus. For Mithra, as well as the Bull, is the demiurgus and lord of generation.ᴾ But he is placed near the equinoctial circle, having the northern parts on his right hand, and the southern on his left. They likewise arranged towards the south the southern hemisphere, because it is hot; but the northern hemisphere towards the north, through the coldness of the north wind.

12. The ancients, likewise, very reasonably connected winds with souls proceeding into generation, and again separating themselves from it, because, as some think, souls attract a spirit, and have a pneumatic essence. But the north wind is adapted to souls falling into generation; and, on this account, the northern blasts refresh those who are dying, and when they can scarcely draw their breath. On the contrary, the southern gales dissolve life. For the north wind, indeed, from its superior coldness, congeals [as it were, the animal life], and detains it in the frigidity of terrene generation. But the south wind being hot, dissolves this life, and sends it upward to the heat of a divine nature. Since, however, our terrene habitation is more northern, it is proper that souls which are born in it should be familiar with the north wind; but those that exchange this life for a better, with the south wind. This also is the cause why the north wind is at its commencement great; but the south wind, at its termination. For the former is situated directly over the inhabitants of the northern part of the globe; but the latter is at a great distance from them; and the blast from places very remote, is more tardy than from such as are near. But when it is coacervated, then it blows abundantly, and with vigour. Since, however, souls proceed into generation through the northern gate, hence this wind is said to be amatory. For, as the poet says,

> Boreas, enamour'd of the sprightly train,
> Conceal'd his godhead in a flowing mane.
> With voice dissembled, to his loves he neigh'd,
> And coursed the dappled beauties o'er the mead:

ᴾ Hence Phanes, or Protogonus, who is the paradigm of the universe, and who was absorbed by Jupiter, the Demiurgus, is represented by Orpheus as having the head of a *bull* among other heads with which he is adorned. And in the Orphic hymn to him, he is called *bull-roarer*.

Hence sprung twelve others of unrivall'd kind,
Swift as their mother mares, and father wind. q

It is also said, that Boreas ravished Orithya,[r] from whom he
begot Zetis and Calais. But as the south is attributed to the Gods,
hence, when the Sun is at his meridian, the curtains in temples are
drawn before the statues of the Gods; in consequence of observing
the Homeric precept, 'that it is not lawful for men to enter temples when the Sun is inclined to the south;' for this is the path of
the immortals. Hence, when the God is at her meridian altitude,
the ancients placed a symbol of mid-day and of the south in the

q Iliad, lib. xx. v. 223, &c.
[r] This fable is mentioned by Plato in the Phædrus, and is beautifully unfolded
as follows, by Hermias, in his Scholia on that Dialogue: 'A twofold solution may
be given of this fable; one from history, more ethical; but the other, transferring
us [from parts] to wholes. And the former of these is as follows: Orithya was the
daughter of Erectheus, and the priestess of Boreas; for each of the winds has a
presiding deity, which the telestic art, or the art pertaining to sacred mysteries,
religiously cultivates. To this Orithya, then, the God was so very propitious, that
he sent the north wind for the safety of the country; and besides this, he is said to
have assisted the Athenians in their naval battles. Orithya, therefore, becoming
enthusiastic, being possessed by her proper God Boreas, and no longer energizing
as a human being (for animals cease to energize according to their own peculiarities, when possessed by superior causes), died under the inspiring influence, and
thus was said to have been ravished by Boreas. And this is the more ethical
explanation of the fable.
'But the second, which transfers the narration to wholes, and does not entirely
subvert the former, is the following: for divine fables often employ transactions
and histories, in subserviency to the discipline of wholes. It is said then, that
Erectheus is the God that rules over the three elements, air, water, and earth.
Sometimes, however, he is considered as alone the ruler of the earth, and sometimes
as the presiding deity of Attica alone. Of this deity Orithya is the daughter; and
she is the prolific power of the Earth, which is indeed coextended with the word
Erectheus, as the unfolding of the name signifies. For it is *the prolific power of the Earth,
flourishing and restored, according to the seasons.* But Boreas is the providence of the
Gods, supernally illuminating secondary natures. For the providence of the Gods
in the world is signified by Boreas, because this divinity blows from lofty places.
And the elevating power of the Gods is signified by the south wind, because this
wind blows from low to lofty places; and besides this, *things situated towards the
south are more divine.* The providence of the Gods, therefore, causes the prolific
power of the Earth, or of the Attic land, to *ascend*, and become visible.
'Orithya also may be said to be a soul aspiring after things above, from οξουω
and θειω, according to the Attic custom of adding a letter at the end of a word,
which letter is here an 'ω'. Such a soul, therefore, is ravished by Boreas supernally
blowing. But if Orithya was hurled from a precipice, this also is appropriate, for
such a soul dies a philosophic, not receiving a physical death, and abandons a life
pertaining to her own deliberate choice, at the same time that she lives a physical
life. And philosophy, according to Socrates in the Phædo, is nothing else than a
meditation of death.'

gates of temples;[s] and, on this account, in other gates also, it was not lawful to speak at all times, because gates were considered as sacred. Hence, too, the Pythagoreans, and the wise men among the Egyptians, forbade speaking while passing through doors or gates; for then they venerated in silence that God who is the principle of wholes [and, therefore of all things].

13. Homer likewise knew that gates are sacred, as is evident from his representing Oeneus, when supplicating, shaking the gate:

> The gates he shakes, and supplicates the son.[u]

He also knew the gates of the heavens which are committed to the guardianship of the Hours; which gates originate in cloudy places, and are opened and shut by the clouds. For he says,

> Whether dense clouds they close, or wide unfold.[x]

And on this account, these gates emit a bellowing sound, because thunders roar through the clouds:

> Heaven's gates spontaneous open to the powers;
> Heaven's bellowing portals, guarded by the Hours.[y]

He likewise elsewhere speaks of the gates of the Sun, signifying by these Cancer and Capricorn; for the Sun proceeds as far as to these signs, when he descends from the north to the south, and from thence ascends again to the northern parts. But Capricorn and Cancer are situated about the galaxy, being allotted the extremities of this circle; Cancer, indeed, the northern, but Capricorn the southern extremity of it. According to Pythagoras, also, the *people of dreams*,[z] are the souls which are said to be collected in the galaxy, this circle being so called from the milk with which souls are nourished when they fall into generation. Hence, those who evocate departed souls, sacrifice to them by a libation of milk mingled with honey; because, through the allurements of sweetness, they will proceed into generation; with the birth of man,

---

[s] In the original, ιστασαν ουν και συμβολον της μεσημβ6ζιας και του νοτου, επ: τη θυρη, μεσημβριαζοντος του θεου, which Holstenius translates most erroneously as follows: 'Austrum igitur meridici symbolum statuunt; cum deus meridiano tempore ostio immineat.'

[u] Iliad, lib. xi, v. 579.   [x] Iliad, lib. viii, v. 395.

[y] Iliad, lib. viii. v. 393.

[z] The souls of the suitors are said by Homer, in the 24th book of the Odyssey (v. 11), to have passed, in their descent to the region of spirits, beyond *the people of dreams*.

milk being naturally produced. Farther still, the southern regions produce small bodies; for it is usual with heat to attenuate them in the greatest degree. But all bodies generated in the north are large, as is evident in the Celtæ, the Thracians, and the Scythians; and these regions are humid, and abound with pastures. For the word Boreas is derived from *Boζa*, which signifies nutriment. Hence, also, the wind which blows from a land abounding in nutriment, is called *Boζζas*, as being of a nutritive nature. From these causes, therefore, the northern parts are adapted to the mortal tribe, and to souls that fall into the realms of generation. But the southern parts are adapted to that which is immortal,[a] just as the eastern parts of the world are attributed to the Gods, but the western to dæmons. For, in consequence of nature originating from diversity, the ancients every where made that which has a twofold entrance to be a symbol of the nature of things. For the progression is either through that which is intelligible, or through that which is sensible. And if through that which is sensible, it is either through the sphere of the fixed stars, or through the sphere of the planets. And again, it is either through an immortal, or through a mortal progression. One centre, likewise, is above, but the other beneath the earth; and the one is eastern, but the other western. Thus, too, some parts of the world are situated on the left, but others on the right hand: and night is opposed to day. On this account, also, harmony consists of, and *proceeds*[b] through contraries. Plato also says, that there are two openings,[c] one of which affords a passage to souls ascending to the heavens, but the other to souls descending to the earth. And, according to theologists, the Sun and Moon are the gates of souls, which ascend through the Sun, and descend through the Moon. With Homer, likewise, there are two tubs,

> From which the lot of every one he fills,
> Blessings to these, to those distributes ills.[d]

But Plato, in the Gorgias, by tubs intends to signify souls, some of which are malefic, but others beneficent, and some of which are

---

[a] Hence, the southern have always been more favourable to genius, than the northern parts of the earth.

[b] In the original, *τοζευει*; but instead of it, I read *πορευει*.

[c] See my translation of the 10th book of his Republic.

[d] Iliad, xxiv. v. 528.

rational, but others irrational.[e] Souls, however, are [analogous to] tubs, because they contain in themselves energies and habits, as in a vessel. In Hesiod too, we find one tub closed, but the other opened by Pleasure, who scatters its contents every where, Hope alone remaining behind. For in those things in which a depraved soul, being dispersed about matter, deserts the proper order of its essence; in all these, it is accustomed to feed itself with [the pleasing prospects of] auspicious hope.

[e] The passage in the Gorgias of Plato, to which Porphyry here alludes, is as follows:— 'Soc. But, indeed, as you also say, life is a grievous thing. For I should not wonder if Euripides spoke the truth when he says: 'Who knows whether to live is not to die, and to die is not to live?' And we, perhaps, are in reality dead. For I have heard from one of the wise, that we are now dead; and that the body is our sepulchre; but that the part of the soul in which the desires are contained, is of such a nature that it can be persuaded, and hurled upwards and downwards. Hence a certain elegant man, perhaps a Sicilian, or an Italian, denominated, mythologizing, this part of the soul a tub, by a derivation from the probable and the persuasive; and, likewise, he called those that are stupid, or deprived of intellect, uninitiated. He farther said, that the intemperate and uncovered nature of that part of the soul in which the desires are contained, was like a pierced tub, through its insatiable greediness.'

What is here said by Plato is beautifully unfolded by Olympiodorus, in his MS. Commentary on the Gorgias, as follows: 'Euripides (in Phryxo) says, that to live is to die, and to die to live. For the soul coming hither, as she imparts life to the body, so she partakes [through this] of a certain privation of life; but this is an evil. When separated, therefore, from the body, she lives in reality: for she dies here, through participating a privation of life, because the body becomes the source of evils. And hence it is necessary to subdue the body.

'But the meaning of the Pythagoric fable, which is here introduced by Plato, is this: We are said to be dead, because, as we have before observed, we partake of a privation of life. The sepulchre which we carry about with us is, as Plato himself explains it, the body. But Hades is the unapparent, because we are situated in obscurity, the soul being in a state of servitude to the body. The tubs are the desires; whether they are so called from our hastening to fill them, as if they were tubs, or from desire persuading us that it is beautiful. The initiated, therefore, *i.e.* those that have a perfect knowledge, pour into the entire tub: for these have their tub full; or, in other words, have perfect virtue. But the uninitiated, viz. those that possess nothing perfect, have perforated tubs. For those that are in a state of servitude to desire always wish to fill it, and are more inflamed; and on this account they have perforated tubs, as being never full. But the sieve is the rational soul mingled with the irrational. For the [rational] soul is called a circle, because it seeks itself, and is itself sought; finds itself, and is itself found. But the irrational soul imitates a right line, since it does not revert to itself like a circle. So far, therefore, as the sieve is circular, it is an image of the rational soul; but, as it is placed under the right lines formed from the holes, it is assumed for the irrational soul. Right lines, therefore, are in the middle of the cavities. Hence, by the sieve, Plato signifies the rational in subjection to the irrational soul. But the water is the flux of nature: for, as Heraclitus says, *moisture is the death of the soul.*'

In this extract the intelligent reader will easily perceive that the occult signification of the *tubs* is more scientifically unfolded by Olympiodorus than by Porphyry.

14. Since, therefore, every twofold entrance is a symbol of nature, this Homeric cavern has, very properly, not one portal only, but two gates, which differ from each other conformably to things themselves; of which one pertains to Gods and good [dæmons[f]], but the other to mortals, and depraved natures. Hence, Plato took occasion to speak of bowls, and assumes tubs instead of amphoræ, and two openings, as we have already observed, instead of two gates. Pherecydes Syrus also mentions recesses and trenches, caverns, doors, and gates; and through these obscurely indicates the generations of souls, and their separation from these material realms. And thus much for an explanation of the Homeric cave, which we think we have sufficiently unfolded without adducing any farther testimonies from ancient philosophers and theologists, which would give a needless extent to our discourse.

15. One particular, however, remains to be explained, and that is the symbol of the olive planted at the top of the cavern; since Homer appears to indicate something very admirable by giving it such a position. For he does not merely say that an olive grows in this place, but that it flourishes on the summit of the cavern.

> High at the head a branching olive grows,
> Beneath, a gloomy grotto's cool recess.

But the growth of the olive in such a situation, is not fortuitous, as some one may suspect, but contains the enigma of the cavern. For since the world was not produced rashly and casually, but is the work of divine wisdom and an intellectual nature, hence an olive, the symbol of this wisdom, flourishes near the present cavern, which is an image of the world. For the olive is the plant of Minerva; and Minerva is wisdom. But this Goddess being produced from the head of Jupiter, the theologist has discovered an appropriate place for the olive, by consecrating it at the summit of the port; signifying by this, that the universe is not the effect of a casual event, and the work of irrational fortune, but that it is the offspring of an intellectual nature and divine wisdom, which is separated, indeed, from it [by a difference of essence], but yet is near to it, through being established on the summit of the whole port; [i.e. from the dignity and excellence of its nature governing the whole with consummate wisdom]. Since, however, an olive is

---

[f] In the original, και τας μεν, θεοις τε και τοις αγαθοις πϱοσηκουσας. But after αγαθοις, I have no doubt we should insert δαιμοσι.

ever-flourishing, it possesses a certain peculiarity in the highest degree adapted to the revolutions of souls in the world; for to such souls this cave [as we have said] is sacred. For in summer, the white leaves of the olive tend upward, but in winter, the whiter leaves are bent downward. On this account, also, in prayers and supplications, men extend the branches of an olive, ominating from this, that they shall exchange the sorrowful darkness of danger for the fair light of security and peace. The olive, therefore, being naturally ever-flourishing, bears fruit which is the auxiliary of labour [by being its reward]; it is also sacred to Minerva; supplies the victors in athletic labours with crowns; and affords a friendly branch to the suppliant petitioner. Thus, too, the world is governed by an intellectual nature, and is conducted by a wisdom eternal and ever-flourishing; by which the rewards of victory are conferred on the conquerors in the athletic race of life, as the reward of severe toil and patient perseverance. And the Demiurgus, who connects and contains the world [in ineffable comprehensions], invigorates miserable and suppliant souls.

16. In this cave, therefore, says Homer, all external possessions must be deposited. Here, naked, and assuming a suppliant habit, afflicted in body, casting aside every thing superfluous, and being averse to the energies of sense, it is requisite to sit at the foot of the olive, and consult with Minerva by what means we may most effectually destroy that hostile rout of passions which insidiously lurk in the secret recesses of the soul. Indeed, as it appears to me, it was not without reason that Numenius and his followers thought the person of Ulysses in the Odyssey represented to us a man, who passes in a regular manner over the dark and stormy sea of generation, and thus at length arrives at that region where tempests and seas are unknown, and finds a nation.

Who ne'er knew salt, or heard the billows roar.

17. Again, according to Plato, the deep, the sea, and a tempest, are images of a material nature. And on this account, I think, the poet called the port by the name of Phorcys. For he says, 'It is the port of the ancient marine Phorcys.'[g] The daughter, likewise, of

[g] Phorcys is one among the ennead of Gods who, according to Plato in the Timæus, fabricate generation. Of this deity, Proclus observes, 'that as the Jupiter in this ennead causes the unapparent divisions and separation of forms made by Saturn to become apparent, and as Rhea calls them forth into motion and generation; so Phorcys inserts them in matter, produces sensible natures, and adorns

this God is mentioned in the beginning of the Odyssey. But from Thoosa the Cyclops was born, whom Ulysses deprived of sight. And this deed of Ulysses became the occasion of reminding him of his errors, till he was safely landed in his native country. On this account, too, a seat under the olive is proper to Ulysses, as to one who implores divinity, and would appease his natal dæmon with a suppliant branch. For it will not be simply, and in a concise way, possible for any one to be liberated from this sensible life, who blinds this dæmon, and renders his energies inefficacious; but he who dares to do this, will be pursued by the anger[h] of the marine and material Gods, whom it is first requisite to appease by sacrifices, labours, and patient endurance; at one time, indeed, contending with the passions, and at another employing enchantments and deceptions, and by these, transforming himself in an all-various manner; in order that, being at length divested of the torn garments [by which his true person was concealed], he may recover the ruined empire of his soul. Nor will he even then be liberated from labours; but this will be effected when he has entirely passed over the raging sea, and, though still living, becomes so ignorant of marine and material works [through deep attention to intelligible concerns], as to mistake an oar for a corn-van.

18. It must not, however, be thought, that interpretations of this kind are forced, and nothing more than the conjectures of ingenious men; but when we consider the great wisdom of antiquity, and how much Homer excelled in intellectual prudence, and in an accurate knowledge of every virtue, it must not be denied that he has obscurely indicated the images of things of a more divine nature in the fiction of a fable. For it would not have been possible to devise the whole of this hypothesis, unless the figment had been transferred [to an appropriate meaning] from certain established truths. But reserving the discussion of this for another treatise, we shall here finish our explanation of the present Cave of the Nymphs.

the visible essence, in order that there may not only be divisions of productive principles (or forms) in natures and in souls, and in intellectual essences prior to these; *but likewise in sensibles. For this is the peculiarity of fabrication.*'

[h] 'The anger of the Gods,' says Proclus, 'is not an indication of any passion in them, but demonstrates our inaptitude to participate of their illuminations.'

'The Oracle'

or A Paraphrastical Interpretation of the answer of Apollo, when he was consulted by Amelius whither Plotinus soul went when he departed this life

I Tune my strings to sing some sacred verse
Of my dear friend: in an immortall strain
His mighty praise I loudly will rehearse
With hony-dewed words: some golden vein
The strucken chords right sweetly shall resound.
Come, blessed Muses, let's with one joynt noise,
With strong impulse, and full harmonius sound,
Speak out his excellent worth. Advance your voice,
As once you did for great Aeacides,
Rapt with an heavenly rage, in decent dance,
Mov'd at the measure of Meonides.
Go to, you holy Quire, let's all at once
Begin, and to the end uphold the song,
Into one heavenly harmony conspire;
I Phoebus with my lovely locks ymong
The midst of you shall sit, and life inspire.

Divine Plotinus! yet now more divine
Then when thy noble soul so stoutly strove
In the dark prison, when strong chains confine,
Keep down the active mind it cannot move
To what it loveth most. Those fleshly bands
Thou now hast loos'd, broke from Necessitie.
From bodies storms, and frothie working sands
Of this low restlesse life now setten free,
Thy feet do safely stand upon a shore,
Which foaming waves beat not in swelling rage,
Nor angry seas do threat with fell uprore;
Well hast thou swommen out, and left that stage
Of wicked Actours, that tumultuous rout
Of ignorant men. Now thy pure steps thou stay'st
In that high path, where Gods light shines about,
And perfect Right its beauteous beams displayes.

How oft, when bitter wave of troubled flesh,
And whirl-pool-turnings of the lower spright,
Thou stoutly strov'st with, Heaven did thee refresh,
Held out a mark to guide they wandring flight!
While thou in tumbling seas didst strongly toyl
To reach to steddie Land, struckst with thy arms
The deafing surges, that with rage do boyl;
Steer'd by that signe thou shunn'st those common harms.
How oft, when rasher cast of thy souls eye
Had thee misguided into crooked wayes,
Wast thee directed by the Deitie?
They held out to thee their bright lamping rayes:
Dispers'd the mistie darknesse, safely set
Thy feeble feet in the right path again.
Nor easie sleep so closely ere beset
Thy eyelids, nor did dimnesse ere so stain
Thy radiant sight, but thou such things didst see
Even in that tumult, that few can arrive
Of all are named from Philosophie
To that high pitch, or to such secrets dive.

But sith this body thy pure soul divine
Hath left, quite risen from her rotten grave,
Thou now among those heavenly wights dost shine,
Whose wonne this glorious lustre doth embrave:
There lovely Friendship, mild-smiling Cupid's there,
With lively looks and amorous suavitie,
Full of pure pleasure, and fresh flowring chear:
Ambrosian streams sprung from the Deitie
Do frankly flow, and soft love-kindling winds
Do strike with a delicious sympathie
Those tender spirits, and fill up their minds
With satisfying joy. The puritie
Of holy fire their heart doth then invade,
And sweet Perswasion, meek Tranquillitie,
The gentle-breathing Air, the Heavens nought sad,
Do maken up this great felicitie.
Here Rhadamanthus, and just Æacus,
Here Minos wonnes, with those that liv'd of yore
I' th' golden age; here Plato vigorous
In holy virtue, and fair Pythagore.
These been the goodly Off-spring of Great Jove,
And liven here, and whoso fill'd the Quire
And sweet assembly of immortall Love

Purgin their spirits with refining fire;
These with the happy Angels live in blisse,
Full fraught with joy, and lasting pure delight,
In friendly feasts, and life-outfetching kisse.
But, ah! dear Plotin, what smart did thy spirite
Indure, before thou reach's this high degree
Of happiness? what agonies, what pains
Thou underwent'st to set thy soul so free
From baser life? She now in heaven remains
Mongst the pure Angels. O thrice-happy wight!
That thou art got into the Land of Life,
Fast plac'd in view of that Eternall Light,
And sitt'st secure form the foul bodies strife.

But now, you comely virgins, make an end,
Break off this musick, and deft seemly Round,
Leave off your dance: For Plotin my dear friend
Thus much I meant my golden harp should sound.[1]

[1] More, *Philosophical Poems of Henry More*, p. 84.

Index

Achilles, 37
Adams, Henry, 7
Adonis, 76–80
Alexander the Great, 103
Alexander, 5, 113
Allston, Washington, 95
Alston, William, 60
Analytic/synthetic distinction, 4–5
Anima Mundi, 21
'Annunciation', 75
Apollo, 226, 228
Aristotle, 1, 45, 58, 139, 186, 208
Aristophanes, 193
Arnold, Matthew, 143
  'Dover Beach', 143
Auden, W. H., 143–4, 230
Austin, J. L., 51
Ayer, A. J., 46–52, 54, 58
  Language, Truth and Logic, 46, 47n,
  50, 52n

Bacchus, 224, 227
Bacon, Francis, 189–90
  Silva Silvarum, 189
Baldwin, Stanley, 163
Balzac, Honoré de, 2, 97
Beard, Charles, 162
Beardsley, M. C., 59
  Verbal Icon, The, 59
Bergson, Henri, 39
Berkeley, Bishop, 1, 2, 3, 6, 7, 8, 10, 20,
  23–6, 46, 84, 85, 96, 114, 190
Blake, William, 9, 15, 39, 40, 58, 74, 81
  'Sick Rose, The', 58
Blavatsky, Helena Petrovna, 40
Bradley, F. H., 2, 39
Brinton, Crane, 162
Brooks, Cleanth, 48–9
  Understanding Poetry (with Robert
  Penn Warren), 48–9
Browning, Robert, 1, 97, 236–7
Buddha, 39, 98, 103, 105
Burke, Edmund, 132
Butler, Samuel, 94
Byron, Lord, 95
  Childe Harold, 95

Cabalists, 12
Caesar, Julius, 29, 107
Cambridge Platonists 21, 23
'Childhood of Mary Virgin', 75
Chomsky, Noam, 234
Cicero, 29
Cimarose, 94
Cleopatra, 144
Coleridge, Samuel Taylor, 2, 10, 45,
  81–105, 108, 112–13, 115, 118
  Biographia Literaria, 10, 81–2, 85, 93,
  94–6
  'Dejection: An Ode', 92
  'Kubla Khan', 92
  Rime of the Ancient Mariner, The, 92,
  118
Collingwood, R. G., 163–4, 169
Croce, B., 2n, 39

Dante, 110, 122
Demeter, 226–8
Descartes, René, 233
Dickens, Charles, 54
  Great Expectations, 54–5
  Pickwick Papers, The, 56
Diotima, 193–6, 206, 209, 214
Dray, W. H., 162–3, 169
Durrant, Geoffrey, 87–93

Eddington, A. S., 7
Einstein, Albert, 28, 186
Eliot, T. S., 144
  'Love Song of J. Alfred Prufrock,
  The', 144
Ellmann, Richard, 13, 24, 26, 65–6, 78–
  9, 121, 167, 239n
Esau, 203

Faerie Queen, The (Spenser), 73
Fichte, Johann, 2n, 10, 13, 14
Fortinbras, 106
Frazer, Sir James George, 43
  Golden Bough, The, 43
Freud, Sigmund, 132, 164, 173, 174
Frye, Northrop, 43

Gentile, Giovanni, 2, 15, 39, 182, 184, 185
Gonne, Maud, 68, 127, 196, 200, 201, 203
Gregory, Lady Augusta, 127, 137
Gregory, Major Robert, 144 (*see also* Yeats, 'In Memory of Major Robert Gregory')
Gyre, 15, 171

Hamlet, 59, 70, 104, 105, 106, 144, 157, 158
Hartley, David, 85, 87, 91, 93, 94, 104
Hartmann, Nicolai, 39
Hearn, Lafcadio, 28
Hegel, G. W. F., 1, 2, 9, 14, 16, 28, 39, 97, 186, 238
Helen of Troy, 107, 167
Hempel, C. G., 50, 164
Henle, Paul, 60
Henn, T. R., 67
Hermias, 224
Hogarth, William, 54
Homer, 223, 224, 226
Hospers, John, 53
Hume, David, 3–4, 46, 184, 189, 192, 201, 230

Iago, 151

James, William, 39
Johnson, Lionel, 148, 152, 153
Johnson, Samuel, 3
Joyce, James, 97, 105, 122
 Anna Livia Plurabelle, 97, 105
 Portrait of the Artist as a Young Man, 122
Jung, Carl, 41, 42, 173, 174
Juno, 75
Jupiter, 223

Kabala, 40
Kant, Immanuel (and Kantian), 1–17, 20, 24, 39, 40, 41, 81, 84, 85, 86, 96, 100, 113–22, 128, 130, 132, 151–2, 190, 228, 230
 Critique of Pure Reason, The, 4, 5, 6
Keats, John, 93, 145, 151, 212
 'Ode on a Grecian Urn', 101, 212
King, Edward, 149

Langland, William, 74
 Piers Plowman, 73

Lavery, Hazel, 136
Lear, 144
Le Corbusier, 54
Leda, 202, 203
Lévi-Strauss, Claude, 233, 234
Lewis, Wyndham, 113–14
 Time and Western Man, 113–14
Leibniz, G. W. von, 4
Locke, John, 1, 3, 85, 86, 96, 184, 230

MacNeice, Louis, 144
McTaggart, John, 2n, 28
Mandelbaum, Maurice, 162
Mantegna, 79
Marx, Karl, 164, 232, 238
Meinong, Alexius, 55
Melchiori, G., 116n, 167
 Whole Mystery of Art, The, 116n
Michelangelo, 75, 107, 111, 167
Milton, John, 105, 145, 149
 'Lycidas', 145, 149
 Paradise Lost, 87
Minerva, 223
Mommsen, Theodor, 29
Moore, G. E., 9, 39, 56, 185
Moore, T. Sturge, 9, 10, 39, 183, 185
More, Henry, 21, 35
 'Oracle, The', 35; quoted 263–5
 'Psychozoia or The Life of the Soul', 21
 'Moses', 75

Narcissus, 227
Neo-Kantian, 8, 10, 16, 39, 40, 41, 84, 85, 102
Newton, Isaac, 87, 128
Nicholas of Cusa, 238
Nietzsche, Friedrich, 2n, 40, 103, 143

Oedipus, 225, 226, 227, 228
'Origin of the Milky Way', 75
Orpheus, 226, 227
Othello, 151

Peleus, 37
Persephone, 226–8
Phidias, 98, 102, 104
Pierce, C. S., 59, 60
Pilgrim's Progress (Bunyan), 73
Plato (and Platonism), 2, 6, 7, 10, 20, 23, 24, 25, 26, 27, 28, 36, 38, 45, 51, 62, 80–1, 114, 122, 186, 193, 196, 197–218 passim, 221, 223, 224–30 passim, 235

Plato–*contd.*
'Parmenides', 28
'Phaedo', 227
'Phaedrus', 224
Symposium, The, 193–6, 206, 214
'Timaeus', The, 227
Plotinus, 23, 24, 25, 26, 28, 36, 37, 40
Poincaré, Henri, 7, 8
Pollexfen, George, 148, 152, 153
Pope, Alexander, 54, 57
'Essay on Criticism', 54, 57
'Rape of the Lock', 57
Popper, K. R., 164
Porphyry, 35, 36, 207, 222, 223, 224;
quoted 226–9, 240–62 (*see also*
Taylor)
Portrait of a Lady, The, 144
Poseidon, 228–9
Pound, Ezra, 97, 105, 225
Cantos, The, 97, 105
Poussin, Gaspard, 36
Pre-Raphaelite, 118
Proclus, 227
Proust, Marcel, 97, 105
Ptolemy, 27, 28
Purcell, Henry, 94
Pythagoras, 98–102, 106, 185–7, 210–
11, 215, 217, 235

Quine, Willard Van Orman, 166, 233

Rajan, B., 68n
Rawley, Dr., 189
Rembrandt, 54
Renier, G. J., 162
Richards, I. A., 48, 49, 51, 52, 58, 230,
231n
Rossetti, D. G., 75
Ruskin, John, 185
Russell, Bertrand, 6n, 9, 13, 39, 46, 48,
55, 184

Schelling, F., 10
Schopenhauer, A., 2n, 28, 39, 40
Semele, 224
Shakespeare, William, 90n, 144
Shelley, Percy Bysshe, 1, 3, 67, 97, 116–
17, 223
Skinner, B. F., 164
Socrates, 193–6, 205, 209, 214
Solomon, 237
Sophocles, 221, 222, 224
Southey, Robert, 95
Roderick, 95

Spectator, The, 94, 104
Spengler, Oswald, 184
Stamp, Kenneth, 162
Stendhal (Henri Beyle), 1, 2, 96 97,
98, 105, 106
Stock, A. G., 126–8, 132
Strawson, P. F., 55, 56n, 129–30, 166
Strong, Eugenie, 118
Apotheosis and Afterlife, 118
Swedenborg, E., 40, 42
Arcana Coelestia, The, 42
*Dreams of a Ghost-Seer Explained by
Dreams of Metaphysics,* 42
Swift, Jonathan, 54, 113–14, 116, 132

Taylor, Thomas, 35, 36, 37, 224, 227
ed. Porphyry's 'On the Cave of the
Nymphs', 35, 36, 207, 222, 224;
quoted 226–9, 240–62 (*see also*
Porphyry)
Thetis, 37
Thilly, F., 12, 13n
Tintoretto, 75

Ulysses, 229
Unterecker, John, 44, 45, 49, 58, 62,
67–8, 77–8
Ure, Peter, 68

Vico, G., 238
Von Hugel, Baron Friedrich, 28
Voltaire, 183

Warren, Robert Penn, 48–9
Understanding Poetry (with Cleanth
Brooks), 48–9
Wellesley, Dorothy, 175
Whitaker, T. R., 68
Whitehead, A. N., 3, 99–103, 182–218,
225, 234
Science and the Modern World, 99,
182–201
Wilson, F. A. C., 40
Wimsatt, W. K., 59
Winters, Yvor, 231
Wittgenstein, L., 46, 51
Wood, L., 12, 13n
Wordsworth, William, 87–93, 101
'I wandered lonely as a cloud', 87–93
Lyrical Ballads, 101
Prelude, The, 91, 92, 101
'Reverie of Poor Susan, The', 87, 90,
91, 93
'Tintern Abbey', 92

Yeats, William Butler, works by
'Among School Children', 57, 58,
185, 191, 192, 193, 194, 196,
quoted 197–8, 199–218, 222, 225,
228, 235
'Ancestral Houses', 127
'At Algeciras – A Meditation before
Death', 32–5
'Beautiful Lofty Things', 127
'Before the World was made', 80
'Bishop Berkeley', 1
'Byzantium', 115–24, 125, 187
'Cold Heaven, The', 60–9, 73
'Colonus' Praise', quoted, 220–1,
222–9
'Crazy Jane', 25, 27, 58, 62
'Dialogue of Self and Soul, A',
quoted 30–1, 32, 35, 40, 206, 214,
215
'Delphic Oracle Upon Plotinus,
The', quoted 19–20, 36
'Easter 1916', 236
Essays and Introductions, 1, 41n, 76n,
106, 111n
Explorations, 8, 42
'Fighting the Waves', 2, 3
'For Anne Gregory', quoted 234–5,
236
'Geneological Tree of Revolution,
The', 11, quoted 238–9
'Her Vision in the Wood', quoted
76–7, 78–80, 103, 123
'Hound Voice', quoted 141, 143
'In Memory of Major Robert
Gregory', 141, 145, quoted 146–8,
149–56, 164–5, 171
'Lapis Lazuli', 40, 112, 125–60, 161,
168
'Leda and the Swan', 56, 57,
quoted 166–7, 168–9, 172, 174,
179, 202
'Long-Legged Fly', quoted 106–7,
108, 123, 161, 179
'Magic' 41, 83
'Michael Robartes and the Dancer',
234
'Mohini Chatterjee', 32–5, 123
'Municipal Gallery Revisited, The',
127, 128, quoted 134–5, 136–8,
140, 152, 153, 156, 161, 164
'News for the Delphic Oracle',
35–7, 123

'Nineteen Hundred and Nineteen',
127, 145, quoted 175–8, 179–81
'Old Tom Again', quoted 19, 24–6
'Prayer for My Daughter, A', 133,
171
'Resurrection, The', 27
'Sailing to Byzantium', 119
'Second Coming, The', quoted
169–70, 171–5, 179
'Secret Rose, The', 65
'Seven Propositions, The', 13, 15,
41
'Solomon and the Witch', 234,
236–7
'Stare's Nest by my Window,
The', 145
'Statistics', quoted, 61, 62
'Statues, The', 96–7, quoted 98–9,
100–6, 119, 123, 167, 179
'Stick of Incense, A', quoted 219,
220
'To a Friend Whose Work Has
Come to Nothing', quoted 139
'To a Young Beauty', quoted 138
'Tom at Cruachan', quoted 19, 24,
37
'Tom the Lunatic', quoted 18–19,
20–3
'Tower, The', 8, 23, 24, 26
'Under Ben Bulben', 29, 32, 106–7,
quoted 108–9, 110–12, 119, 123,
165, 179
'Vacillation', 32
'Veronica's Napkin', quoted 120–1,
122
Vision, A, 10, 11, 14, 15, 17, 29, 113,
116, 164, 187
'Why Should not Old Men be
Mad?', 145
'Wisdom', 218, quoted 219, 220
Wheels and Butterflies, 2, 3
'Witch, The', quoted 71
Words for Music Perhaps, 18
'Words upon the Window-Pane,
The', 3, 29
Yeats–Moore Correspondence, 7n, 9n,
15n, 22, 39, 114, 115, 116, 182n,
183

Zarathustra, 98
Zeus, 167, 168, 172, 201, 202
Zwerdling, Alex, 66–7

ACKNOWLEDGMENTS

The author and publisher would like to express their thanks to M. B. Yeats and the Macmillan Companies of London and Canada, also to The Macmillan Company, New York, for their permission to include poems quoted extensively or in entirety from W. B. Yeats's *Collected Poems* (1963 reprint of 1950 2nd ed.) as follows: from *Last Poems* – 'Long-legged Fly', 'Under Ben Bulben', 'Lapis Lazuli', 'Why Should not Old Men be Mad?', 'News for the Delphic Oracle', 'The Statues', 'The Municipal Gallery Revisited', 'Hound Voice', 'A Stick of Incense' (Copyright 1940 by Georgie Yeats, renewed 1968 by Bertha Georgie Yeats, Michael Butler Yeats and Anne Yeats); from *A Full Moon in March* – 'A Needle's Eye' (Copyright 1934 by The Macmillan Company, renewed 1962 by Bertha Georgie Yeats); from *Words for Music Perhaps* – 'Tom the Lunatic', 'Tom at Cruachan', 'Old Tom Again', 'The Delphic Oracle upon Plotinus' and from *The Winding Stair* – 'A Dialogue of Self and Soul', 'Mohini Chatterjee', 'Statistics', 'Her Vision in the Wood', 'Byzantium', 'Veronica's Napkin', 'For Anne Gregory' (Copyright 1933 by The Macmillan Company, renewed 1961 by Bertha Georgie Yeats); from *The Tower* – Fragment I, 'Leda and the Swan', 'Nineteen Hundred and Nineteen', 'Among School Children', 'Wisdom', 'Colonus' Praise' (Copyright 1928 by The Macmillan Company, renewed 1956 by Georgie Yeats); from *Michael Robartes and the Dancer* – 'The Second Coming' (Copyright 1924 by The Macmillan Company, renewed 1952 by Bertha Georgie Yeats); from *The Wild Swans at Coole* – 'In Memory of Major Robert Gregory', 'To a Young Beauty' (Copyright 1919 by The Macmillan Company, renewed 1947 by Bertha Georgie Yeats); from *Responsibilities* – 'The Witch', 'To a Friend Whose Work has Come to Nothing' (Copyright 1916 by The Macmillan Company, renewed 1944 by Bertha Georgie Yeats) and 'The Cold Heaven' (Copyright 1912 by The Macmillan Company, renewed 1940 by Bertha Georgie Yeats).